The Global Grapevine

The Global Grapevine

Why Rumors of Terrorism, Immigration, and Trade Matter

GARY ALAN FINE

BILL ELLIS

OXFORD
UNIVERSITY PRESS

2010

OXFORD
UNIVERSITY PRESS

Oxford University Press, Inc., publishes works that further
Oxford University's objective of excellence
in research, scholarship, and education.

Oxford   New York
Auckland   Cape Town   Dar es Salaam   Hong Kong   Karachi
Kuala Lumpur   Madrid   Melbourne   Mexico City   Nairobi
New Delhi   Shanghai   Taipei   Toronto

With offices in
Argentina   Austria   Brazil   Chile   Czech Republic   France   Greece
Guatemala   Hungary   Italy   Japan   Poland   Portugal   Singapore
South Korea   Switzerland   Thailand   Turkey   Ukraine   Vietnam

Copyright © 2010 by Gary Alan Fine and Bill Ellis

Published by Oxford University Press, Inc.
198 Madison Avenue, New York, NY 10016

www.oup.com

Library of Congress Cataloging-in-Publication Data
Fine, Gary Alan.
The global grapevine: why rumors of terrorism, immigration,
and trade matter / Gary Alan Fine, Bill Ellis.
    p. cm.
Includes index.
ISBN 978–0–19–973631–7
1. Rumor.   2. Globalization—Social aspects.
I. Ellis, Bill, 1950–   II. Title.
HM1241.F56 2010
302.2'4—dc22 2009039712

9 8 7 6 5 4 3 2 1
Printed in the United States of America
on acid-free paper

To
Linda Dégh
and
W. F. H. Nicolaisen
* * *

Mentors and Scholars

Contents

Acknowledgments

Every book involves teamwork. We thank Caroline Carr of the Russell Sage Foundation, who unerringly discovered some of the most intriguing Web sites cited in this book. Kate Gleeson and Gianna Mosser provided much needed editorial support as we compiled draft after draft. We are grateful for Carol Mann, our agent, and James Cook, our editor at Oxford University Press. We also thank Gillian Bennett, Joel Best, Simon Bronner, Véronique Campion-Vincent, Irfan Khawaja, and Jay Mechling for their advice in the preparation of this manuscript. In support of his part of the research toward this book, Bill Ellis received a Sabbatical Grant in 2005–2006 from Penn State, which also generously provided travel funds so that he could present preliminary findings at several meetings of the American Folklore Society. Gary Alan Fine appreciates his fellowships at the Russell Sage Foundation in 2005–2006, the Rockefeller Foundation Bellagio Center in 2008, and King's College at the University of Cambridge in 2009, when portions of this manuscript were written and presented. Both authors thank their students at Penn State University, Hazleton Campus; George Mason University; and Northwestern University for sharing many of the rumors they had heard among their families and peers about these topics, especially for Ellis's Penn State students who provided much valuable information about reactions to the Illegal Immigrant Relief Act controversy of 2006–2007. Dorothy Noyes also made it possible for Ellis to present a revised and expanded version of his research into the Hazleton controversy under the auspices of the Ohio State Center for Folklore Studies. Ellis especially appreciates the support of Margaret Yocum of George Mason University, who made it possible for him to teach an upper-level course in contemporary legend in spring 2007, during which many of the theoretical and interpretive ideas in this volume were tested and refined. Both authors gratefully acknowledge the immense tolerance of their families during the several years in which this book was being prepared.

The Global Grapevine

Introduction

Rumor: Plausible and Credible

In a world so frighteningly diverse, we can conclude that anything is possible. What can we believe and by what standards do we judge? Were Israeli secret agents responsible for the carnage on September 11? Do border-jumping Mexicans deliberately spread deadly flu? Are children's toys manufactured in China maliciously poisoned with lead? Are Caribbean cabana boys waiting to spread AIDS? Once we had only our own backyard to fear, but now, borrowing from the sonnet of the great English poet William Wordsworth, we find that the world is too much with us. The comforting and snug local communities that we once knew have been overwhelmed by a splintered and intimidating global community. Whereas in the past the American nation was a mighty fortress, many citizens feel that today its walls have been breached. Anywhere is everywhere, or so it seems.

We hope to engage those beliefs that have come with increased globalism. Specifically, we examine some of the rumors and legends that circulate about the risks of our interconnected world. It is easy to take rumors and legends for granted: we hear and read variations on them on a daily basis. Because they are so much part of our commonplace life, we often minimize them as merely funny and peculiar claims. But that is precisely the point: because they are so much a part of our daily routine, they have real impact. What we think determines how we see the world around us and invisibly influences our political and personal choices. Rumors and legends affect how we live our lives.

Whether the concern is terrorism, immigration, or international trade, Americans—along with citizens of other advanced nations—see threats from abroad. (In this book, we often speak of Americans, although some of the examples are from European sources and much of the analysis applies to Western nations generally.) Nations that were proud of their accomplishments, history, patriotism, and personality find these sources of pride under threat from those who are defined as strangers. Unwashed masses seem to threaten our clean lives. Our comfort zones are continuously shrinking. So long as we can maintain our daily habits, we feel comfortable and secure, but when our familiar world changes, due to globalizing forces, we become disoriented. We first see new features of our lives as "strange" and "incomprehensible." It is tempting to perceive such perplexing factors as signs of a loss of control or a threat to our livelihood or our families. What begins as puzzlement and annoyance can become a profound fear coupled with a readiness to accept accounts of conspiracy and moral decay. By bringing the unexpected close to home, the anxieties and uncertainties created by globalism become crystallized as rumors, legends, and subversion myths. These are claims that we are prepared to accept either with certainty or provisionally, but for which we have little concrete evidence.

Yet, in truth, was the United States ever the insular fortress many politicians invoke? Its original inhabitants, their land taken from them by stealth and force, their numbers decimated by epidemics caused by contact with the European newcomers, justifiably feel that their culture was destroyed by contact with foreigners. But the continued vitality of America has been based on its ability to absorb and accommodate wave after wave of immigrants from colonial times to the present. And it is not only America that is under siege, as other nations have had to cope with the impact of Americans and their culture for decades. While localities and regions have not entirely lost their unique flavor, the expansion of multinational companies, global franchises, rapid immigration, and travel opportunities increase the similarities among places and societies. What made places special threatens to melt into an international soup. As the world has become more tight-knit, both Americans and those influenced by our culture have become nervous about these changes.

The concern extends further because these changes affect Americans individually and collectively. Henry Luce, the publisher of *Time* magazine, referred to the twentieth century as the American century. Will the twenty-first century also be America's century? Will the changes brought about by political violence, immigration, and trade diminish America's standing in a global economy and undermine its authority as the world's preeminent political and military power? The fact that Americans spread so many rumors about this topic suggests that we doubt our own future. One consequence of the creation of a global social system is that Americans are more aware of once-distant others. Increasingly, we confront strangers in political, economic, or cultural arenas. Some of the information gleaned is accurate; some is wildly, fantastically inaccurate; and much is based on uncertain and imperfect sources. These claims may be amusing, frightening, or both, but the fact that many are accepted reveals how ready people are to believe and shape their actions based on what they have been told. As a result, rumors demand attention. Sometimes we share rumors about terrorist cells planning a new attack on a shopping mall; other times we mutter about illegal immigrants receiving special treatment; and on still other occasions we worry about the importation of illegal drugs or frightening new diseases spread from abroad. Through its ability to make audible the unspoken, rumor provides an opportunity for people and communities to explore how their nation is changing.

Our goal is to show how rumors that concern global politics matter. Specifically, we describe four major rumor themes that emerge repeatedly: rumors about terrorism, immigration, international trade, and tourism. Here Americans confront others who are culturally and socially different from themselves, often residents from the so-called third world—Arabs, Africans, Asians, or Latinos. As we point out, some of these rumors need to be confronted and challenged for their political implications, and all need to be questioned. Thinking back half a century, we find an America that had sharply limited the number and types of immigrants allowed to enter the nation, a result of the nativism of the 1920s. The Immigration and Nationality Act of 1965 changed our nation in profound ways, permitting an increased number of migrants, particularly non-Europeans. Shifts in the need for labor for low-wage jobs encouraged workers to cross our borders without proper papers or government approval: a tide of undocumented workers or illegal aliens, depending on one's perspective. Whether we are comfortable with this reality, America is multiracial and multicultural, a rainbow of hues. The rumors and legends that we share address our concern with these "outsiders."

Rumor, Legend, and the Balance of Truth

The complexities of modern life, coupled with the growth of the media, including Internet sources, find contemporary societies awash in news. For better and worse, we live in a world in which there is simultaneously too much information and too little. Many groups present the *truth* about what is happening around us in an attempt to persuade us. Such truth claims frequently have an uncertain provenance: when we doubt their claims, they may be labeled "rumors" or "urban legends." And when they harmonize with our belief system and we trust their source, we accept them, act on them, and share them. And in sharing them we announce that we are a part of the community of talk. While we believe that people must have some trust in the content of what they perform, sharing rumors is an easy way of participating in social groups—local, national, and sometimes global.

Rumor is a term that is used in a variety of ways in popular talk. For social scientists, *rumor* is an expression of belief about a specific event that is supposed to have happened or is about to happen. This claim may pique our interest but lacks what the larger political system considers *secure standards of evidence*, a concept to which we will return. *Legend*, a related, overlapping term, often refers to a more elaborate expression, typically told as a story or narrative that spreads widely, changing in detail with each teller but expressing a similar scenario. In other words, a rumor often is a generalization, stating (for instance) that immigrants "do" something, while a legend is a specific example, alleging that at a particular time and place immigrants "did" or "are about to do" something. The boundaries between the two are hazy, however, and even folklorists and social scientists who study both find themselves hard put to draw a sharp boundary.[1]

Nevertheless, consensus has emerged among experts that the proper study of so-called "legend" or "rumor" was not the infinitely varying narrative texts collected by observers, but rather the *social process* that generated them. Observing the process of legendry, rather than the narratives themselves, became the proper topic of contemporary legend research. In this sense, it became unnecessary to decide if a given text were a legend or "just" a rumor. This insight made analysis of the material possible emphasizing whether legends are "true" (some are, some aren't, and some can't be called either true or false) and whether those who tell legends believe them (some surveys suggest—surprisingly—that skeptics are more likely to pass on legends than true believers). If one attraction of both rumors and legends is that they can be told, discussed, and transmitted in the absence of a clear standard of proof, or even a clear conviction of its credibility, then surely academic research need not begin and end with simple debunking of a widely circulated legend. Rumor and legend are both the products of a distinctive type of speculative political discourse that contributes to a lively— and often healthy—civil society. Since it is impossible to maintain a clear distinction between rumor and legend, for the sake of convenience we typically use rumor to refer to either.

As a form of knowledge, rumor strives to organize a confusing world. These claims arise under circumstances that are perceived as important and ambiguous, and in which the parties to the rumor have low critical ability to judge the information transmitted.[2] As we discuss further in chapter 1, rumor develops from *politics of plausibility* and *politics of credibility*. The two are closely related, but, unlike rumor and legend, they are distinct. We may not find a given story *credible*; that is, we may find the source of information dubious (and the use of the "friend of a friend" as the authority has been noted for decades). However, many people will nevertheless discuss and pass on rumors because they contain a *plausible* claim. If we believe that a story or assertion makes intuitive and cultural sense, given how we conceive of our world, we are likely to accept the rumor as at least *potentially* true.

Some rumors connect to the hearers' underlying beliefs, which they maintain so devoutly that exploring or questioning the claim seems unnecessary. These stories are *too good to be false*. A context defined by war, disaster, or crisis may give them incredible power. We recall, for instance, the instinctive way in which even well-educated, liberal-thinking news commentators were quick to report that blacks housed in the Superdome in the wake of Hurricane Katrina were engaging in rampant acts of rape, murder, looting, or even cannibalism, even though no firsthand evidence of any such disorder ever emerged. In other words, our fundamental argument is that rumor shapes how people think and then respond to the world around them, sometimes justifying prejudice and sometimes motivating and justifying social reform. Spreading rumors and legends is a fundamentally political act with the power to alter social structures—for the better, but also for the worse. Rather than treating legend texts as a subliterary genre, we should see them as "maps for action, often drastic action," and pay attention to how they motivate political change.[3]

Rumor's Role in Times of Crisis

The study of rumor has had a lengthy and distinguished history. Whenever threats were seen to public order, rumor followed, often followed by disorder and loss of life or property. By the twentieth century, rumors became the focus of scholarly attempts to understand how they became widely known and what their consequences might be.[4] This research, like the claims they scrutinized, had political motivations. Rumor reveals much about what people are saying and thinking, often behind closed doors. To understand when and where rumor appears has helped governments control public sentiment. Sometimes these efforts limit public anxieties, and at other times governments increase public fears to support their own policies. For instance, in 1990, the Kuwaiti royal family, driven from power by an invasion by neighboring Iraq, paid the American public relations firm Hill and Knowlton to generate and circulate horror stories about the atrocities committed by Saddam Hussein's troops. The resulting claim, that Iraqi soldiers had stripped hundreds of premature babies out of incubators in Kuwaiti hospitals, was instrumental in gaining American support for a counterinvasion to drive Iraq out of the country, despite warnings that the story was an obvious fabrication.[5]

But rumors are used by activists as well to challenge and resist government action. Widespread rumors speak to general fears and activist groups understand how to use rumors to crystallize political movements to demand changes. In the early twentieth century, for instance, Upton Sinclair, in his novels, such as *The Jungle*, included stomach-wrenching stories about food contamination, including a far-traveled legend about human beings accidentally being ground up into sausages or rendered into commercially marketed lard. The sources of these stories may not have been credible, but even the English "Sweeney Todd" scare stories had a long urban history before they emerged in Victorian London. Still, they were plausible enough to gain passage of much-needed federal legislation mandating food safety.

Shortly after the Pearl Harbor attacks in 1941, President Franklin D. Roosevelt signed executive orders allowing the military to round up some 120,000 Japanese Americans, two-thirds of whom were American citizens, and incarcerate them in internment centers. The move was supported at first by most Americans, who felt, like Lieutenant General John L. DeWitt, the internship program's administrator, that "There is no way to determine their loyalty." Though many Japanese Americans had enlisted and served honorably as U.S. soldiers,[6] DeWitt vehemently insisted, "A Jap is a Jap."[7] The camps were not closed until the war was near its finish. Among those interned at the time was Tamotsu Shibutani, the son of Japanese immigrants, who had been studying sociology at the University of California, Berkeley. He took extensive notes on his experiences, which he later used in his graduate work at the University of Chicago and which became the basis of his classic rumor text, *Improvised News*.

Shibutani knew from personal experience the crucial role that rumors play when crisis disrupts people's normal routines. He argued that at such times, people engage in "extemporaneous rumoring," an emotional and extreme form of informal news exchange. Shibutani found, and most rumor experts agree, that even in the most extreme situations people gather together to analyze and discuss the content of rumors in terms of their plausibility. He found that in most cases, the rumor process tended to favor plausible information and filter out the claims that are beyond what is seen as likely.[8] People place themselves in the position of those whose actions they are attempting to predict, as true for Japanese American internees and for Americans after September 11. Rumors are often wrong, but they are rarely insane. We play the roles of others, and sometimes ignorance or prejudice leads us astray.

As Shibutani intuitively understood, wars, economic dislocations, and disasters provide the kindling for the flame of hearsay, and much rumor scholarship has examined these moments of tension and threat. It has been argued by the psychologists Gordon Allport and Leo G. Postman[9] in the 1940s that rumors arise out of an *effort after meaning*, attempting to create understandings of what has happened and predictions of what will happen at moments in which facts are hard to come by. People simplify stories, elaborate those parts of particular interest, and assimilate (or change) the content to those beliefs that they already hold. It is easy to see how cataclysmic events such as Hurricane Katrina or the attacks on September 11 provide occasions in which rumor thrives. The existence of some "news" provides security, even when the forecast is bleak.

Rumors that address similar themes that we hear today—political conspiracies, dangerous food, or unpredictable illnesses—have been documented for over two millennia. The standard definition of rumor is that it lacks secure standards of evidence. These claims develop from unofficial communication, and the information can turn out to be true or false. A rumor sometimes reports accurate information; it is not always false or a lie, but it is considered at least possible, and thus worth discussing. In turn, official sources need not always tell the truth; they sometimes spread disinformation. Governments and other institutionalized sources can be wrong or even deliberately lie, but scholars do not consider their statements to be rumor, only propaganda. That is, these sources are in the position to know the truth, whether or not they choose to find it or, having found it, conceal it from the public. Nevertheless, disinformation or propaganda, to be successful, likewise depends on the politics of credibility and plausibility.

For instance, the George W. Bush administration based much of its justification for the 2003 invasion of Iraq on the claim that Saddam Hussein was developing and stockpiling weapons of mass destruction. After the invasion, it eventually became clear that these weapons did not exist. American authorities excused themselves by noting that the intelligence gained by overseas agents often came from sources with dubious credibility, and could have been exaggerated or invented for reward. Saddam himself had implied that he had a more dangerous arsenal than in fact was the case in order to deter attacks from neighboring countries like Iran. But he, too, was hardly a credible source on the matter. In the end, however, the decision was made because the claim was, in the eyes of President Bush, a *plausible* one.

Of course, once members of the public forget the original source of the material and claim it themselves, what had been disinformation can easier enter the world of rumor. It was telling that when a team of psychologists surveyed a sampling of Americans a year after the start of the war, they found, to their surprise, that a third of them said they recalled news reports saying that weapons of mass destruction had in fact been found. When tentative news stories about such finds are repeated often enough, the psychologists concluded, they can create false memories in a substantial number of people even when the original stories are subsequently discredited.[10] Despite echoes from the past, many rumors about the world political system are recent in origin. With the changes in the American economy and population, political rumors are becoming increasingly insistent and require response. The reactions to the terrorist attacks on the Pentagon and the World Trade Center on September 11 reveal just how powerful rumor can be at moments of intense uncertainty and demands for community. As the smoke was billowing and as the towers collapsed, the mass of Americans—in Kansas, in Kentucky, and in Queens—improvised their way to an imperfect understanding of the terror. While interpreting responses to the attacks on September 11 will be a central feature of this volume, the rumors that emerged in aftermath of the terrorist attacks on New York and Washington are only dramatic examples of the general category of rumor about how the world impinges on America.

Rumors: Speaking the Unspeakable

Rumor fills several important roles for societies, and unraveling their meaning allows us to reveal social concerns. First, the examination of rumor uncovers the concerns—some hidden, some explicit—of citizens. Rumor allows a community to discuss and debate issues that may be embarrassing, discomforting, or disturbing. We can address these beliefs, because we can act as if we are talking about real events, not personal beliefs. Rumor allows us to discuss hidden fears and desires without claiming these attitudes as our own. We project these concerns by asserting that *it actually happened* or is *about to happen*, presenting ourselves as mere reporters of current events. While we might be blamed as the messenger of unpleasant news, such a position is more comfortable than being condemned as a provocateur or a bigot. Even to an unsympathetic audience, the claimed truth of rumor (however incorrect it may be) provides a potent defense. Rumor permits concealed sentiments to enter public debate, gaining an often sympathetic audience for assertions that might otherwise be deeply troubling. While these sentiments are not always pleasant, they can be more effectively dealt with if they are made public than if they are kept in the closet.

In a previous book, *Whispers on the Color Line: Rumor and Race in America*, Fine (along with his coauthor, African American folklorist Patricia Turner) focused on rumors that were spread by communities of black and white Americans. Racial rumors were one way in which Americans could express their fears in ways that were covert, in that the rumors claimed to be accounts of actual events, either those that had happened or those that were planned. To claim that the government wished to commit genocide against its African American population might be treated as paranoid, unless one could point to facts (but actually rumor) that supported the ugly belief. Likewise, for whites to warn about black sexuality is racist, unless the speaker can point to a horrific crime when white virgins were raped as a gang initiation. Rumor purporting to be fact permits dangerous attitudes to enter conversation. Further, the examination of rumor reveals patterns through which information is spread. Who tells whom, and how? With the expansion of the Internet as an information bazaar, the dynamics of knowledge diffusion has changed substantially. Rumor can now spread with remarkable speed by means of the Internet, and can be exposed as false just as quickly. The availability of debunking information, however, does not automatically stop its spread, as there may be reasons besides credibility that might motivate one to pass along a rumor. Returning to the understanding of racial rumors, blacks and whites often communicate only to members of their own racial group, both because they often do not share informal moments and because they are afraid of how others will respond. These are racialized pools of knowledge, sheltered from those of different backgrounds.[11]

The shock that many white Americans felt when they learned of the beliefs of Barack Obama's minister, Rev. Jeremiah Wright, indicated just how separate blacks and whites can be in their beliefs. For whites, the idea that AIDS might have been genetically engineered by bioweapons experts might seem ludicrous; but for blacks who are aware of a history of government-paid physicians deliberately allowing diseases to go untreated in order to study their effects on black patients, the claim is all too plausible. Of course, it is not the case that all blacks or all whites have common race-based beliefs, but the divisions are sufficiently wide that communication between the races may be fraught with pain and misunderstandings. Many blacks do not share beliefs about the government and large corporations with their white colleagues for fear of being labeled paranoid, and whites avoid talking about black crime and poverty because they wish to avoid being seen as racist. By uncovering networks of private talk, the student of rumor can reveal the structure of society.

The fabric of rumor involves not only hidden beliefs but also real changes in attitudes, and it serves as a barometer of these changes. We recognize the changes in America as a "rainbow society," the changes in transportation that permit international travel, and the reality that products sold in one nation are produced elsewhere, often places with very different economic climates. Industrial and agricultural products increasingly are imported from nations of the developing world. Rumor provides a record of such changes, admittedly in dramatic and transformed forms. As we describe in the next chapters, Americans' reactions to the attacks on September 11 through rumor reveal just such a record of beliefs.

As is the case with rumors that deal with race relations, a fierce etiquette exists in talking about multiculturalism and globalism. We create a brittle *culture of tolerance*, through which we decline to express our deep beliefs, sugar-coating them in happy talk. As Attorney General Eric Holder bravely noted, all too often Americans are cowards when talking with each other about issues of race, unwilling to confront our unpleasant beliefs.[12] The politics of tolerance is evident in considering global threats as well as in talk of race. *Whispers on the Color Line* demonstrated how the insistence on surface tolerance produced discourse that skirted fundamental racial honesty. We called for a painful, but honest, dialogue. The same is true when discussing global transformations. Polite talk often distorts debates on immigration, terrorism, trade, and tourism. How can we advance public policy when people will not address what shapes their anxieties? In this book, we analyze rumors that deal with each of these central topics that express fear and hope about an interconnected world. The first three themes have been salient concerns, contributing to contentious political debates. Tourism, less politically sensitive, also appears in rumor, sometimes humorously, but occasionally reflecting fear as well.

Immigration

When migration occurs in substantial numbers, new residents inevitably shape the culture and economy of the receiving nation. Whether this is for good or ill is a difficult and divisive question. The same issue has been faced by every previous American generation. The Irish arriving in the 1840s and 1850s brought with them a dedicated workforce that enabled the construction of railways and mined the coal needed to fuel them and made the steel to maintain them. Their penchant for brawling and engaging in violent protests also brought on them the suspicion that an Irish workforce could turn on their bosses with bloodshed. Nevertheless, most Americans, Irish or not, now see their contribution as one that enabled the country to advance economically and culturally. In the short run, the conclusion depends on one's values, preferences, and position in society. Some benefit from a rise in immigration, while others lose.

Immigration is not a problem in the United States alone. Many nations in the European Union find themselves saddled with a nativist or anti-immigration party—most dramatically Jean-Marie Le Pen's National Front movement in France—but similar movements and parties operate in

Germany, the Netherlands, Denmark, Austria, and elsewhere. The United States lacks such a party, perhaps a function of the stability of the two-party system and the difficulty of forming new political movements, or perhaps because of the ideology that the United States should properly be a "melting pot," a nation of immigrants, a perspective that is widely shared and made visible in the Statue of Liberty. These features of American politics weaken the belief that our borders should be closed to continued immigration. However, the absence of a political party that espouses such a belief does not mean that anti-immigrant sentiment is absent. When legislation was introduced in 2007 intending to address border security and create a permanent status for those who crossed American borders illegally, opposition from both the Left and the Right kept it from even coming to the floor for a vote, demonstrating the difficulty of productive dialogue and consensus.

In addition, the effect of migrants on a nation—legal or not—is complex, and their immediate and visible effects may be quite different from the unintended or latent consequences of migrant presence. However, these are matters that demographers, economists, and political scientists address. Our concern in examining rumor as culture is to understand what people think has been and will be the consequences of immigration. The strange habits and cultural traditions that these "strangers" hold can easily be twisted into accounts of events that have actually happened or are about to happen.

Terrorism

Like immigration, terrorism involves attitudes to those who stand outside the nation. Most immigrants are not—and are not seen as—terrorists, but terrorists who aim for targets within the United States have been able to enter the country through improper means and, being here, are able to enact their violent plans. This does not deny what has been called "home-grown terrorism"—particularly evident in Great Britain—but even here most citizens see the perpetrators as foreign, no matter the nation of their birth. For many, ethnicity is seen as being a more important indicator of patriotism than one's actual citizenship.

One of the more remarkable aspects of the aftermath of September 11 is how the attacks managed suddenly and convulsively to alter the perspectives of most Americans—a seismic shift—and how those attacks led to decisions that negatively impacted the lives of most Americans. We speak of a pre–September 11 mindset and a post–September 11 mindset. Many citizens willingly accepted a greater inconvenience of air traffic, larger government deficits, a loss of personal privacy, and even, for some, a chilling effect on freedom of speech and religion. Few Americans believed that these crimes should be treated as police matters, investigated after they occurred. Citizens rejected the idea that accepting the occasional attack was a cost of living in a free society. Our concern is not to determine whether these changes in our everyday lives are necessary, but only to remark that they occurred with great speed and without extensive debate. These political transformations demonstrate the potentially cataclysmic effects of events on the public mindset and on government action. Given dramatic circumstances, mass opinion and public policy can shift overnight.

The power of terrorist acts to sow uncertainty and to change worldviews provides an opening for rumor. Rumor responds to the plausibility of events, and terrorism alters what people see as plausible. Further, terrorism creates a situation that is important and frequently ambiguous. Insecure and panicking people desperately and hurriedly search for explanations; their need is so great that they are often reckless about what they believe and spread. People act with a lowered critical ability.[13] It is tempting, as many commentators have noted, to assume that a "terrorist" is a certain kind of person, a clandestine warrior committed to the destruction of our country, rather than a member of a group who, for any number of motives, political, personal, or psychological, carries out an act intended to create terror. Today, in a world in which terrorism is or is felt to be a live and insistent reality, a threat that may disrupt comfortable routine at any moment, understanding rumors about terrorist acts is of critical importance for understanding social change.

International Trade

A third domain of rumors dealing with global contacts involves international trade. Forty years ago the United States was primarily a manufacturing nation. Most of what we consumed, we created—cars, televisions, and food. Psychologically, we knew that it was our countrymen, our fellow citizens, who produced what we used. Perhaps not everything was of high quality, but the psychology of nationalism provided an implicit guarantee. Over the past two generations, this has changed substantially. For decades, the United States has maintained a large trade imbalance. America imports more than we export; much of what we consume—sneakers, avocados, video-games, motorcycles, pet food, toys, tuxedos—is manufactured elsewhere, and no longer only in the industrial nations of Europe and Asia, where often their manufacture increased the status of the product. Increasingly the tags on our products read Indonesia, Mexico, China, Peru, the Dominican Republic, or Guatemala as the country of origin. Surely in future decades more products will be grown or manufactured in the nations of Africa. This trend has benefited American consumers, although not American workers.

Psychology is linked to nationalism. As a general rule, we award our fellow citizens much unexamined trust. We assume the quality of products produced in the United States; the same cannot be said of many products that are produced abroad. Citizenship often implies trust in our country-men, but who are these foreigners and how might their interests differ? Some measure of racism and ethnic bias affects the answer, even as our own citizenry rapidly changes. Are these uneducated Asians, blacks, or Hispanics really able to produce high-quality goods? For a period during the 1970s and 1980s, many Americans came to believe that products from Japan were superior to American goods, but that was the exception. We purchase shirts from Haiti and sneakers from Vietnam because we have little choice and because the price is right. It is here that rumor intrudes. The claim that these foreign products—natural or manufactured: bananas, beer, or micro-waves—are dangerous is treated as plausible. We may assign the danger to the presence of exotic vermin (snakes or scorpions) concealed in the prod-uct, the incompetence of foreign workers to produce safe products, or the malicious desire of these envious or bitter foreigners to do us harm. Rumor suggests that evil outsiders deliberately conspire to import danger, some-times with the connivance of our own fellow citizens. Given the power of the American military and police, how did our borders become a sieve, allowing all manner of poison to slip through?

Tourism

While products are imported into American markets, Americans increas-ingly enjoy visiting foreign lands. The amount of international travel—for business and leisure—has increased enormously. Even middle-class Americans routinely travel to foreign resorts, and often these locales are located in the third world: Cancun, Montego Bay, Barbados, Rio, Phuket, or Bali. The delicious exoticism of the destinations is part of their charm. We desire to "get away," to experience an unusual locale. However, that very exoticism provokes concern. Our tacit ability to navigate a known landscape is undermined. To be sure, many of these resort destinations tame or domesticate the exotic character of the place, but some risk remains. The threat derives both from the local flora and fauna and from the native population. The natives are themselves tourist attractions for visitors from the industrialized West. It is precisely their "otherness" that makes them both enthralling and dangerous.

The strangeness of the landscape and the people encourages the perception that hidden perils are present. Anything is possible, and this increases the plausibility of stories that play off these worries. This anxiety, perhaps barely expressible, provides a space for rumor to develop. Rumors warn travelers of their potential naïveté, being unable to recognize the risks to their lives and property. Thieves are rife, hotel attendants are not to be trusted, lovers are diseased, and animals and plants can cause havoc if one is not watchful. In short, one is not in Kansas anymore.

Hunting Rumor

To study rumor is to accept a challenge. There is no central repository that tracks rumor. Rumors come and go, sometimes noticed and often ignored. Rumors are occasional, evanescent, and often private. People may be embarrassed or reticent to admit that they spread rumors, making interviews problematic. As a result, researchers often "stumble upon" rumor. The examination of rumor is an area that demands multiple methods and much good fortune. As rumor scholars, we rely on shards of evidence, bits and pieces of hearsay wherever they can be found. To be sure, interviews, observations, or even experiments can on occasion provide useful data. Perhaps most critical is the ability to keep one's eyes and ears open to beliefs that sound plausible yet are unlikely, given other rumors that have circulated. As we go about our daily routine, we listen for the latest rumor. Even if we cannot easily predict where rumors will emerge, they are widely spread. We never lack for rumor.

Sometimes an event occurs such as September 11 after which, because of its importance and ambiguity, rumors multiply. In the days and weeks—and months and years—after the attacks in Washington and lower Manhattan, we knew that rumors would blossom and fade. As a result, we monitored news sources, inquired of friends, surveyed students, and trolled through Internet Web sites. Sometimes we struck gold; sometimes the rumors that appeared were the old ones that had been making the rounds. Once we heard of the rumor about a planned attack on a shopping mall ("Mall-o-Ween," to be discussed in chapter 1), we knew that we had to keep track of the story as it grew and developed until such time as it was no longer seen as interesting. Because of its timeliness, the Internet (such as chat rooms, discussion groups, or dedicated listservs, as well as more formal Web sites, such as Snopes.com or About.com) proved invaluable. We could discover the rumors, denials, and jokes that were based on the rumor, as well as deliberate hoaxes. In many ways, the presence of electronic communication has changed the ability to examine rumors, providing easy access to wild claims. We were archeologists who found excavation sites at our office desks.

With regard to the rumors about immigrants, Bill Ellis worked at a small campus in Hazleton, Pennsylvania, during an especially intense panic caused by the alleged threat of undocumented workers. His quarter century of experience in the area familiarized him with the rumors that had already become entrenched in this working-class Rust Belt community (see chapter 4). In addition, he attended a church that was located only one street away from the epicenter of the rumors. Ellis gathered rumors as they emerged, from fellow church members, from area acquaintances, and from the students in what was quickly becoming an ethnically diverse campus, giving this local account a particularly rich texture.

We found other accounts, such as rumors about the adventures of tourists, from discussions with friends and students as well as through systematic review of newspapers, a task made much easier because of Web sites that collect news articles, such as search engines like LexisNexis and Google. Whenever possible, we looked for a wide range of variations rather than taking a single text as definitive. Remembering that rumor can serve as a verb, not only a noun, we were interested in the process of fact finding that such material represented, not their literal truth. Even if the media do not collect rumor with the detail or the context of the social scientist, these published or broadcast accounts served admirably as an indicator of public interest. By publishing these rumors, even while debunking them, the media documented their currency and often provided important context that showed what factors gave them credibility. No source is sufficient by itself, but taken together, they present a reasonably accurate picture of the rumors in circulation. We cannot provide a "census" or a random sample of rumors, but we hope that available evidence, coupled with a careful and cautious analysis of what these rumors mean, permits a greater appreciation of how rumor matters in our interconnected world.

The Plan of the Book

First, a note about language—and perspective. Writing to a wide audience poses challenges that writing to a small group of academic specialists lacks. In making this case, we try never to forget the diversity of Americans and their perspectives, as well as those of other Western citizens. There is no one set of beliefs that everyone holds—or should hold. But the use of pronouns like "we" and "you" can imply political and social boundaries, even as they also assert community. For this reason, while the authors call themselves "we" and write for an imagined "you," we also try to balance a shared recognition and a common concern with an understanding that readers in a healthy democracy come from many backgrounds and have many divergent political opinions. So for ease of reading we speak to an imagined "you," an audience that is conventionally middle class and perhaps even somewhat prone to naïve or stereotypical thinking. This is no more than a useful and temporary conceit, one that provides a starting point and impetus for our discussions. We no more believe that all of "you" think the same way, just as the authors know that "we" do not always agree on all points of our interpretations. For this reason, we have taken care at various points to emphasize the wide scope of opinion and the broad spectrum of what readers might reasonably accept as plausible. Overall, we keep in mind that "Americans" are men and women from many backgrounds, with various experiences, who embrace widely different claims about the world.

The first chapter, "Rumor and September 11: Understanding the Unthinkable," analyzes how the rumors that emerged in the immediate aftermath of the attacks helped to shape the American reaction to those global threats. These rumors channeled how Americans interpreted their changed world and provided a window into American fears, pride, and fantasies. As we describe, they illuminate American identity, its centrality, and its diversity. The main strands of rumor provide a wedge by which we can better understand attitudes toward terrorism. We speak of rumor as a form of focused attention, a means by which people in confusion and dismay search for meaning. A compelling need exists to process the events that had so forcefully impressed themselves, and dozens—if not hundreds—of rumors emerged during this period. The fact that these communications among diverse individuals focused on the same set of events provides an opportunity to discover what themes Americans considered plausible as they surveyed a shattered world order. We focus on two particularly dramatic examples to demonstrate how rumor addresses terrorism. One claims that Arab Americans publicly celebrated after the Twin Towers collapsed, and the second asserts that a terrorist warned a girlfriend or a benevolent citizen of danger, showing gratitude even during this most desperate time. These stories undercut the moral legitimacy of those who were assumed to have sympathy with the deadly act, but also revealed that the terrorist was not so different from others. In the second chapter, "A Riot of Conspiracies," we return to rumors about violent, terrorist attacks, but broaden the discussion to include rumors about conspiracies. Terrorism has a lengthy, if not distinguished, history, and rumors that deal with national attacks are not recent. In examining conspiracy rumors, we discover that groups create rumors to address their own wishes and fears. Some believe that the Arab community in America was responsible for the attacks, others name the Israelis, and still others name the American government. Each group uses information that they consider to be plausible—sometimes accurate, sometimes not—and organizes these facts to support what they wish—or need— to believe. Conspiracy theories, whether for terrorism, warfare, or politics, often gain an enthusiastic audience. Chapters 3 and 4, "Migrants: Disease in the Body Politic" and "'There Goes the Neighborhood': Latino Migrants and Immigration Rumors," change topic, addressing what rumors tell us about American attitudes toward immigration. Chapter 3 provides a historical account of the dilemma that the American nation is of several minds about immigration. Although Americans are rhetorically open to "huddled masses, yearning to breathe free," we have long worried about the effects of widespread immigration. Immigration and its surrounding fears have consistently featured in American political discourse, even during the colonial period. Rumor relates to threats to the body politics, often using the metaphor of disease. Chapter 4, using the case of Hazleton, Pennsylvania, brings this debate up to the present, describing the heated deliberations on contemporary immigrants, largely, although not exclusively, from Latin America. When a nation must incorporate strangers—others who are perceived as fundamentally different in attitudes, culture, values, or religion—native citizens are likely to assume, or fantasize, what these groups might plausibly do and whether governments and businesses may undercut popular will for their own interests.

Chapter 5, "Tourist Troubles: The Travels of Global Rumor," addresses the desire of American travelers to visit distant lands, and how rumors reveal our mixed feelings about the exotic. These travels remove people from their tight, comfortable cocoon, forcing them to interact with others who they would not meet during their mundane routines. This strangeness leads tellers and audiences to accept accounts of events that might otherwise seem highly implausible and in the process draw boundaries among nations. Yet, in contrast to issues of terrorism, migration, and trade, tourism typically has less dire consequences, and many of these stories contain as much humor as fear. The line between a joke and a warning is not always clear, but like rumor, jokes reveal popular attitudes. To some extent, these narratives satirize fellow citizens who are bumbling and naïve, even while others, such as those pointing to acquiring AIDS through a romantic interlude, are deadly in their implications. In chapter 6, "The Menace of International Trade," we address how rumors about dangers from foreign products reveal economic anxieties. These products can be either natural—fruits and plants—or manufactured. Produce may hide deadly stowaways like insects or reptiles. Other stories focus on manufactured products. Whether through incompetence or malice, foreign workers produce harmful or disgusting products. The foreign brewery workers who urinate in the vats of beer to be exported to the United States are one dramatic example of the set of rumors that we address in greater detail. Given American attempts to police our borders, how do such products reach our cities so easily? Although we grant trust to our fellow citizens, the same does not apply to workers from overseas. We plausibly imagine that these workers look with envy and bitterness at the power and wealth of the American economy and may wish to wreak revenge through mercantile sabotage. Chapter 7, "Global Trafficking in Bodies," extends our focus beyond our shores to examine the impact of rumors that suggest that organs or bodies are being harvested in third-world nations, often by Americans or their agents. In some instances, these rumors recount middle-class Americans discovering their kidneys stolen, and in others, westerners pilfer the organs of impoverished children. While some of these rumors are told within the United States, others are used to contain or contest American influence. With the growth of organ transplantation as a legitimate and even essential medical operation, many find it plausible that those with power, wealth, and opportunity will kidnap and murder for their personal benefit. The stories are spread within the context of American political and economic dominance. These stories—horrible and frightening—warn about the need for global justice. Rumor can serve as what James Scott refers to as a "weapon of the weak."[14]

In the conclusion, "Whispers on the Borderline," we highlight the implications of how global rumors might be interpreted. One cannot wish uncomfortable stories away; they must be confronted. Rumors reveal how people see their world. To enforce a discourse of surface tolerance serves to submerge such beliefs; private conversations are never confronted and true tolerance is harder to achieve. Suppression makes prejudice harder to be challenged. We must bring these claims to the surface in order to discuss the underlying concerns that justify them.

We stand at a moment where the idea of "fortress America" is implausible. The United States is part of a global system, and we must embrace this undeniable reality while protecting ourselves from the challenges of political violence, fully open borders, and unbalanced trade. If free speech, migration, and extensive trade are valuable, most see the need for some limits. Rumor points to the public understanding of these limits. Ultimately, rumor alerts us to the pitfalls of the future, the challenges of the present, and the failures of the past.

1

Rumor and September 11

Understanding the Unthinkable

It is 8:48 A.M. on September 11, 2001, and the world is about to change forever. Whatever Americans may be expecting from this cloudless, sunny day, they are surely not prepared for the terror, anguish, and horror as American Airlines flight 11 slams into the north tower of the World Trade Center in lower Manhattan. This crash is followed shortly by a second jetliner, United Airlines flight 175, hitting the south tower. These assaults kill nearly 3,000 passengers, workers, rescuers, and bystanders. The attack on the Pentagon and the crash of United flight 93 in rural Shanksville, Pennsylvania, add to the death toll. Amidst the confusion and chaos, anger and tears, rumor blooms.

The shattering destruction of the World Trade Center and the Pentagon was the most traumatic event in American life over the past half century, dwarfing the murders of President John F. Kennedy and the Reverend Martin Luther King Jr. Not since Pearl Harbor had our homeland been assaulted. New York City residents stood transfixed as they watched their imposing skyline crumble; other Americans stared at television screens that repeated the images in a hypnotic loop. In a matter of hours, an event that would have seemed preposterous was now an insistent reality and defied understanding.

Terror leaves its victims with a powerful desire to comprehend their broken world. We question beliefs once taken for granted. We worry that changes are so rapid that we cannot cope; our core beliefs are in flux.[1] Terrorist groups recognize this vulnerability, of course; their acts are aimed to provoke this mental dislocation. Since the destruction of trust is the intent of terrorism, everything taken for granted in society—public spaces, transportation, even food and water—becomes a potential terrorist target and therefore a possible source of peril to the community under attack.

By the evening of September 11, many Americans feared that another terrorist attack might occur in the days and weeks ahead. The subsequent discovery of anthrax being sent through the mail furthered this belief, creating even more fertile conditions for rumor to grow and spread. The terrorist attacks on September 11 were a textbook case of the "power of the deed," shaking public confidence and undermining the routine bonds of trust that cement individuals to each other and help us to accept life as routine.

The core of any rumor is a proposition for belief: an assertion about how the world is (or was) or how it will soon be. It is, in the phrase of social scientists, a "truth claim." But we hear many truth claims and not all of them are rumor. Rumor specifically refers to those claims that are not backed by authoritative information. That is, these claims are spread outside "official" sources of information. Those who have the authority to know—governments, for example, or those who participated in or planned the events themselves—do not communicate rumor, because their information is based on official knowledge. In this sense, Osama bin Laden and George W. Bush are brothers: what they claim about September 11 is not rumor. These men are in a position to know, so their statements come to their followers' attention as immediately credible.

This is not to say that authoritative information is always true: Osama bin Laden, George W. Bush, and the subordinates from whom they obtain information are fallible and sometimes manipulative, and they are as prone to believe and spread unsecured truth claims. Bin Ladin, like many Islamic extremists, may have heard, believed, and acted on conspiracy theories about a dangerous Jewish cabal that allegedly controls world politics. President Bush may have based his decision to invade Iraq on a mélange of Middle Eastern gossip and innuendo, channeled selectively to him by a tightly knit conduit of neoconservative staffers committed to the rightness of the cause. The ensuing fiasco has produced a series of "tell-all" exposés of the back-corridor discussions that led to the decision to declare war; these made it clear that the tight clusters of co-workers in the Bush administration certainly relied on rumor to make sense of the September 11 attacks and their motives, much as did other Americans. The point is that when such information was accepted by the administration and was presented to the media by official spokespeople such as General Colin Powell and Vice President Richard Cheney, it was no longer rumor. It may have included lies and "disinformation" or it may have been sincerely mistaken, but it was not rumor because it was presented and circulated in the media as authoritative information.

Communities, however, often do not have such authoritative knowledge, and when disaster strikes, whether natural or man-made, members of the public search for information on their own, a process that, following psychologists Gordon Allport and Leo Postman, scholars describe as "effort after meaning." Rumors that come to prominence during times of disaster allow researchers to understand the collective beliefs of a community. Sometimes these claims are false or even malicious, but rumors can also be partially or entirely true. We need to recognize that, just as authoritative information can be false, informally circulated information can be accurate. Although we cannot easily measure the amplitude or velocity of how rumors spread after the September 11 attacks, journalistic reports indicate that the tally of rumors in the aftermath of September 11 was as great as in the aftermath of any disaster.

Rumors circulated that groups of Arab Americans publicly celebrated the attacks; an Islamist terrorist warned his non-Arab girlfriend to stay away from the Twin Towers on September 11; Arabic taxi drivers disappeared from the streets of lower Manhattan; workers were miraculously saved; and politicians knew all along. Predictions of specific days when another attack would occur (July 4, Halloween, the Friday after Thanksgiving) were rife, usually with some symbolism attached to the date. These and other rumors surfaced as people tried to make sense of the disaster. After the anthrax letters were sent, rumors warned of poisonings, including Coca-Cola, toxic samples of perfume or lotion, deadly sponges, or diapers. Others revealed that U-Haul trucks, UPS driver uniforms, or Costco candy had been stolen, all for nefarious purposes. The routine items in our lives had become frightening.

After the attacks, Americans questioned how to live in a world where desperate and determined others wanted to destroy them. This new sense of fear and uncertainty caused people to examine how to understand this enemy, and rumors about the terrorists flourished. Whether true or false, their influence on society was profound. Immediately after the attacks, Arab Americans fell under scrutiny and attack as people heard rumors and vented their anger and fear. At the same time, it would be wrong to assume that the presence of a rumor suggests firm belief in its content. Many claims are held provisionally by both tellers and listeners, and this is particularly true in the case of assertions about what might happen next. A claim that a second terrorist attack may take place on a future date cannot be disproved authoritatively until the date actually passes, so such claims fall into a liminal category: neither true nor false.

In the hours after the bombing of the Alfred P. Murrah Federal Building in Oklahoma City by Timothy McVeigh on April 19, 1995, rumors spread wildly that the bombers were Arab or Muslim. No facts were presented, but the claim made compelling sense, particularly in light of the earlier bombing of the World Trade Center in 1993. The attack fit a *template*,[2] a category of belief explanations. In time, most Americans became persuaded that the Oklahoma City attack was homegrown and created a new template, where the bombing surfaced from a desire for revenge among the Far Right for the FBI attack on the Waco, Texas, compound of the Branch Davidians in 1993 and the earlier FBI killing of right-wing survivalists in Ruby Ridge, Idaho. Once story lines become set and the past and present converge, new rumors become plausible.

Rumor and the Politics of Plausibiity and Credibility

Trust is essential to belief, but who, what, where, when, and how do we trust? To determine our response to claims made by others, we judge those who communicate and what they communicate. As an everyday practice, we engage in the *politics of credibility* and the *politics of plausibility*. These concepts are tied to public trust within civil society.

Sharing information about important developments draws people together in a communication network. The presence of rumor takes us to the heart of what it means to have a public sphere, a space of common discourse in which the community judges whether claims are to be accepted and whether they deserve a response. Even in authoritarian regimes, such as China or the former Soviet Union, as long as people were allowed to gather they could and did spread rumor without end.[3] It is not only democratic regimes that have had a vibrant rumor culture. As citizens in authoritarian states were just asking about what had happened, they had at least some protection from claims that they were subverting the state. When individual perception of what is "true" becomes the topic of conversation, the group explores, tests, and refines their conclusions about the social world around them. As Bill Ellis has argued, the performance of these claims involves "the communal exploration of social boundaries."[4]

In short, rumor is built around a political impulse, sometimes explicit in its content, which warns about an emerging menace. More often, though, the act of transmission implicitly is a political act: striving for knowledge that citizens feel they have a right to know, and challenging how local institutions handle their affairs. Even when not specifically about politics, rumor involves the *power* of knowledge and the *authority* of the speaker, and thus we speak of the politics of plausibility and credibility. Rumor claims whom and what should be trusted, allowing strategies of action to be formulated. Plausibility and credibility are distinct concepts, in that *claims* can be more or less plausible, deserving trust, while *persons* are judged to be more or less credible or trustworthy.

Both plausibility and credibility are situated within the politics of everyday life. Even if rumor seems an individual matter of diffusion and response, these judgments are tied to relations and trust integral to the organization of a social system. Rumors may be plausible but not credible: we may say we doubt the speaker, but it is just the sort of thing that we could believe *might* happen given the people and situations described. Or rumors could be credible but not plausible: they could come from a source that we normally trust, but which contain details that we suspect or know are not so. But if a rumor is to flourish in public discourse and become a part of our collective memory, it needs to be *both* credible *and* plausible.

God and Satan: Rumors of Hope and Evil

We begin our discussion of the aftermath of September 11 with two rumors—both magical—that appeared shortly after the attacks: "The Building Surfer" and "Satan in the Smoke." One reflects on the possibility of hope, the other on the presence of evil. These rumors, odd as they might seem to skeptical readers, reveal the politics of plausibility and the politics of credibility. After such barbarous attacks, anything seemed possible.

Surprisingly, given the trauma of September 11, some of the first rumors to solidify were those that expressed hope. Perhaps even on such a dark and fateful day, God was at work. Shortly after the smoke cleared, one of the earliest rumors was of a man trapped in the falling tower, who slid down the edge of the collapsing building to his safety, cheating death. This is a powerful wish-fulfillment rumor—a type of rumor that permits us to believe that our dreams might come to pass—with one of our heroes able to survive in seemingly impossible circumstances. Is the claim plausible? At the moment it was, and would remain so for those who saw God's hand at work. The story of "The Building Surfer" spread widely in the days and weeks after the attack. Sometimes the man who survived was described as a fireman, other times just an everyman caught up in the tragedy. The specific method by which the survivor used a piece of debris as a ski varied from story to story, but it was important to explain how the escape took place so that the details would bolster the story. The floor from which the escape took place differed according to the memory of the narrator; sometimes it was designated as the 71st floor, or sometimes the 82nd or the 92nd floor,[5] but every narrator named a specific floor. It is verifiably true—and often emphasized—that a Port Authority police officer, Sgt. John McLoughlin, was in fact pulled from the rubble of the Twin Towers the day after the collapse, and that his survival was reported at the time as a near miracle. "It's wonderful," a rescue worker told a *New York Times* reporter, adding, "None of us can imagine how he survived." Another said that the officer had been on the 82nd floor of the South Tower when it fell, although later investigation showed that he had in fact been on the ground floor.[6] McLoughlin's story was so inspirational that filmmaker Oliver Stone made his character (portrayed by Nicholas Cage) the focus of his 2006 movie *World Trade Center*.

Although McLoughlin and a handful of others experienced "miraculous" and sometimes inexplicable survivals, typically from lower floors, "The Building Surfer" claim reflects public wishes rather than definitive fact, even while the wish was based on a set of "facts," providing the plausibility structure for which listeners searched. Such a rumor was spread by the public on its "best behavior," suggesting that survival was possible, even in the most trying circumstances.

A second early rumor also reflected the titanic battle between hope and fear. If the destruction was set in motion by forces of evil, who but Satan should be held responsible? Some of a religious mindset suggested the attacks had been masterminded by the devil himself, and it was "proven" that Satan's visage could be seen in photographs of the smoke and fire of the burning towers. For these believers, the devil was an active presence in human affairs and this claim was plausible. Several photographs were circulated on the Internet as proof. The image shown here, taken by Mark

Phillips, a freelance photographer who had been working with the Associated Press for many years, was especially memorable. The fact that Phillips was a professional photographer with a good reputation—affording credibility—legitimated the image in the minds of many. Attempting to maintain his credibility from those who would attack him, Phillips vehemently denies having altered the photograph in any way,[7] and he subsequently received e-mails from people who found that it validated religious beliefs they held deeply. A correspondent in Hoosick, New York, responded:

"Satan in the Smoke" © Mark D. Phillips/markdphillips.com

Your photo of the World Trade Center burning with the image of the Devil is truly amazing. Thank you for sharing it with the rest of the World. Frightening as it is, the Devil apparently likes to take the credit for anything that happens evil in our World. He uses others to do his deeds and enjoys basting [basking?] in the credit of its outcome. It will make those of us who do believe in God that much stronger and united against the Devil and his associates. May God bless our America and may it always be the Land of the Free no matter what others will do to discourage it. Thank you for sharing this photo with us.[8]

Phillips's image fits in with a tradition of "miraculous photography," which has a long history in American folklore.[9] Additional e-mails received by Phillips after the photo was published show that such groups took the photograph quite literally as a message from the other world, a view that depended on previous strongly held beliefs. "For the last several years I have taken numerous pictures in the sky which have revealed many saintly images as well as many beastly images," one correspondent told Phillips, concluding, "I belive [sic] God unveils these spiritual images to us for the many that need signs that Heaven and Hell exist as well as there in [is?] a great spiritual battle going on for souls."[10] Others claimed to see other divine beings and symbols. "Just above the face of evil," another e-mail said, "I clearly see a cherub with wings unfurled holding our National Symbol, the bald eagle. It may appear to some that the cherub is releasing the eagle. No matter how that is seen, the image clearly shows Light overcomes Evil."[11] Soon the photograph was actively circulated in a religious context, bolstering the image with a priest or minister's blessed credibility. An e-mail to the photographer said, "It was at last Sunday's mass in church that I learned of the photograph you took. Our priest mentioned it in his homily and then showed us the photograph as we were exiting church." The terrorist attack, the correspondent added, "is truly the work of the devil and your photograph confirms it. God Bless you."[12] Rumors that depended on plausibility and credibility had come full circle to confirm the beliefs.

While many people saw the image as no more than a coincidental trick of lighting, the face of Satan against the doomed Twin Towers provided, as John Groch observed, "an apt metaphor for various interpretations of September 11th, both those that were offered in the heat of the moment and those that emerged later." Evangelicals could use the image to blame the attacks on secularists, feminists, and homosexuals; right-wing commentators could castigate liberal politicians, while left-wing commentators, relying on the metaphor in the smoke, like filmmaker Michael Moore, could blame the failings of President Bush.[13] We return to these attempts to understand the causes of September 11 in discussing conspiracy theories.

Rumor and Crisis

The study of rumor helps us understand that thinking is always socially influenced, a key claim of what is called "cognitive sociology." What we think is neither universal nor idiosyncratic, but is tied to what others in our community think. We think in line with what we have been taught by those around us.[14] In addition, thought operates through *social mnemonics*, techniques by which we remember what our group believes to be important.[15] So when we consider rumors, we instinctively use our sense of how the world works and use the touchstones we're comfortable with to decide that one rumor is believable while another is ridiculous, even if the factual bases of both are equally dubious. For example, the belief, as we shall discuss, that groups of Arab Americans celebrated the attacks seemed reasonable to many Americans, but to those in the Arab American community, the belief was both offensive and impossible to credit.

As rumor scholars, our purpose is not to describe the details of the attacks. We do not question the widely shared chronology of that dark day, although we note that it is possible, as doubters Thierry Meyssan or Webster Tarpley,[16] among many others in the so-called 9/11 Truth Movement, have done, to construct an alternative history and to treat the official truth claims of the U.S. government as doubtful and grounded in organizational self-interest. In contrast, we explore the process by which, through identification, narrators and audiences define some truth claims as worth communicating. What we define as being worthy of sharing then, in turn, affects what actions we are likely to accept in response, shaping public attitudes and even state policy. As noted before, those who determine such policies may pass on unsecured information to the public to prime them for a preferred response.

After September 11, two widely spread rumors and their variations (known as rumor complexes) circulated. Because of the fact that they were widespread and seemed plausible to many, both rumors revealed how society tried to understand the terrorist attacks. Because of their promi-nence and the key ways they revealed how Americans attempted to under-stand the attacks, we use these cases as the central examples of the chapter (we discuss conspiracy rumors related to September 11 in chapter 2).

The first involves the claim that on September 11, groups of Arab Americans publicly celebrated the attacks. Substantial evidence exists that some Arabs in East Jerusalem welcomed the destruction, and this was caught on film by Reuters and broadcast on CNN, although there was a (false) rumor spread by a Brazilian student that the footage was originally from the 1991 Gulf War.[17] However, the rumor that we examine involves actions within the United States by American citizens or residents.

The second rumor is the widely spread story that an Islamic terrorist warned his American (i.e., non-Arab) girlfriend (or some other woman who had done him a kindness, such as providing change in a store[18]) to stay away from the Twin Towers on September 11 and then to avoid some other public space, such as the mall on Halloween,[19] in order to save her from ter-rorist attack.

"The Celebrating Arabs"

Within hours after the attacks on the World Trade Center, rumors began to circulate across the United States about Arab Americans "dancing in the streets," celebrating the destruction.[20] Rumors claimed that such merriment occurred in cities and towns in Maine, Massachusetts, New York, New Jersey, Pennsylvania, Florida, Michigan, and California. When taken together, this suggests a widespread celebration. These rumors were first shared on talk-radio as callers reported celebrations they claimed to have witnessed; in short order the claims spread to the Internet, and soon were discussed on television and in local newspapers and general interest maga-zines.[21] A year later the stories were still reported on national television, and were widely known on college campuses.[22]

Some evidence suggests that a few Arab American adolescents briefly relieved their political frustrations in front of a library in largely Arab South Paterson, New Jersey, in a way that some might have defined as celebrating. As a result, it is possible to claim that the story is true as reported (some "Arabs" were "celebrating" in "the streets of America"), but false in light of how the statement was generally interpreted, suggesting widespread joy. There were no organized demonstrations, but perhaps only a handful of adolescents briefly yelling. Even if the story was "true," those spreading it did so in the absence of secure evidence.[23] If a few teens were momentarily boisterous, this does not quite constitute "Arabs celebrating in the streets of America." No evidence demonstrates an organized or sustained jubilation because of the terrorist attacks.[24] When the stories were specific enough to be checked by journalists, they could not be verified. Consider three representative cases:

ORCHARD LAKE, Mich.—At lunchtime at the Sheik, a big Middle Eastern restaurant, American flags hang in the windows and around the dining room. "I love America," says the owner, Dean Hachem, who arrived here from Lebanon 24 years ago and became a U.S. citizen in 1985.... Half a year ago, the Sheik would have been humming at this time of day.... But on a recent Wednesday, the place was silent. Just three of the 40 tables were occupied. "That e-mail destroyed my life," says Mr. Hachem. The e-mail in question was written on Sept. 11. It told the story of a nurse at Henry Ford Hospital who came for lunch at the Sheik that day and saw Arabs who worked in the restaurant "cheering as they watched TV footage of our American tragedy."... It ended: "Do not patronize this restaurant and please pass the word to everyone you know!" The e-mail quickly spread to thousands of homes in Detroit suburbs. A stunned Mr. Hachem denied that the incident occurred and invited people to see his security tapes.... No one could be seen celebrating.[25]

Threats against Dunkin' Donuts employees who were rumored to have celebrated Tuesday's attacks led to a decision to close the Cedar Grove [New Jersey] store temporarily, a store spokesman said. Police later said a store video proved there was no truth to the rumor, which they said provoked threats against the employees— one Asian Indian and two Americans.[26]

As Central Floridians crawled through morning traffic Thursday, a talk-radio host told his listeners that Muslims at "the mosque on Goldenrod" were celebrating Tuesday's terrorist attacks on America. A talk-show caller related the tale of a melee at the University of Central Florida prompted by rejoicing Arab Americans. Neither incident occurred. There were no celebrations. And there was no fight.[27]

Because of the potential threats of violence and retribution, the press and local officials frequently made intense efforts to squelch such rumors. In spite of their denials, and though the rumors seemed implausible and bigoted to some, they persisted because, to others, the idea of a joyous festivity made sense. Even if there were no overt cheering, might the rumor be true in a lesser sense? Might not smiling, nodding, or an ambiguous comment constitute a celebration? Might disloyal Arabs in this country show no visible reaction, and yet be silently, secretly joyful inside themselves?

"The Grateful Terrorist"

A second rumor complex painted a somewhat more benign vision. In one form of this rumor, as much about gender politics as about terrorism,[28] a young woman was warned by her boyfriend, a man of Arab (or Afghan) ethnicity, that she should avoid a location on a particular date. Often the rumor announced a pair of warnings—the first was to avoid flying on September 11 and the second to avoid malls on a later date, such as Halloween. As a result of the latter warning, the story was sometimes labeled "Mall-O-Ween." When the rumor included a pair of warnings, the telling was situated between the two, with the first attack justifying the foreshadowing of the second. As the rumor became solidified, often the depicted woman was not a girlfriend, but simply a woman who had helped or acted kindly,[29] a change that increases the opportunity for identification.

Occasionally the rumor was retrospective, focusing on the September 11 warning, and sometimes it was prospective, giving the warning for a date and time in the near future, such as Halloween; often it was equally weighted. Unlike the rumor "The Celebrating Arabs," this rumor lacked even a shred of factual basis. The Federal Bureau of Investigation claimed that the story was not credible;[30] the fact that they responded suggested its wide diffusion. Consider two examples:

> My friend Colleen arrived for a facial when FBI agents were leaving Murad on Sunday, October 7, 2001. They were there to interrogate a girl who worked there to find out if she knew anything. The reason for their lead was she was best-friends with a girl who was dating an Arab man, who disappeared and was involved in the terrorist attacks on the WTC. He disappeared this summer and left her a note, saying the following in the effect of: "I have to go away

and will not be able to see you again. Please do me a favor and do not fly in any planes on September 11, 2001 nor shop at any shopping malls on October 31, 2001."[31]

My friend's friend was dating a guy from Afghanistan up until a month ago. She had a date with him around 9/6 and was stood up. She was understandably upset and went to his home to find it completely emptied. On 9/10, she received a letter from her boyfriend explaining that he wished he could tell her why he had left and that he was sorry it had to be like that. The part worth mentioning is that he BEGGED her not to get on any commercial airlines on 9/11 and not to go to any malls on Halloween. As soon as everything happened on the 11th, she called the FBI and has since turned over the letter.[32]

The rumor was taken seriously by public authorities, who vigorously denied it, and the story soon vanished. The shopping mall legend was intense but relatively short-lived: Bill Ellis's survey of message boards showed that its circulation was most intense during the two days of October 9 and 10, after which it vanished from discussion quickly, chased by official debunkings from the FBI and other law enforcement and media sources.[33] More significantly, it seems to have developed few distinct variants, indicating that its circulation was primarily through the Internet.

Along with the presentation of a terrorist who is grateful to a lover, folklorist Diane Goldstein[34] suggests that a central theme of this story was guilt for having foreknowledge of the coming tragedy and not passing on the warning. In some odd sense, the terrorist acts ethically—it is the woman who fails her community. In this sense, the story is about the need for all citizens to help their community in fighting terrorism whenever they receive information. This theme is stated explicitly in the coda of the Internet legend, where the supposed initiator of the thread says that the motive for e-mailing the story was that "with one of his warnings being correct and devastating, I'm not willing to take the chance on the second and wanted to make sure that people I cared about had the same information that I did."

However, most crucial is the legend's depiction of the mind of a terrorist and the implicit trust that exists between lovers. This story humanizes the terrorist, making him more like us and allowing us to engage in sympathetic role taking.[35] We see that on occasion political motives can be overcome by concern or affection: if we were planning a terrorist attack, we might warn those about whom we care deeply. We might be a person who hates society but still loves individuals. This theme is also central in another "grateful terrorist" legend that proved far more widespread and durable. It concerns a person—typically a woman—who encounters a Muslim in a public place and performs a small act of kindness. In some versions, the good neighbor gives this man a small sum to make up for a shortage of change in a store or fast-food restaurant; in others, she returns his wallet. In return, the man who was helped hints about the timing or location of the next terrorist attack.

Recycling Rumor

Although the attacks on September 11 are unique events, drawing out new rumor forms, in fact, rumors are often recycled. People rely on those narrative templates that have proved to be plausible and durable in the past. Rumors appear, are spread, and then disappear—ignored—until similar circumstances make the stories appropriate once again. And, indeed, the rumor of "The Grateful Terrorist" was a recycled tale. The legend type predates September 11, as it circulated in Great Britain at least a year and a half earlier, focusing on the Irish Republican Army. This rumor reproduction suggests our crisis may not be as unusual as it first appeared. One version reports:

> A director of her husband's firm's wife's friend was in McDonald's in the Trafford Centre (large new shopping mall in Manchester). A man with an Irish accent behind her in the queue rather threateningly asked her for a pound coin. She complied, to get rid of him. He got his food, and afterwards said, "You did me a good turn, so I'll do you one. Don't come here during March." She went to the police, who showed her a book of photos of known IRA operatives. On the second page was the man she'd seen in McDonald's.[36]

The story, updated to make the mysterious person Arab or Middle Eastern, re-emerged at the end of September in the industrial Midlands region of Great Britain. A common version read:

> This person was at a supermarket check out in Stafford 3 weeks ago [i.e., September 3, 2001]. In front of her was a man, who when

he took his items to the till, was 7p short. The cashier told the man to put an item back, this person then stepped in and gave the man a 10p to make up the difference. When the person made their way outside the man was waiting to say thanks. He made a big issue out of the gesture, saying people don't help each other any more, and he wanted to do something to say thank the person. All he said was: Stay out of Birmingham in 6 weeks.[37]

As before, the legend ends with the grateful man later being identified as a terrorist from a police book of mug shots. Barbara Mikkelson observed that other versions referred to a variety of British towns, including Coventry, Tamworth, Milton Keynes, and Chester.[38] The site also varied widely, ranging from Harrods to a cheap goods store, from a petrol station to the local McDonald's. Over time, however, the commonly found version focused on London, typical in that rumors often target large companies and/or large cities, making the tale more relevant or compelling for its audience.

My friend's girlfriend's friend was walking in Hyde Park. She noticed a man of Middle Eastern appearance getting up from a seat and walking away. As he got up he dropped his wallet. She picked up the wallet and ran after him and returned it to him. The man turned and thanked her, he then said "Thank you for doing this good deed. One good deed deserves another, stay out of London on Thursday." He walked away.[39]

As these British examples show, the legend shows wide variation, indicating multiple reworkings in oral circulation and private e-mails. Constant in all, however, is the moment in which the other reveals his human motives for passing on the warning: recognition that the small favor puts him in debt to the Good Samaritan. The small kindness received exhibits that the two were, after all, neighbors, so the terrorist could no longer withhold his foreknowledge of the coming attack.

As variations of this rumor spread to the United States in 2002, the warning became attached to Coca-Cola products, but the core narrative continued to vary widely, indicating continuing oral circulation. Rumors that are spread in written form typically have more stability in that future communicators or audiences can refer to these core, stable texts, sometimes passing them on directly. When a rumor is spread by word of mouth, narrators must attempt to remember the story and may shape it to appeal to their audiences. These features will introduce variation into stories that are primarily oral. Thus, rumors that reveal considerable variation are typically those that are spread face to face, even if the accounts may also be spread on Internet chat rooms or Web sites. However, despite the variations, the motive for the terrorist's gratefulness remained central to the narrative, and even was elaborated. A text set near Lumberton, North Carolina, read:

> A coworker of mine told us that her stepmom was at the grocery store in line behind an Arab man. He was short $.75 on his grocery so the stepmom gave him the money. He replied "Why did you give me this? All Americans are pigs." Anyway she just ignored the comment but when she left out of the grocery store he was waiting for her in the parking lot. He came up to her and again asked her why did she give him the money. She stated that she would have done it for anyone. He replied, "I cannot repay you but I will tell you this: do not drink any Coca-Cola products after July 3rd." This is very scary, so please be very careful. After 9/11 we can't take anything for granted.[40]

Here the motif of mutual humanity is expanded: the terrorist initially sees Americans as inhuman. The American, however, embraces the man's humanity, saying that she would have done the same for anyone, regardless of ethnicity. The terrorist, surprised by the Samaritan's act of charity, can no longer place her at risk. This story conveys that charitable behavior, even against people one has been encouraged to distrust, is the proper defense against hate. The fact that the story is set in a small community like Lumberton, North Carolina, reminds us that terrorists may be all over and that moral kindness can be widespread as well. The link to September 11 is explicit in a number of texts:

> When she [the Samaritan] was in the parking lot loading her groceries into her car, this same [Middle Eastern] man came over to her and said, "I just want to thank you for what you did in there, it was very generous of you. Since September 11th, people have not been very nice to people like me. I want to tell you something, because I think you are a good person and I don't want you to get hurt...after July 11 do not drink any Coca-Cola products."[41]

After paying for her groceries she [the Samaritan] left the store. While walking toward her car the man came back up to her and her daughter. He told her that this was the nicest thing anyone had done for him since September 11th. He said that he mostly got the cold shoulder and rudeness from people and that he was so touched by what she had done. He thanked her again and said that because she had done such a nice thing for him he felt he needed to do a nice thing for her and her family. He then said, "Don't drink any Coca Cola products after September 2002" and he walked away without another word.[42]

These texts humanize the man who is the object of the Samaritan's charity, despite his knowledge of a horrific attack. They depict him as the victim of prejudice because of the widespread lack of trust felt toward Middle Easterners in the wake of September 11. Yet, this lack of trust is apparently justified, as this Arab shares knowledge of a plot to harm Americans by tampering with a widely consumed commercial product. Hence the two elements, foreknowledge and mutual trust, are inextricably related, as seen in the short coda that is typical of many comments added by those who passed on the narrative out of neighborly concern.

"What Kind of Person Could've Done This?": The Role of Rumor in Understanding the Terrorist

When challenged to understand how the September 11 terrorists could have justified the attacks, many Americans are perplexed. Terrorism—and those who engage in such action—seems mindless. These actions are bewildering within the pragmatist confines of American political culture. Yet, it is not accurate to suggest that terrorists—in this case Islamic radicals—are mindless; indeed, they may have "too much" mindfulness, placing their political goals and ideology before mundane social life, treating their ideals as more important than the lives of others. Yet, from the American perspective, the acts themselves, requiring killing for ideology or belief, become literally senseless. The ideology of terrorism—the demand to have society change in ways they desire—is so alien to how Americans prefer to think of themselves that understanding these forceful and committed men, holding such seemingly un-American values, proves a challenge. As a result, Americans are often open to all kinds of strange explanations to make plausible sense of these crazy actions; their critical ability to judge rumor is significantly

lowered. It is difficult for many Americans to imagine themselves as terrorists, but we continually try, because that role-playing is the only way that we
can give meaning to these acts. The willingness to believe and to spread
rumor is based on the ability to take on the role of another. In times of strain,
such an attempt is crucial in that if we can understand those whose actions
impact our lives, we are more likely to predict what will happen.

The problem of interpretation bears on the apparent tension between
explaining something and understanding it. On the one hand, faced with a
cataclysmic event like September 11, we wish to *explain* the event, to figure
out *why* it happened. We might proceed as scientists, trying to examine the
event objectively and dispassionately, suggesting that the terrorists' actions
were compelled by their strategies, interests, and goals, shaped by their
upbringing, experiences, and social pressures. The problem becomes that in
explaining the event in this way, we avoid ascribing moral responsibility,
but crisis demands a moral interpretation. By treating terrorists as rational,
aimed at achieving some reasoned end, morality is pushed to the side as the
action is explained by different interests than our own. Yet, we cannot forget
that the actions of a few killed thousands of innocent people. To those who
hold the terrorists in contempt, for others to treat the terrorists' actions as
rational—and thoughtfully oriented to achieve some policy—is deeply
offensive, no matter how well it explains what happened.

The two rumors endeavor to avoid the rationality problem by suggesting
that we must come to know the terrorists and their supporters. We must
attempt to provide them with identity, either in moral outrage or in sympathy. The rumor of "The Celebrating Arabs" treats these revelers as less than
fully human, denying them moral standing. We identify them from the outside as so committed to their ideologies that they welcome destruction and
are willing to display these horrific beliefs in public. Their motivation is political without moral concern for individuals. From the perspective of much of
the public, this lack of concern is beastly, and these celebrants were often
described in animalistic terms, denying them decency. Such a view, meeting
hatred with hatred, seemed appropriate, at least in the first days of shock and
fury. Such angry and prejudicial rumors were easy to find in the early days.

In contrast, we can try to understand the terrorist as being like "us"—
marginalizing his ideological fervor. We may identify with our foes, and
perhaps even sympathize with them. Through this lens, they become familiar—perhaps too familiar—and we assume that they will share our motivations. We desire to see the world though the eyes of the terrorist, from the

inside, a challenge in the heated emotions of the time. Could Americans after September 11 identify with the perspective of a person whose acts were detested? Who can embrace *that* point of view after what the terrorist has done? This strategy seems a form of *psychological treason.* This seems to explain, despite the urgency of the "Why" question, the indignant response of many Americans to the very idea of asking such questions about September 11,[43] and audiences sometimes reacted angrily to those who offered explanations, even when the explanations were unsympathetic.[44]

This moral and psychological strategy was impossible as a general practice, but became more feasible when a story—that of "The Grateful Terrorist"—permitted identification. Rumors often have this effect. By describing a "real" event, audiences cannot deny its existence, and they are challenged to fathom those responsible. This form of identification called for role taking, contributing to a more sympathetic—and perhaps more subtle—understanding of human action. The rumor of "The Grateful Terrorist" promoted identification and it permitted a more nuanced and sophisticated attempt to provide answers.

Often rumors are told with moral messages—to accept the reality of the events described suggests that one accepts the lesson of the story. "The Grateful Terrorist" rumor asserts that one of the terrorists acted as we might have if we were in similar circumstances, attempting to mitigate the tragic dimensions of a foreordained event. As described earlier, the story of "The Grateful Terrorist" was not an entirely novel narrative, but is parallel to earlier versions that reflected the paradox of understanding how evil people can perform caring actions, a long-held moral conundrum. The question—the epistemological dilemma, as philosophers would refer to it—is whether we should identify terrorists as people like us or whether they are so different, so perverse, that we can only treat them as beasts. As this pair of rumors suggest, in practice both views have some validity and both attempt to comprehend the inexplicable. Can we identify with a terrorist in his own terms—from the inside—or are we forced to understand him from the outside, denying moral responsibility?

September 11 Rumors and American Identity

Our responses to September 11 in the form of rumor are linked to our political culture and our pragmatic attitudes that insist that beneficial outcomes must trump ideology. With this view that rejects ideological action in the face of consensus and majority rule, we frequently struggle to understand those who would kill "innocent victims" for a cause, forgetting for a moment that governments may engage in similar actions. However, when the deaths are caused by those we define as strangers, operating outside of government authority, many Americans reject admitting that there might be any justice to their cause. In denying the terrorists rationality, we are thrown back on interpreting their actions in light of their identity: a rich source of rumor.

The American credo is that all persons are to be treated as equal. Yet, terrorists challenge this view by refusing to admit that they might be wrong or that majorities should have sway. As a result, in the American mind, terrorists are thought to be like us, only different, and we like them, but dissimilar. We view terrorists by means of the folk psychology by which we judge ourselves: what would we do if we were terrorists? We engage in role taking to understand our environment and to permit us to act effectively.[45] Such a stance helps us explain and helps us predict. Yet, we hit a wall whereby we cannot understand what might compel such killing, except for depravity. We waver between identifying the terrorist as responsible and considering him as debased. This tension is evident in the distinctive themes of the two rumors.

The first rumor complex, "The Celebrating Arabs," alleges that being a terrorist (or terrorist supporter) is an all-encompassing, master status, involving a consistent system of thought. This rumor assumes that one cannot but help at this moment of triumph to display one's political allegiance, positioning many terrorist sympathizers as ready to announce their beliefs. Within the confines of one's community, one expresses deeply held opinions, views that might be strategically hidden or shaded on other occasions, suggesting that attitudes and behavior will be consistent. If we supported Arab terrorist attacks, might we celebrate? Perhaps after such a "success," we too, would dance in the streets, reveling for the moment. And when misfortune comes to some icon of the "axis of evil," does not each one of us quietly smile in *Schadenfreude*? This rumor suggests that one is defined by one's ethnic and political position; if one supports the Palestinian cause, one will support the actions of those who use violence for such purposes. We believe that we can understand people's behaviors by how they stand on a core issue—in this case support for Palestinian statehood. The complexity of Arab American politics is erased, ignoring that Osama bin Laden might not speak for all Arabs. Support for a rock-throwing demonstration or a suicide bombing will *naturally* be translated into support for acts of macroterrorism, even those that occur outside of the battle zone. Connected is the belief that it is impossible to read the beliefs of an Arab American. An outsider to the community cannot uncover the *true* belief of these cryptic ethnic outsiders, and as a result of this puzzle, many Americans find it reasonable to assume that anyone (any Arab or Muslim, at least) can have terrorist sympathies, ready to emerge at the appropriate moment. Terrorist supporters celebrate because they are *that kind of person*, as we imagine that we might be *if we held those beliefs*. We imagine that we would display our beliefs, even if we—as outsiders—find those beliefs offensive.

The second rumor complex forces a different sort of imagination of the terrorist worldview. The first set of rumors does not examine terrorists, but rather terrorist supporters. The second set of rumors forces us to imagine that we are involved in planning the attack. It suggests the primacy of personal affection over politics, humanizing the terrorist by indicating his tender feelings, at least on the interpersonal level. Personal relations can transcend politics. The "Afghan Boyfriend" version, told after the fact, indicates that a terrorist might place the operation at risk to save a girlfriend. Perhaps love does conquer all. The "Samaritan in the Store" version, told *before* an attack, suggests that terrorists share our feelings of gratefulness and neighborliness when a good deed has been done. Even a momentary act of charity may compromise the "victims as pigs" mindset necessary to carry out violence against the innocent. That this rumor takes the most despicable of all social actors and makes him compassionate suggests how difficult it is to admit the existence of pure evil.

And yet the rumor can have it both ways. We can imagine an audience reading or hearing a story about a misunderstood Arab American talking to a person in the store and nodding with multicultural empathy to passages like this (from a text quoted earlier):

> He told her that this was the nicest thing anyone had done for him since September 11th. He said that he mostly got the cold shoulder and rudeness from people and that he was so touched by what she had done. He thanked her again and said that because she had done such a nice thing for him he felt he needed to do a nice thing for her and her family.

Then, like so many successful urban legends, the story blindsides the audience with the climax: "Don't drink any Coca-Cola products after September

2002!" Indeed, the Middle Eastern terrorists hidden among us remain committed to their inhuman cause, even if they have human feelings.

Of course, what these examples suggest about the importance of role taking is true of many rumor topics, not just about terrorist attacks. Whenever we attempt to explain the inexplicable, we rely on our ability to know one another—or to believe that we do. Audiences accept that seemingly bizarre claims are plausible because they can imagine performing similar behaviors. Even if convinced that one would not do such things, one can imagine the mindset that might produce such horror. The rumor audience takes the role of the other, and given these assumptions of character, the story becomes believable.

Rumors in Action

Texts do not just sit, but are used. They are strategic communication. People do things with words.[46] In their talk, people attempt to anger, motivate, amuse, or question their audience. Understanding rumor in conversation is essential to treating rumor as a form of politics and in figuring out how rumors can be contained or channeled. We listen to people as well as stories. People justify their own beliefs by presenting a legion of facts to which they point to support their conclusions. The events specified in the rumor do cultural work, although in different ways: one rumor is retrospective ("The Celebrating Arabs") and the other is prospective ("The Grateful Terrorist").

Using "The Celebrating Arabs" in Conversation

The first rumor provides *concrete* support for a set of political beliefs and fears, whether or not those claims are justified. In the days and months after the rumor spread, it was used to make political points beyond its boundary. Typically, the rumor justified the allegation that the Arabs among us lusted for our destruction. How did this become plausible? When most Americans imagined what we might do if we were committed to the destruction of the state of Israel or the imposition of radical Islam, this seemed like a plausible reaction. In other words, it made sense for Arabs to be celebrating in the streets of New Jersey.

Consider a few uses of this claim. The narrators' critical ability was lowered because the story was *too good to be false*. In a column in the *New York Post*, Fred Siegel,[47] professor of history at Cooper Union, wrote:

> Here in New York, it was easy to get angry listening to Egyptians, Palestinians, and the Arabs of nearby Paterson, N.J. celebrate as they received word of the murderous attacks in New York and Washington. But Mayor Giuliani...rightly warned that it would be wrong to take their anger out on the city's Arab and Muslim residents.

This piece was eventually posted on a Web site of supporters of the then-Israeli Likud party leader and now prime minister Benjamin Netanyahu, where it was included, presumably, because it fit the self-image of Netanyahu and his supporters: tough but not brutal. This claim later appeared in a 2001 Rosh Hashanah sermon delivered by Rabbi Stanley Asekoff[48] of Temple Shalom, a conservative Jewish synagogue in West Orange, New Jersey. Asekoff borrows from Siegel, slightly altering the meaning of one of Siegel's sentences:

> Now we understand why some Egyptians, Palestinians, and Arabs were celebrating in Paterson, New Jersey. Now we understand why owners and workers at Arab owned Dunkin' Donut Shops in Cedar Grove and Caldwell were dancing in their parking lots stomping on American flags.

He repeats "Now we understand why" throughout the sermon—a phrase that suggests that we comprehend how these supporters of terrorism think. We move from the events themselves to their motivations, meaning that we can imagine what it must be like to be them. While this is a divisive or wedge-driving rumor,[49] it depends on an assumption of the character and intention of those who stand outside the moral boundaries of the community.

A third example comes from a progressive writer, Drew Limsky,[50] a New York journalist and novelist. He notes in a commentary for the *Los Angeles Times:*

> Many on the left, as well as some religious leaders, must assume that if we don't strike back, the terrorist will have the kind of epiphany that one finds in literature: They'll follow our noble lead, suddenly see the value of human life and look for other careers. But life isn't literature.... There is nothing in recent history to suggest that Sept. 11's carnage sated the bloodlust of the Islamic terrorist network, nor the appetites of their sympathizers who were filmed dancing in the street in places like Paterson, N.J.

Limsky's claim legitimates a political stance. The rumor depends on knowing the mind and predicting the actions of others. The rumor with its implicit psychology provides a basis for action. "Dancing in the street" reveals terrorist-sympathizing bloodlust. Our claimed knowledge of terrorists' minds connects the public celebration and their internal ferocity. The predatory imagery—bloodlust, appetite—connects to the claim of what really causes their behavior.

These quotations and many others, both public and private, in the weeks after September 11 fit a political dialogue that permits many to feel that they can understand those very different from themselves. Professional debunkers—police, public officials, and journalists—are politically and rhetorically situated as well. They claim not to have seen "anything"— anything that would constitute a celebration. Of course, absence of evidence is never evidence of absence. In a political climate in which threats exist and in which individuals feel threatened, suggesting that the absence of evidence means evidence of absence makes strategic sense. It's better to claim that no demonstration occurred. Robert Grant,[51] a spokesperson for Paterson's mayor, underlines the politics of his denial, impugning the tellers' motives:

> Scott and Todd [two local disc jockeys] of WPLJ not only allowed callers to relate fabrications about the Middle Eastern community of Paterson, they validated the information. . . . What they did was hand a bullhorn to the guy yelling fire in the packed theater. . . . There was no attempt on the part of most of the electronic media to determine the validity of these accusations, and they were passed along as fact. It is the biggest hoax on the airways since Orson Welles said we had been attacked by Martians in the 1930s.

In another report, Grant proclaims, "If I had the ability to charge them [the media persons] with hate crimes, I would do it in a minute."[52] He imagines the motivations of those who transmit the stories, alleging that they are haters and hoaxers.

Using "The Grateful Terrorist" to Protect and Secure

The second rumor complex has a different relationship to action. It seems less overtly political. It does not deny the violence of the terrorist, but by constructing the terrorist as well meaning toward a lover or Samaritan, it legitimates the accuracy of the warning, permitting tellers to feel that even though they would not spread most "rumors," this one is believable. The action of the terrorist, in conjunction with his relationship, justifies the rumor, and the presence of the dual warnings allows audiences to respond. To return to the two texts of the grateful terrorist and his girlfriend presented earlier, the writers conclude:

> This is not an e-mail that I've received and decided to pass on. This came from a phone conversation with a long-time friend of mine last night. I may be wrong, and I hope I am. However, with one of his warnings being correct and devastating, I'm not willing to take the chance on the second and wanted to make sure that people I cared about had the same information that I did.[53]

> Don't know about you but I live across the street from a shopping mall, and my in-laws do too. Given my daughter is usually at their house on a Wednesday afternoon, right near the mall, am thinking of where else to go. Halloween may not be so Happy. Please send this to anyone that you know. Let's hope this isn't for real, but since it was actually left in a letter to a loved one from one of the people involved in the attacks of September 11, 2001, I am not taking it too lightly.[54]

In each case the writer places herself in the position of the terrorist by sharing information with those that she cares about. In so doing, the writers simultaneously accept the claim ("With one of his warnings being correct and devastating," "It was *actually* left in a letter") and distance themselves from it ("I may be wrong," "Let's hope this isn't for real") in case the foreknowledge is misleading. Here are facts from a real person whose self we can understand even if his background is different from our own, and even as we reject his politics.

Doubters emphasize that this claim of the terrorist's motivation is implausible and they deny its validity by linking it to a tradition of similar dubious stories. Barbara Mikkelson of the rumor-debunking Web site Snopes.com claims, "This story fits neatly into the genre of a number of similar rumors about helped terrorists or compassionate Arabs who are moved to offer specific warnings about upcoming attacks, and thus should most likely be dismissed as more of the same."[55] The story's traditional basis becomes the justification for doubting the terrorist's motivation. These global warnings seem all too common.

Again, the teller becomes the target of doubt. In other words, the doubter suggests that she can understand the motives of the teller just as the teller can understand what it is like to be a terrorist. Barbara Mikkelson suggests:

> The rumor has traveled as far and as quickly as it has because one special part of it speaks very strongly to what we deeply want to believe: that there is a way to protect ourselves from terrorism.... For the cost of avoiding one venue on one day, a lot of comforting false security is provided to a populace desperate for it. The horrible truth about terrorists is that they can strike in any place at any time.... Power (the power to avoid, in this case) is thus returned to a people left feeling unspeakably helpless in the face of fearsome and deadly unpredictability.[56]

By role taking, the analyst makes claims about the terrorist ("they can strike in any place at any time") and the teller ("feeling unspeakably helpless"). The ability to embrace the role of another makes rumor effective.

And yet an interesting variation on the legend shows what might happen if the differences between people are not as great as they seem. Soon after the "Samaritan in the Store" variant began to circulate in Great Britain, an antilegend was spread that humorously deconstructed the claims Mikkelson reports about unpredictable terrorists and helpless tellers. These jocular texts criticize those that suggest that Muslims are not to be trusted. They remind us that the line between rumor and humor, warning and satire, is not always clean, a theme that emerges in many examples.

The beginning of this text was clearly inspired by the "Don't go to McDonald's," but the point of view has been changed from the "friend-of-a-friend" to a first-person account, suggesting that the story, when completed, is to be treated as fictional:

> Yesterday I was on the Underground traveling on the Northern line. An Arab-looking man got off the train and I noticed that he had left his bag behind. I grabbed the bag and ran after him, caught up with him at the top of the escalator and handed him back his bag. He was extremely grateful to me and reached into his bag

which I noticed contained bundles of banknotes.[57] He offered me a reward, but I refused. So he looked round, made sure nobody was looking and whispered to me: "I can never repay your kindness, Sir, but I will try to with a word of advice for you. Stay away from Aberdeen Steak Houses." I was terrified. "Is there going to be an attack?" I whispered.

Many of those who encounter this narrative for the first time read only this far before responding that this story was yet another version of the by-now-familiar hoax. The "Arab-looking man" with the bag of banknotes, we infer, must be working as a bag man for a well-financed terrorist cell. However, the text is transformed into a parody of the legend, which ended instead with a punch line that explodes the tension:

> "No Sir" [the stranger] whispered back "I went there yesterday evening—the food was shit and the dessert selection extremely limited." Thank god he warned me, he could well have saved me from unnecessary suffering.[58]

Instead of guilty knowledge of future acts of terrorism, the advice is groaningly mundane: it implies that visiting a mediocre restaurant chain is a greater threat than international terrorism.

The antilegend was an immediate success. The politics of the original legend could be leavened by humor. By the following morning it had been featured on BBC radio, and eight days later versions had been posted on at least 25 additional message boards, with private e-mail and listservs spreading it further. Those who passed it on freely varied the details of the text, mostly to locate it in their own regions or countries, including the United States. Some versions returned the focus to McDonald's. Others mentioned Pizza Hut, Hard Rock Café, and Texas Steak House, all international chains.

As this version came to the United States, the details of the punch line varied, but not its way of deflating the threat of the story by showing the "terrorist" as having a mind exactly like the "narrator." The most common American version relies simply on a common regional stereotype:

> Yesterday, a woman was on the Subway traveling downtown. A person of Arabic appearance got off the train and the woman noticed that he had left his bag behind. She grabbed the bag and ran after him, caught up with him at the top of the escalator, and handed

him back his bag. He was extremely grateful to her and reached into his bag which appeared to contain large bundles of banknotes and white powder. He looked round, made sure nobody was looking and whispered to her: "I can never repay your kindness, madam, but I will try to with a word of advice for you: Stay away from New Jersey." She was terrified. "Is there going to be an attack?" she whispered. "No, ma'am" he whispered back. "It's a shit hole."[59]

Each story plays off the assumptions of terrorists to demonstrate that the potential attackers have similar values as other citizens.

Comfort in Moments of Crisis

In moments of chaos, the future seems cloudy and uncertain. At these moments, people often embrace a proliferation of rumor to help explain the turmoil. Rumor involves a collective effort after meaning, a desire to tame uncertainty. Yet, as collective action, it involves improvisation by those who take the bits of information that are available and couple these with expectations of what might happen in such circumstances. As such, rumor is improvised news, providing stability, comforting even when the conclusions are dark or mistaken.

The unexpected trauma sparked by enemies of America led to a set of rumors—including "The Celebrating Arabs," "The Grateful Terrorist," and others to be discussed in chapter 2—treating the terrorist and his supporters as central. We argue that people strive to understand the terrorist figure through role taking. Audiences take the claims made by rumor and attempt to determine if these claims fit their understanding of human nature—more specifically, their imagination of the kind of person that a supporter of terrorism is likely to be. Sometimes the image can be sharply drawn with the audience member ("The Celebrating Arabs"); at other times the image suggests that in many ways terrorists are just like others ("The Grateful Terrorist"). Whichever it is, by situating the terrorist within moral understanding, the fearful uncertainty of the moment can be overcome.

Terrorism and its numerous associated rumors provide a stark reminder of connections that transcend nations and peoples. They remind us that trust—and mistrust—characterizes the relationship of citizens and their society, as well as a broader transnational community. With the rise of totalitarian and colonial nations in the first half of the twentieth century, the solidification of the Cold War and the growth of nuclear proliferation in the last half, and the explosion of Islamic terrorism and American hegemony at the end of the century and the beginning of the twenty-first, rumor is not only a local matter but also a strategy of talk that attempts to tame the fear of an impinging world.

2

A Riot of Conspiracies

In the days after September 11, many Americans were startled to learn that one of the fonts used in Microsoft Word indicated that the giant company was involved in—or at least supporting—the attack on the World Trade Center. It is true that some joked that Bill Gates was the devil, but this rumor pushed his "evil" to extremes. The rumor suggested that if you were to type "NYC" in 72-point type, change the font to Webdings, and then change the font to Wingdings, symbols would appear that revealed Microsoft's corporate intentions: a skull and crossbones, a Jewish star, and a hand giving the thumbs-up sign. "Death to Jews—OK!" What could be more persuasive? The story had been around—and had been debunked—since 1992 by comedian Penn Jillette, among others. But after September 11, the story was revived and Microsoft had to deny it again, as some people suggested that the giant computer company was revealing its true feelings to those in the know.

Political rumors in the aftermath of disaster typically follow a pattern: crisis management, blame, and conspiracy. The immediate events and their results must be processed by the public. First, people must compose themselves and search for what is likely to happen next. They are confused, even frightened, asking others what they have heard, comparing notes, ready to take action. This is the process of *improvised news*, described by the sociologist Tamotsu Shibutani. People hope to get through the day, demanding to know what threats are upon them and how to respond. So, immediately after the attacks on the morning of September 11, rumors spread about fires on the National Mall in Washington, attacks on the White House, and plots in other major cities. Claims were spread that box cutters were discovered on other flights, where they had been placed to help other hijackers.[1]

Once this period has passed, and some measure of stability has returned, rumors change their focus. We feel safer, but now we desire to learn that justice has been meted out. People search for inspiring stories about tragedies and triumphs, providing the event with moral meaning and emotional resonance. At this point, they also pin blame on those who are obviously responsible, painting these villains in dark shades. The accounts are structured as battles between forces of good and evil. Stories are told about those who miraculously escaped, sliding down the towers, or about the discovery of an undamaged copy of the Bible in the wreckage of the Pentagon. We also find that political rumors emerge, often instinctive efforts to assign blame and punish those who are responsible.

Shortly after September 11, rumors spread about the terrorists and those in Al Qaeda who had planned the attacks, treating them as fully responsible and completely evil, and suggesting what other attacks were planned: as we described in chapter 1, widely known rumors from this period depicted joyous Arab Americans as well as a planned attack on shopping malls on Halloween. Given the tragic events, it is no surprise that Americans speculated about the future. These questions were met with a set of answers in the form of rumors that predicted a string of dire attacks. People searched for clues and their standards of proof decreased as additional attacks seemed likely. Just as trust in the ability of government to provide protection decreased, the readiness to accept uncertain sources of information increased. The emotional reactions give rise to claims that target those outsiders such as Arab Americans, Muslims, or swarthy foreigners who seem to have some of the features of the terrorists. Of course, not everyone embraced these fears, but enough did so as to place at risk those imagined to be perpetrators.

In the third stage, rumors become more elaborated and nuanced. The emotion may become more subtle and other themes are raised. On the one hand, the stories of the attacks themselves become more complex, even humorous, such as the account of the adulterous husband spending September 11 in bed with his lover. When his cell phone rings during his tryst, he assures his wife that he is busily working at his desk in the Twin

Towers, not realizing that she, along with most Americans, has just seen his office crumble into ruins.

But other stories are more explicitly political. Once the immediate crisis has passed—the hot moment has cooled—larger issues emerge, and people use rumor to look past the obvious villains and identify the hidden conspirators who are, as they believe, truly responsible. The members of the damaged society are forced to consider how to forestall future threats—and they do this in light of those beliefs that make sense to them. This is where conspiracy theories enter. The immediate perpetrators—the airplane hijackers—may have simply been tools of more subtle cultural villains, who know they will benefit from the changes in society caused by terrorism. In the case of Pearl Harbor, Americans knew full well that there were networks of foreigners devoted to finding ways of attacking again: Japan, supported by Nazi Germany, was openly at war with us. In the case of the September 11 attacks, we found ourselves at war again, but one of a different kind, where the networks were secret, existing covertly among us. It was, for many people, quite plausible that others, ostensibly our friends, might in fact be enemies working from within, often in the highest places. We may not have had credible proof of these conspiracies, but they nevertheless inspired passionate beliefs.

Understanding Conspiracy Theories

Conspiracy theories are not precisely rumors, but they are constructed out of rumors. They rely on what scholars call a cultural grammar—a nexus of belief—combining plausible elements into what has been termed a "totalizing discourse."[2] Sociologists have spoken of these folk attempts to understand the world as "quasi-theories."[3] Given accepted public knowledge, these beliefs take disorder and make it orderly by fitting the situation into widely held assumptions of human motivation. In other words, conspiracy theories can explain large swaths of an otherwise ambiguous world; they are transcendent explanations, unlocking a closed world with a cleverly forged key. The power of a conspiracy theory is that it connects rumors with documented, official facts. The facts provide a basis for belief in other claims that are not as clearly supported. By pointing to hidden enemies with their penchant for evil, conspiracy theories seek to *humanize* the crisis and propose scapegoats for the damage that has been caused. With human responsibility, individuals can potentially be caught and punished and evil can be rooted out. In this startling way, conspiracies make even the worst events manageable by suggesting that with sufficient commitment we can identify scoundrels and prevent them from attacking again.

Broad conspiracy rumors are so easy to come by, and those who assert them are so certain in their ire and outrage, that we are likely to wonder what the narrator has to gain. Why are they sharing such ugly facts: to warn us about real dangers or because they want to cause us fear? To give weight to the credibility of our source, we judge their likely motives. Is the source disinterested? In examining many rumors, but particularly those that allege wide conspiracies, we stand on the rocky shoals of potential deceit. When we impute motives to a speaker, we open the possibility for a challenge to the plausibility of the text through questioning the speaker's credibility. As Gary Alan Fine and Patricia Turner remarked, "Motive is the worm in the apple of belief."[4] Does the narrator have a reason to deceive or to shade information? The apparent motivation of a speaker influences how audiences interpret a text. This connects to what the philosopher J. L. Austin[5] speaks of as the "illocutionary force" of an utterance. What is the person attempting to do in making the claim? What kind of statement is it by virtue of likely motivation? A joke? A lie? An entertaining account? Is the speaker's intent to foment revolution against a dishonest government or to impel us to take sides in a political battle? Recognizing this, speakers often attempt to channel the assumptions of their audiences by presenting *motive talk*, providing their own assessments of their motivation.[6] Conspiracy theorists often do this by grounding their claims in their belief in God, justice, or democracy. What ultimately matters is how the claim is taken. For this reason, folklorists have come to consider the audience reaction to a rumor as just as central to its meaning in context as the bare text itself.

In reacting, audiences draw upon assessments of *interest* and *history*. Most audiences are predisposed to accept the claims made by others, unless compelling reasons suggest caution. In considering the credibility of the speaker, we often ask whether there is something to gain or hide, and whether the person has provided poor information in the past, a problem for those who see deceit everywhere. The sky never stops falling. Political commentators, lovers, and parents know that they must interpret with care the claims of those who attempt to persuade them, while movement activists, swains, and children know full well that once they are caught presenting false information, what they say later on will be treated with greater caution. Each performance shapes a narrator's credibility. If *everything* is the fault of the Jews, the Arabs, or the oilmen, those who are not already convinced may stop listening.

A Surfeit of Conspiracies

The French rumor researcher Véronique Campion-Vincent sums up the appeal of conspiracy theories by stating, "Conspiracy theories try to explain a complex and seemingly random environment through the adoption of a simple model of causality, but they simultaneously reinforce the in-group's cohesion through the designation of enemies."[7] As noted, much of their power lies in the ability to explain large numbers of discrete facts, including those emerging in current events in an efficient and emotionally satisfying way. For those who embrace them, they make sense in that they support— apparently with detailed evidence—claims that one is ready to believe. Conspiracy theories rarely persuade one to dislike a group for whom one had no animosity, but reinforce and specify prejudice and disdain. Conspiracy theories are always located within contexts of belief. As sociologist David Bromley notes, conspiracy theory presents a history of the crimes, a space where conspirators act, and a counterculture of deviant values.[8] At the same time, conspiracies are tied to the history, space, and culture of those troubled by these perversions. For instance, those who mistrust Jews will be prepared to judge the evidence in anti-Semitic conspiracy claims as plausible, while those without this anger dismiss the claims as bogus. Put another way, conspiracy theories are not a single claim about a specific event but are integrated theories that make sense of a large number of otherwise confusing and disorienting facts. These theories result from what the French philosopher Alain de Benoist termed "the seductiveness of simplification in an increasingly complex universe."[9]

Conspiracies and Evil Elites

A conspiracy theory begins with a simple core premise: that history is consciously shaped by an evil elite—take one's pick which one. Once one selects the villains, the rest of the explanation will follow. The choice of villain provides the structure or backbone for the interpretation of facts. Plausibility in this case depends on the belief that no other cultural grammar explains the factual record so fully or effectively. A conspiracy theory makes sense of what has happened in the past and provides strategies to prevent it from happening again.

Those who investigated the assassination of President John F. Kennedy learned full well how adaptable villains can be. Besides the immediate perpetrators—Lee Harvey Oswald and Jack Ruby—possible assassins were discovered in every dark corner of the political community. A similar reaction took place in the wake of September 11. In interpreting such tragedies one asks, "Who benefits?" or *Cui bono?* While these beliefs are disturbingly common, not everyone is equally susceptible to conspiracy rumors. Psychologists find that high levels of anomie, authoritarianism, and powerlessness along with low levels of self-esteem correlate with belief in specific conspiracies.[10] One must treat such findings (often based on data collected from undergraduate students) with care, as beliefs in conspiracies are widely spread in American society and elsewhere.[11] Few citizens lack a favored conspiracy, and some may be correct.

As we describe in chapter 3, rumors explaining social strain have often targeted outsiders and foreigners. However, as Campion-Vincent has observed, many current conspiracy theories now suspect the allegiance and honor of political elites. She notes that in the wake of a damaging flood that occurred along the banks of the River Somme in spring 2001, many inhabitants assumed that governmental agencies had deflected surplus water from the Seine into their region, sacrificing an economically backward region to benefit more prosperous and better connected ones.[12] Similar complaints have encouraged conspiracy theories current among African Americans, such as the somewhat more diffuse complex of rumors and beliefs that Turner[13] has documented as "The Plan," exemplified most dramatically in the conspiracy theories and rumors that emerged after Hurricane Katrina; refugees explained that politicians deliberately blew up the levees in New Orleans as a form of urban renewal or even genocide. People with grievances are prone to see as plausible those explanations that target those evildoers who had already been under suspicion. These theories begin with clear facts: the flooding of the Somme canals or the destruction of black neighborhoods in New Orleans. These indisputable, verifiable facts help to make conspiracy theories compelling. Yet, the theory takes these facts and weaves a web of explanation that is of questionable value.

Conspiracies of Terror

As we have emphasized, believers in the plausibility of conspiracies often question the motivations of those that they mistrust. In the aftermath of the September 11 attacks, communities gathered around three types of explanations: one suggesting that Arabs, not just a few terrorists, caused this attack and were planning others as part of a jihadist war; a second blaming the Israeli Mossad and powerful Jews in general; and a third suggesting that the attacks were either known about or caused by the U.S. government. While the first explanation gained the widest public support in the United States, the others gathered communities of believers as well, and the final explanation proved to be very hardy indeed.

The Arab Conspiracy

The preponderance of evidence suggests that the planned attacks on September 11 were the handiwork of 19 members of Al Qaeda. No evidence has been presented of a larger conspiracy beyond these individuals, although they surely received tactical support and training from others (Zacarias Moussaoui, the so-called 20th hijacker, was not actively involved in planning the attacks). However, the absence of an established infrastructure of terror beyond the 19 individuals is disturbing to many Americans. Could these men have acted without local assistance? Where are those hidden helpers?

One branch of this rumor suggests that numerous Arab Americans had been aware of the attacks before they happened and chose not to warn authorities, presumably because they supported jihad. After the fact, people claimed to notice that Arabs were surprisingly absent on the morning of September 11. For instance, Internet accounts suggested:

> A man who worked in the World Trade Center and survived the attack recounted this to a friend of mine. The man had a routine which included commuting to the World Trade Center from New Jersey every morning. As part of his regular commute he passed by the entrance to the Millennium Hotel next to the world trade center. The circle in front of the hotel is always full of taxis waiting for fares from the hotel. On September 11th there was not one taxicab in the circle. The man only remembered it because it

was such a strange sight seeing no cabs where there are usually a dozen or so.[14]

I heard from a coworker that at ferry terminals in south Manhattan, numerous cabs normally line up to transport arriving ferry passengers to their local destinations but that early on September 11, 2001, virtually no such cabs were available—the suggestion being that Middle-Eastern cab drivers had received notice that they should avoid the area that morning.[15]

Similar narratives claimed that Arab-run office shops, newsstands, and flower markets were closed the morning of the attack. One brief account made the threat more explicit: "On the morning of Sept. 11th, a Middle-Eastern-looking newspaper vendor handed a man back his change and said, 'Here's your change...have a good day; it's the last day of your life.'"[16] The implications were obvious: Arab Americans had been warned in advance and waited with anticipation. As a result, the conspiracy was much larger and deeper than had been imagined. The mutual trust that should have been evident in a society that promoted itself as a melting pot was an illusion. The reality that taxi drivers are a very diverse community, not only composed of Arab Americans, made the rumor of disappearing taxi drivers especially perplexing. Were Indian, Haitian, Nigerian, Serbian, and Salvadoran cabbies warned as well?

This rumor suggests that the attacks were not merely the work of a few angry and isolated terrorists, but were supported by a larger community, a community that had an information network separate from the rest of society. Three years after the attacks, this belief still resonated among large segments of the country. A poll conducted by Cornell University's Media and Society Research Group revealed some disturbing statistics about common beliefs about fellow American citizens who were Muslims. Almost half of those polled felt that Islam more often encouraged its followers to commit acts of violence than other religions: the percentage increased to nearly two-thirds among those who described themselves as "highly religious." In 1941, in the wake of Pearl Harbor, the federal government actually confined Japanese Americans in internment camps to prevent them from engaging in conspiracies, and in 2004, a disturbing number of citizens found the same approach attractive. The poll showed that 42% of "highly religious" persons agreed that all Muslims should be required to register their home addresses with the government, and nearly half of all those polled felt that at least one of their civil liberties should be suspended.[17]

The Israeli Conspiracy

As is often the case when conspiracies are considered, Jews (and now Israelis) are often named as perpetrators. Beliefs in conspiracies by Jews have been integral to Western history for millennia. In this respect, the third millennia seems little different from the first two.

In chapter 1, we discussed the rumor that suggested that Satan's face was visible in the smoke of the burning World Trade Towers. A frequently forwarded e-mail that distributed Phillips's photograph seemingly revealing the devil interpreted the vision as evidence that the true evil was not the destruction of the Twin Towers, but the work of those economic elites who had inhabited them. "Don't these photos of Satan at the World Trade Center catastrophe tell us that the current seat of Satan's power is the World Trade Center?" this message began. "Don't these photos depict Satan being awakened from his hiding place in the World Trade Center? For it is the international bankers who operate from the Fed, the CFR, and the World Trade Center who create first, second, and third world debt."[18] Indeed, conspiracy theorists pointed to unusual stock trading in the period immediately prior to September 11. Far more options were traded in the stocks of United Airlines and American Airlines than was usual. Investors throughout August and during the days immediately before September 11 placed large numbers of "puts" on these two—and apparently only these two—airlines. These were bets that their stock would fall rapidly. United and American were the two airlines that terrorists hijacked, and of course their stock dropped dramatically. The existence of these puts (25 to 100 times the normal value) was noted at the time.[19] Puts were also placed on Morgan Stanley and Merrill Lynch immediately before the attacks, two companies that were heavily damaged. Perhaps, conspiracy theorists proposed, these elite traders knew something that they kept secret for their own benefit.

After a lengthy investigation,[20] the National Commission on Terrorist Attacks upon the United States (the 9/11 Commission) found that these trades were innocuous, not connected with the attacks, only mere fortuitous investments.[21] Whether one finds such conclusions plausible is a matter of personal taste and confidence in the morality of those who shape the economy and those who evaluated the attacks.

Believers in an elite conspiracy can easily understand these iconic refer-
ences, which refer to one of the longest-lived complexes of anti-Semitic
belief in the modern world. "International bankers" is a hoary phrase going
back to a mysterious group of conspirators described in a document titled
Protocols of the Meetings of the Learned Elders of Zion, which purports to be
a set of lectures given in the 1890s, presenting the agenda of a select group
of Jewish financiers who had been planning for centuries to achieve world
domination over the "goyim," or Gentiles.

Historian Norman Cohn[22] has reconstructed the origins of this document
in detail: it was probably written in France in 1897 or 1898, at the height of the
prosecution of Alfred Dreyfus, a Jewish army officer who had been convicted
of treason based on falsified evidence. The text plagiarized large sections from
an 1864 satire written by Maurice Joly, a French liberal. The *Protocols*, however,
were not published until 1903 (in a Russian translation in the St. Petersburg
anti-Semitic newspaper *Znamya*), and they became enormously popular in
1920 when an English translation appeared in Great Britain and was promoted
by the American industrialist Henry Ford. Even though the document has
been conclusively and repeatedly demonstrated to be fraudulent, for many
over the years—Christians, Orthodox, and Muslims—the claims have seemed
plausible. Today, the *Protocols* are still taken as gospel in many Arab communities, where the article regularly appears in government-controlled media. In
many societies Jews hold more economic, cultural, and political power than
would be predicted by their proportion of the population. From this, the claim
that their success is a function of conspiracy seems reasonable to those who
feel resentment. Certainly it did in Czarist Russia, Nazi Germany, Henry Ford's
Midwest, and currently throughout much of the Middle East, where it has
been dramatized on Egyptian and Lebanese television.[23]

The key idea, which is that some core elite of wealthy conspirators is
secretly causing crises to the detriment of democracy and morality, has
been a constant part of some branches of evangelical religious thought.[24] If
one sees the Jews as engaged in a fundamental battle for dominance with
Christians, such a desire for control makes sense. These individuals see Jews
being implicated in the crucifixion of Christ as an example of their conspiracy, sustained by their professions as money lenders, and later they were
said to control banks, governments, and international organizations. In
short, the World Trade Center was already the site of Satan's evil, and so
perhaps its destruction was a well-planned event, not from outside, but
from the evil already residing within the site.

The *Protocols* provided an answer to the terror on September 11. In this scenario, Jewish bankers constitute a secret, satanically inspired cadre working to divide existing political parties and nations, promote unnecessary international conflicts, and generally upset the status quo in which Jews hold power. By promoting chaos, representatives of the Elders infiltrate and expand their control of responsible positions in governments and institutions. As Protocol 10 puts it, "it is indispensable to trouble in all countries the people's relations with their governments so as to utterly exhaust humanity with dissention, hatred, struggle, envy and even by the use of torture, by starvation, by the inoculation of diseases, by want, so that the 'goyim' see no other issue than to take refuge in our complete sovereignty."[25] Further, if the international bankers' goals were opposed by any government, Protocol 7 states, "we shall show our strength . . . by terrorist attempts." As a last resort, the Elders threatened to make use of an ultimate weapon, "a maneuver of such appalling terror that the very stoutest hearts quail," as dictated in Protocol 9. This weapon will be used in "the undergrounds, metropolitans, those subterranean corridors which, before the time comes, will be driven under all the capitals and from whence those capitals will be blown into the air. . . ."

Those aware of passages like these from the *Protocols* could easily explain the attack on the financial services industry supposedly filled with Jews. If the bankers were actually behind the World Trade Center attack, it was plausible to assume that evil elites would indeed "take measures to protect our own." In a mirror image to the claim that Arabs were not to be found in lower Manhattan on September 11, a rumor spread that Israelis (or Jews) did not show up at their jobs at the World Trade Center on the date of the attack.

The fact that a particular rumor is not demonstrably true does not, however, mean that it ceases to be plausible to many people. Conspiracy theories assume that the perpetrators of a conspiracy require secrecy to achieve their goals. So an effort to halt the circulation of a rumor based on a conspiracy theory, paradoxically, demonstrates that it *is* true. The British Fascist Nesta Webster, one of the strongest proponents of the accuracy of the *Protocols*, stated this directly in 1921:

> The truth is, then, that the Protocols have never been refuted, and the futility of the so-called refutations published, as also the fact of their temporary suppression, have done more to convince the

public of their authenticity than all the anti-Semite writings on the subject put together....the only conclusion that we can draw is either that the Protocols are genuine and what they pretend to be, or that these advocates put forward by the Jews have some interest in concealing the activities of Secret Societies in the past.[26]

Writing in prison at about the same time, Adolf Hitler said that the best proof that the *Protocols* were authentic was that the *Frankfurter Zeitung*, Germany's leading liberal newspaper, "moans and screams [about them] once every week."[27]

Although the standard claim was to blame the Jews as a religious group, today the nation of Israel is often blamed specifically. Given the political discord and violence in the Middle East, many claim that any act that might adversely affect the reputation of Arabs is part of an Israeli conspiracy. These rumors fit the belief that Arabs could not be behind these dreadful events, but that Israelis might, desiring to drive Americans more firmly into the arms of Israel. Although the claim that the Mossad, the Israeli Secret Service, was somehow behind the attacks on September 11 might strike many as curious—or worse—those who accept the belief, including many Muslims in the Middle East and elsewhere, assert the plausibility of the story by asking who benefits from the deed. In this case, by involving America in the Middle East, Israelis might be seen as beneficiaries of the terrorist attack. Considering the world scene on September 12, it may have appeared that radical Islamic states were under attack from public opinion and American policy. Any Arab militant act, however justified in the cause of national struggle, could be linked to the destruction at Ground Zero. Given this, many saw the Mossad as a plausible villain. From this perspective, Mossad's only concern is to promote the interests of the state of Israel, already seen as an illegitimate, authoritarian, or rogue state in the mind of many Arabs.

Perhaps we should be grateful that many Arabs found it so implausible and offensive that other Arabs might be behind such horrific attacks, even if Osama bin Laden presumably admitted the deed in November 2001. (Some suggested that this confession was not made by the real Osama, but by an actor, or that Osama himself is not the mastermind of the attacks but only a stooge paid by the West.) This rejection of responsibility echoes the belief among Holocaust deniers that Hitler could hardly have committed a crime of such iniquity. The idea that Arab militants could not commit such an unspeakable act led to an O. J. Simpson–like search for the "real" villains.

According to the U.S. Department of State, conspiracy theories that suggested that Israel was somehow responsible appeared within 24 hours of the attack. The Syrian government-owned paper *Al Thawra* apparently was the first to make the claim that Jews were absent from lower Manhattan on September 11 in their edition of September 15. The rumor filled a social vacuum and continued to grow both in the United States and in the Middle East to such an extent that the U.S. State Department felt called upon to deny it:

> Shortly after September 11, 2001 false rumors began to circulate claiming that 4,000 Jews, or 4,000 Israelis, had failed to report for work at the World Trade Center (WTC) on 9/11, supposedly because they had been warned to stay away by Israeli secret services, which were allegedly responsible for the attack. The claim is totally false.[28]

Nevertheless, proponents of the rumor presented evidence that, if accepted on its face, provided some support. For instance, on September 12, the Internet edition of the *Jerusalem Post* reported that, "The Foreign Ministry in Jerusalem has so far received the names of 4,000 Israelis believed to have been in the areas of the World Trade Center and the Pentagon at the time of the attacks."[29] Since it turned out that 4,000 Israelis were not killed, where did they go? The figure was transformed into the belief that these individuals had been warned in advance by the Israeli government.

In fact, many Jews and some Israelis did die in the attacks, and the proportion of Jews killed matched their proportion of the population of New York City. Of course, conspiracy theorists, firm in their belief that Jews dominate the financial services sector, argue that a higher proportion of Jews should have been working there, and so a discrepancy in the death toll nevertheless does exist. Still, whether the proportion killed was precisely in line with the proportion of Jews who worked at the World Trade Center on September 10, there is no evidence that a warning was distributed (and none of the thousands who supposedly received the warning have reported it). There is no evidence that either Jews or Muslims were warned in advance. But, as conspiracy theorists often emphasize, absence of evidence does not disprove the theory. It simply demonstrates how united the enemies of America are in suppressing the proof of their guilt.

A second piece of evidence of the possible role of Israelis in the destruction of the towers was the odd case of five Israelis who were arrested after the attack. The Israeli newspaper *Ha'aretz* immediately reported the case in some detail:

> Five Israelis who had worked for a moving company based in New Jersey are being held in U.S. prisons for what the Federal Bureau of Investigation has described as "puzzling behavior" following the terror attack on the World Trade Center in New York last Tuesday. The five are expected to be deported sometime soon. The families of the five...said that their sons had been questioned by the FBI for hours on end, had been kept in solitary confinement for three days, and had been humiliated, stripped of their clothes and blindfolded....[The FBI, a mother said, felt] that he was working for Mossad....The Foreign Ministry told the families that the FBI had denied holding the five and that the consulate had chosen to believe the FBI....They are charged with illegally residing in the United States and working there without permits....They are said to have been caught videotaping the disaster and shouting in what was interpreted as cries of joy and mockery.[30]

Some months later the issue re-emerged when ABC News suggested that these men were Israeli espionage agents working on a mission in the United States:

> Maria says she saw three young men kneeling on the roof of a white van in the parking lot of her apartment building....The men were taking video or photos of themselves with the World Trade Center burning in the background, she said. What struck Maria were the expressions on the men's faces. "They were like happy, you know...They didn't look shocked to me. I thought it was very strange," she said. She found the behavior so suspicious that she wrote down the license plate number of the van and called the police....The arresting officers [at 4:00 P.M.] said they saw a lot that aroused their suspicion about the men. One of the passengers had $4,700 in cash hidden in his sock. Another was carrying two foreign passports. A box cutter was found in the van. But perhaps the biggest surprise for the officers came when the five men identified themselves as Israeli citizens....The case

was transferred out of the FBI's Criminal Division, and into the bureau's Foreign Counterintelligence Section...One reason for the shift, sources told ABCNEWS, was that the FBI believed Urban Moving [the company the men worked for] may have been providing cover for an Israeli intelligence operation. Eventually, *The Forward*, a respected Jewish newspaper in New York, reported the FBI concluded that two of the men were Israeli intelligence operatives....No one has been able to find a good explanation for why they may have been smiling with the towers of the World Trade Center burning in the background. Both the lawyers for the young men and the Israeli Embassy chalk it up to immature conduct.[31]

Added to this was the claim that Israel had been aware of the attacks several hours before they occurred. On September 27, 2001, the *Washington Post* reported:

Officials at instant-messaging firm Odigo confirmed today that two employees received text messages warning of an attack on the World Trade Center two hours before terrorists crashed planes into the New York landmarks....Alex Diamandis, vice president of sales and marketing, confirmed that workers in Odigo's research and development and international sales office in Israel received a warning from another Odigo user approximately two hours prior to the first attack....Soon after the terrorist attacks on New York, the Odigo employees notified their management, who contacted Israeli security services. In turn, the FBI was informed of the instant message warning.[32]

This information suggests some measure of Israeli involvement in the events of September 11, evidence of which most Americans are unaware. Although rumors quickly developed that the Mossad was responsible for the attacks, this is highly unlikely given bin Laden's claims of responsibility (unless he, too, as some theories suggest, is secretly an Israeli agent or stooge).

Once again, it is not our aim to suggest what might "truly" have happened on September 11, but rather to examine how beliefs develop in the absence of secure evidence, building on what audiences consider to be plausible. Perhaps—and this is not certain—Israeli intelligence knew about the plot in advance and did not, or did, inform the American government. Those who accept this view would endorse the analysis in the *Sunday Herald*, a Scottish newspaper:

> To those who have investigated just what the Israelis were up to that day, the case raises one dreadful possibility: that Israeli intelligence had been shadowing the al-Qaeda hijackers as they moved from the Middle East through Europe and into America where they trained as pilots and prepared to suicide-bomb the symbolic heart of the United States. And the motive? To bind America in blood and mutual suffering to the Israeli cause.... There was no suggestion whatsoever from within American intelligence that the Israelis were colluding with the 9/11 hijackers, simply that the possibility remains that they knew the attacks were going to happen, but effectively did nothing to help stop them.... Mossad...was spying on Arab extremists in the USA and may have known that September 11 was in the offing, yet decided to withhold vital information from their American counterparts which could have prevented the terror attacks. Following September 11, 2001, more than 60 Israelis were taken into custody under the Patriot Act and immigration laws. One highly placed investigator told Carl Cameron of Fox News that there were "tie-ins" between the Israelis and September 11; the hint was clearly that they'd gathered intelligence on the planned attacks but kept it to themselves.[33]

This is then transformed into the claim that the Israelis were behind the attack, suggesting an oddly racist belief that only the Israelis—and not the Arabs—would have the competence to bring off such a complex plot. These claims were spread widely on anti-Semitic, Holocaust denier Web sites, "Progressive" anti-Zionist Web sites, and militant Islamic sites. The claims of Israeli (or Jewish) involvement fit a set of beliefs that made sense to some individuals and was offensive to others.

The American Conspiracy

The belief that the American government was responsible for the destruction of the Twin Towers (and the Pentagon) is a growth industry. Numerous books, pamphlets, and Web sites have placed evidence before the American public "demonstrating" the involvement of the American government in the attacks on September 11. Perhaps Osama bin Laden was a braggart when he took credit for the attacks, perhaps the tapes are faked, or—gasp!— perhaps he is an American agent putting on a performance to justify our search for cheap oil.

While most of those who have argued for U.S. culpability have been marginal political actors, Iranian President Mahmoud Ahmadinejad wrote to President George W. Bush, "Sept. 11th was not a simple operation. Could it be planned and executed without coordination with intelligence and security services, or with extensive infiltration? Of course, this is just an educated guess. Why have the various aspects of the attacks been kept secret?"[34] Whether Ahmadinejad's guess is educated, he is surely correct that the operation was not simple. In such circumstances, there is simultaneously an absence of definitive information and a surfeit of tangential information. Is the information available the right information, and is it legitimate?

As in all such complex and traumatic events (Pearl Harbor, the Holocaust), skeptics point to potentially useful pieces of information that are "mysteriously" absent, have vanished, or are being held back (whether for malicious reasons or for legitimate ones, such as national security). The fact that the Defense Department did not release the images of the jet hitting the Pentagon led to speculation that no such pictures existed. The early skeptical volume by Thierry Meyssan, *Pentagate*, makes a similar case.[35]

The absence of desired information under conditions of suspicion and lack of trust in the credibility of institutions that are supposed to provide secure information generates rumor. However, too much information also can provoke rumor. With the proper critical perspective, individuals can pick and choose information, searching for those claims that support their beliefs. One rumor suggested that FEMA had disaster relief teams in New York City the night before September 11 based on what may have been a verbal slip by a FEMA spokesperson, Tom Kenny, who referred on CBS News to Monday (September 10) when he supposedly meant Tuesday (September 11). If his statement was accurate as he stated it, it would appear to suggest that FEMA knew that an attack was coming.[36] Here was a piece of evidence that either means nothing or suggests quite a lot, depending on one's level of trust in government authorities. There is not just one piece of evidence for deliberation, but in an event with so much complexity, one can troll through a wealth of information that supports a preferred viewpoint. While some individuals who had been politically neutral may be persuaded (as surely happened with attempts to understand the assassination of John F. Kennedy), many of those who embrace these uncertain claims are predisposed to believe. They stand in a particular relationship to forces of authority and power that make certain sources highly credible and certain claims especially plausible.

THE TRUTH MOVEMENT. The general questioning of the standard explanation is known as the 9/11 Truth Movement,[37] a community that covers numerous differences and disagreements. These individuals agree on the fact that the truth of that day has not been fully told, and they embrace what others would describe as rumors—or lies or fantasies. With regard to a governmental conspiracy, two types of beliefs are common, beliefs that go by the acronyms of LIHOP and MIHOP.[38] The former stands for Let It Happen on Purpose, and suggests that the American government was aware of the attacks prior to their happening but chose not to repel them because they fit vital policy goals. Here, the claim is that the U.S. government wished to invade Afghanistan and perhaps Iraq, gaining control of Middle Eastern oil, and the attacks legitimated this desire. This resonates with claims that were made after Pearl Harbor that the Franklin D. Roosevelt administration knew of the Japanese attack but was willing to accept the death and destruction of much of the Pacific Fleet because it permitted the United States to intervene in the war against Hitler, despite the protest of noninterventionists. Both beliefs presume an absence of trust in the claims of government leaders.

Those who believe in MIHOP—Made It Happen on Purpose—go a step further. These critics suggest not just that the government didn't stop painful events that were in their interests, but that they actively caused them. This belief suggests that a widely spread conspiratorial network exists that wishes to make the attacks appear to be the work of Arabs. This requires a greater belief in the malevolence of governmental policy makers than many Americans can accept, and it requires that unofficial and unsecured information be taken as truth.

Both LIHOP and MIHOP beliefs have many strands, but each involves a systematic questioning of what is seen as legitimate information by others, all the while embracing questionable sources. These beliefs typically excuse Arabs from blame or treat them as patsies, while various versions combine the blame of the American power elite with the blame of Israel.

The Conspirator in Chief: Bin Laden Rumors

One actor stands at the core of the conspiracy to commit the attacks on September 11, at least in the story as told by those who accept the official version, and he is a target of much rumor. This is, of course, Osama bin Laden. Bin Laden was not a figure who had been well known to most Americans prior to the attack, despite his likely involvement in other acts of violence. This lack of awareness perhaps suggests the lack of seriousness that terrorism was given before that September Tuesday. The shadowy bin Laden was an ambiguous figure, but a dangerous one, and in such situations rumor works to clarify meanings, even if such clarification is more symbolic than definitive.

Here we present two sets of rumors, one that specifies the basis of bin Laden's hatred of America and the second that examines the extensive reach of his wealthy family. These stories help to explain his conspiratorial plans and his ability to achieve them. As is so often the case, people feel comfortable when they can personalize political movements, and so rather than seeing Islamic terrorists as a network or Al Qaeda as an organization, people attribute the cause of the attacks to bin Laden himself, even if his operational authority is uncertain. This personalization of politics allows us to focus our hatred on a prominent actor and to treat him as the conspiratorial front of the destruction.

Why should Osama bin Laden harbor such an intense hatred for America that he would command his followers to crash airplanes into the heart of the American economy and military? What is his motive? One might reasonably suggest that the explanation is tied to ideology alone, but this is not effective to discredit the attacks and rather raises the battle to a struggle between opposite belief systems. To prevent a clash between equals, Al Qaeda's mission needed to be made frivolous. The primary rumor in this regard, and one that might have begun as a deliberate and humorous hoax, one that satirizes beliefs in masculine dominance, is the claim that bin Laden's hatred for America stems from an American girl giggling at his tiny penis. Snopes.com reports the following texts:

I heard a rumor that Osama bin Laden has underdeveloped genitals because of a medical accident that happened to him as a baby.
Supposedly, an American woman laughed at him before they had
sex and ever since then, he has become bitter at Americans.

Have you heard the one about Osama going to school in
Chicago, dating an American girl, and getting laughed at by her
because of the small size of his penis?[39]

At about the same time, an extremely popular e-mail message
described what might be the "ultimate revenge" for September 11.
Beginning by warning that killing bin Laden would only make him a martyr among Muslim extremists, the message suggested that special military
forces should "covertly capture him, fly him to an undisclosed hospital
and have surgeons quickly perform a complete sex change operation.
Then we return 'her' to Afghanistan to live as a woman under the
Taliban."[40] Dr. Susan Block, a proponent of RAWA, an organization working to achieve equal rights for women in Afghanistan, described the scenario as "a marvelous idea":

> It's a joke, of course, but it rings with a delicious sense of sexual
> justice. Plus, it helps heal that awful castrated feeling so many of us
> Americans have felt since our biggest phallic buildings were so
> painfully cut down. In that sense, it's a sort of sick but somewhat
> therapeutic anti-terror vengeance fantasy.[41]

Both the rumor and the joke acknowledge how the attack was seen, symbolically, as a thrust against the nation's sense of self—to the nation's
body—and suggests that the proper response is to respond similarly to
our primary tormentor. Whether serious or jocular, the scenario strips
bin Laden of the image of the masculine warrior, infantilizes him, and
trivializes him. The fact that there is no record of bin Laden having been
in the United States, much less having sexual relations with an American
woman, doesn't stand in the way of a compelling image. While explaining
bin Laden's motivations, it emphasizes that his hatred is not rational and
suggests that once bin Laden is surgically removed, radical Islam will
vanish.

A second set of stories addresses the extensive economic power of
bin Laden and his family. They have the resources to carry out the
attack:

Subject: BOYCOTT

What can you do to help stop Osama bin Laden? How about boy-
cotting his products so his cash flow starts to dry up? Pretty simple,
if you ask the people at the *Wall Street Journal*. Today's WSJ out-
lines, in great detail, how Osama gets his millions from his father's
company...Saudi Binladin Group (SBG) headquartered in Jeddah.
This group has annual revenues of FIVE BILLION US greenbacks,
some of which goes to Osama to pay off his many puppets who are
stupid enough to go around blowing themselves up for a few bucks
and some geek named Mohammed. I don't know about you, but
I am interested in learning more about how Osama gets his millions. And if there's a way we can slow down his cash flow, he'll
eventually run out of extra funds to pay out to those idiot diaper-
heads. DID YOU KNOW that Binladin gets a bunch of its income
from partnerships with General Electric? GE holds a stake in a
power equipment company in Saudi Arabia that is majority-owned
by the Binladin family. GE also supplied equipment to several
Saudi power plants built by the Binladin Group. Money in Osama's
pocket. DID YOU KNOW that the Binladin group is also part
owner of the Saudi distributor of Snapple beverages? Yes, Cadbury
Schweppes PLC, which owns Snapple, contributes to Osama's
secret cache of terrorist efforts. Don't buy GE products. Don't buy
Snapple or Schweppes beverages. Don't pay those ridiculous prices
for Cadbury chocolates. All that extra mark-up simply goes toward
helping Osama anyway. Pass the word. Do something. Forward
this baby.[42]

Understandably, such claims inflamed the emotions of rumor narrators.
While the claims are apparently inaccurate as they relate to Osama bin
Laden himself, the bin Laden family is one of the wealthiest and most powerful families in Saudi Arabia and runs the Binladin group, which, among
other things, does serve as a distributor for foreign products in Saudi Arabia.
However, the assumption that Osama bin Laden himself is extremely
wealthy (and presumably invests his money in Western, capitalist enterprises) seems eminently plausible to many. Among the most prominent
claims that have circulated is that Osama bin Laden owns Snapple (the
Binladin group at one time distributed Snapple), that he is a principal

owner of Citibank (apparently this is Saudi Prince Alwaleed bin Talal), or that he is involved with General Electric (again the Binladin group).[43] Possibly bin Laden has investments, but this is shrouded in mystery, as well they might be, given that they would be confiscated by the American government.

The Conspiratorial Tongue

We point to how people make sense of the contours of their lives after a terrorist attack. They search for blame—a focus to attribute their anger—and often discover it. September 11 helped to sharpen our indictment. To be sure, we selected those villains that we had previously mistrusted, but the terrorist attacks gave additional power to our complaints. In this, President Bush had it right as regards rumor. There is a pre–September 11 mindset and a post–September 11 mindset. What was once taken for granted was questioned; everything was askew. Conspiracy beliefs had the power of making sense of this cognitive chaos. We felt that we were confronted with strong and mysterious forces, whoever they were: Arabs, wealthy Saudis, Jews, businessmen, Israelis agents, or conniving American politicians. Rumors of terrorism, even more than most rumors, are populated with "bad guys," fulfilling our desire for psychic revenge. Given a split and divided community, the character and the position of these bad guys vary. Conspiracies propose plausible assessments of who might have caused such a deadly attack so blame can be apportioned appropriately.

Assuming the existence of conspiratorial groups suggests that they will continue to shape our lives. Our operating assumption, despite the rhetoric of madness, is that our enemies are competent and strategic, and are capable of the most dramatic crimes. Challenging their control will not be easy. In an odd and paradoxical way, rumors about terrorism provide our foes with a respect that they otherwise might not deserve. By examining rumors about conspiratorial control, we do much to understand what anxieties are afoot in society: they provide a reading of the dark quarters of our mind.

3

Migrants

Disease in the Body Politic

On May 1, 2006, Latino activist groups sponsored "A Day without Immigrants," a political rally held in numerous American cities, intended to demonstrate the value of Spanish-speaking communities to the United States. Protesters were upset by a legislative proposal passed by the U.S. House of Representatives that would make residing illegally in the United States a felony, and that demanded more security fences along America's border with Mexico. In Los Angeles, it was estimated that between 1 and 2 million people protested in two separate marches; in Chicago, over 400,000 demonstrated. At one school in a Latino neighborhood, 85% of the students were absent. Tyson Foods and Cargill Meat Solutions, large poultry and meatpacking companies employing large numbers of Hispanic workers, shut down their plants. Recent immigrants—legal and not—were asked to stay away from work and to refrain from patronizing businesses, demonstrating how essential migrant communities were to the American economy. Despite the competition for jobs, march organizers argued that the economic benefits to the country from these workers were substantial, and claims in Los Angeles were that the boycott cost the Los Angeles economy $52 million or 4.3% of the daily economic activity.[1] Massive public demonstrations and marches promoted Latino American pride and protested punitive immigration legislation. Although the event was well intentioned, it set off a counterresponse of rumors against

Latinos, which bolstered the very stereotypes that the demonstrations intended to challenge.

A widespread rumor held that while retail sales dropped 4.3%, this loss in income was more than made up by a 67.8% drop in shoplifting. Other, more detailed sets of statistics, circulated by e-mail, claimed that California police records showed similar dramatic reductions in auto thefts (82%), vandalism (73%), violent crime (alternately 28% or 48%) and drug-related offenses (54%, "not including the area surrounding the march [in Los Angeles]"). "Looks like the immigration rally was well worth it," one e-mail chuckled drolly, while another concluded, "They should protest every day!"[2]

Latinos have become the target, not just of Anglo-Americans, but also of the descendents of other ethnic migrants, who now find their niche threatened by groups that, like their grandparents, are competing for their jobs and for space in neighborhoods they had settled. Once people feel acclimatized and accepted in American society, they often feel that new migrants are a threat to their own economic security, community safety, and social comfort. This is strikingly true of the children and grandchildren of immigrants who may forget the travails of their family. Of course, to be fair, many previous generations of immigrants, arriving by ship, less able to avoid border checkpoints, make the point that their families entered legally. On the other hand, these earlier arrivals were allowed to enter and reside in this country indefinitely with fewer legal restrictions. Today, many "illegal" immigrants enter legally, but later become "illegals" when their temporary work visas expire before they receive formal authorization to remain and work toward citizenship. Increased restrictions on the numbers of aliens allowed to enter annually, caused by tightening federal regulation in the previous century, has made what once was an easy process complicated, filled with legal pitfalls.

But in some ways the situation of immigrants has not changed. Earlier waves of migrants were targets of stereotypes that portrayed newcomers as the purveyors of disease, immorality, and even disloyalty. Many of these images remain active in contemporary American culture, as shown by the rhetoric generated by the most recent waves of immigration from Latin America and elsewhere.

A Culture of Mistrust

Mistrust of the effects of outsiders has a long history. Nation states are imagined communities, treated as publics with distinctive character, history, and culture.[3] When we think of India, Sweden, Brazil, or France, certain powerful images come to mind. Swedes are stolid, Indians tied to social castes, Brazilians fun loving, and the French are, well, French. While it may be stereotyping, the citizens of these nations are identified with particular kinds of characteristics, and they, too, define themselves in particular ways. It is understandable that an influx of people who are seen as fundamentally different would be imagined to be dangerous to the very idea of the nation. The traditions and values that individuals hold as core to the meaning of their lives are seen as threatened and the health of the community is imagined to be endangered.

New residents, like new ideas, can provoke a defensive response metaphorically akin to the physical body's immune reaction. As an unknown, seemingly exotic factor, migrants provoke curiosity, and so rumors about their behavior and intentions become plausible. They might be capable of anything. Even as recently as spring 2009, when the world was preparing for the effects of a pandemic of swine flu, Mexicans and Mexican Americans were bracing for potential racism because the flu was initially believed to have originated in Mexico and hit residents there particularly hard, causing what was initially reported as 148 deaths in the first days of the outbreak (the numbers were later found to be inflated). Michael Savage, the host of *Savage Nation*, a conservative talk show reported to be the third most popular syndicated feature on American radio, responded to the news with outrage. "Make no mistake about it," he told an estimated audience of 8 to 10 million listeners. "Illegal aliens are the carriers of the new strain of human-swine avian flu from Mexico." Chiding the Barack Obama administration for not closing the U.S./Mexican border immediately, he suggested that the virus could be an artificial bioweapon manufactured by Islamic terrorists and deliberately planted in Mexico, knowing that it would quickly spread through the United States along with immigrants. Border jumpers, Savage told his audience, are "perfect mules for bringing this virus into America," using a slang term for foreigners hired to smuggle drugs across the border.

Neil Boortz, another popular conservative talk show host, agreed that it was possible that the virus was not a natural product but a weapon aimed at the United States. "What better way to sneak a virus into this country than give it to Mexicans?" he commented, adding, "I mean, one out of every 10 people born in Mexico is already living up here, and the rest are trying to get here."[4] Officials at the Pilsen Wellness Clinic in Chicago warned that the public should not tie Hispanics to this disease.[5] Fortunately for all concerned, though this epidemic caused fatalities like any new influenza outbreak, it eventually proved to be much less severe than expected.

But the linkage of disease and Latino ethnicity was clearly present in many people's minds, giving this claim immediate plausibility to many listeners. Four years previously, Bill O'Reilly, the prominent Fox News commentator, had let pass a caller's claim that immigrants were themselves "bioweapons." On his radio show, he took a call from a listener, who remarked:

> The point of my call today is I'd like to take a different look at illegal immigration. I believe that it has the same impact as a major terrorist attack. And here's what I mean. If you take the sum total of the economic consequences of illegal immigration, and also consider that the illegals crossing the border, that are coming across with, say, tuberculosis, syphilis, leprosy—each one of those people is a biological weapon. And, I believe that illegal immigration is— equals and surpasses the impact of 9-11.

"You might be right," O'Reilly responded, adding that there were an estimated 11 million illegal immigrants on the loose, and "Nobody knows the condition they're in." While some 3,000 people were killed in the September 11 attacks, he mused, "I think you could probably make an absolutely airtight case that more than 3,000 Americans have been either killed or injured, based upon the 11 million illegals who are here."[6]

This claim, while extravagant, was hardly new in American political culture. A century before Latinos threatened the American public as "illegal aliens,"[7] the public saw Asians as a menacing migrant population. The Asian Exclusion League, a nativist group formed in 1905, called for stricter controls "to prevent or minimize the immigration of Asiatics to America," and even as prominent a newspaper as the *New York Times* described Chinese immigrants as "befouled with social vices, with no knowledge or appreciation of free institutions or constitutional liberty, heathenish souls and heathenish propensities." If measures were not taken swiftly, the *Times* warned, "we should be prepared to bid farewell to republicanism."[8]

Cecil B. DeMille's 1923 silent version of *The Ten Commandments* depicts the flamboyant director's first cinematic vision of Moses leading the Israelites out of Egypt and receiving from God's hand the famous code of ethics. In the lesser-known second half, we learn of DeMille's view of the commandments' relevance to contemporary life, as embodied by two brothers, Dan and John McTavish, and their devout, Bible-reading mother. John, the good son, devotes himself to a simple life as a carpenter, while Dan, an agnostic, doubts the old-fashioned Mosaic code and strives to get ahead at all costs. In contrast to his brother, DeMille underscores Dan's unethical behavior—his covetousness, misappropriation of funds, profane language, and disrespect for his mother—all violations of the Ten Commandments.

Finally, a mysterious, ethnic woman appears slinking ashore in a harbor. This is "Sally Lung, a Eurasian," a title card tells us, wanted by authorities because she carries the dreaded disease leprosy. Dan McTavish, predictably, falls into her clutches, and, mindless of the consequences, she takes him to bed. When his unethical business dealings catch up with him, he comes to Sally's bedroom, seeking comfort and help. Cynically, she laughs and points to one of the news clippings, and he realizes that she has deliberately infected him.

DeMille's film, like most silent movies, communicates through powerful visual icons that were immediately recognized by his audience. After the shadowy scene in which she slips into the country illegally, Sally Lung immediately appears in the provocative dress of the "vamp." A well-known short poem by Rudyard Kipling, "The Vampire" (1897) had briefly made "vampire" (or "vamp" for short) a slang term for a sexually loose, predatory woman, usually imagined as a foreigner. Theda Bara created a sensation when she appeared as "The Vamp" in "A Fool There Was," a 1915 silent film inspired by Kipling's poem (and using its first line as the title). The studio, capitalizing on the controversy over her performance, claimed that she was born in Egypt of French-Italian parents. (In fact, she was born to a Jewish immigrant family in Cincinnati. Her father was Bernard Goodman.) Nita Naldi (born Anita Dooley in New York City), who played Sally, like Bara capitalized on the ethnic implications of her stage name, and DeMille emphasized her foreignness by filling her boudoir with oriental decorations, along with smoldering incense sticks. Sally is one of the many tainted "vamps," or sexually dangerous foreigners, featured in the popular culture of the Roaring Twenties, a moment of concern about immigration. The scene of a diseased migrant slithering ashore to infect society was a potent symbol of the dangers that migrants posed to the American body politic.

The image remained lively in American folklore up to contemporary times. CNN commentator Lou Dobbs, who frequently addressed issues of immigration, caused a sensation in April 2005 by presenting, then defending, a claim that diagnosed cases of leprosy had skyrocketed, from an average of about 20 per year for 40 years to 7,000 new cases in the past 3 years alone. Challenged about the accuracy of the data, Dobbs stubbornly refused to back down, insisting, "If we reported it, it's a fact." The affair quickly passed, explained as an innocent misinterpretation of a clumsily worded newspaper article,[9] but the furor showed that the link between foreigners and "loathsome," incurable diseases was still lively.

Immigrants as Virus

Even before DeMille's iconic film, migrants to the United States had been described as a virus that sapped a nation's strength. Concern was perhaps more symbolically expressed than practically resolved when, in the past, immigrants were given medical exams or quarantined in isolated, "sterile" places like Ellis Island, not yet ready to be incorporated within the nation. Today, these procedures are no longer employed, but we brood about the unchecked transmission of swine flu, bird flu, AIDS, or even the Ebola virus by means of foreigners entering our country. With increased international air travel, such transmission is all too plausible. All manner of germs may be transmitted by those flying on airplanes, a theme of the early spread of AIDS in the depiction of the infamous international traveler Patient Zero,[10] the sexually active gay man, an airline steward, whose international adventures were claimed by some epidemiologists to have spread the HIV virus in the late 1970s.

Americans are not alone in these fears, and may, in fact, be less prone to worry than other nations. Unlike many European countries, we have no nativist party that has as its primary goal to close the borders, reduce immigration, and preserve national (and sometimes imaginary) traditions. But it is not only Western nations that worry. China recently shed the stigma over the SARS epidemic by refusing entry to Mexican travelers and quarantining healthy Mexican citizens, when swine flu appeared to presage a global epidemic.[11] To admit a third-world person often seems equivalent to embracing all of the conditions of the third-world environment from which he or she emigrated.

Diasporas and Healthy Societies

Throughout human history, populations have migrated from their ancestral homeland, a characteristic of many groups, but none more than Jews, who have for millennia been forced from their homes by proclamations or by pogroms, becoming wandering strangers. This phenomenon of mass migration is known as a *diaspora*. Originally the term refers to the dispersal of Jews in the sixth century B.C. after the destruction of the First Temple in Jerusalem, coupled with forced exile of Jews to Babylonia. The term *diaspora* has come to refer more broadly to any group that has migrated from their traditional homelands. Diaspora studies are now found on many college campuses, as the movement of people is defined as characteristic of modernity and as a way of capturing the soul of an ethnic or religious group. Migration can be voluntary or forced, and it can result from prejudice, political oppression, or economic opportunities.

Understandably, such movements of people can threaten the traditions, and even the well-being, of their new communities. Land is rarely empty, and migration creates new neighbors and sometimes—as when Europeans settled Native American lands—leads to the spread of diseases to which the hosts lacked immunity. While nations should properly consider infectious disease in admitting visitors, these fears echo dramatically with cultural images of the *nation* as a body that is subject to disease. According to this long-held metaphor, not only do individuals become ill, but so do nations.

The idea of a healthy body as a metaphor to describe a nation goes back to ancient times, when Plato began his *Republic* by contrasting a "healthy" society, based on principles of self-control, with a "feverish" or even "festering" society that has been corrupted by lavish self-indulgence. Aristotle relied on a similar analogy between the state and body in arguing that the state occurs prior to any individual, suggesting in *Politics* that "if the whole body be destroyed, there will be no foot or hand…"[12] European political philosophers such as the sixteenth-century Englishman Thomas Hobbes likewise saw the state as being an artificial person. In the introduction to *The Leviathan*, Hobbes sees sovereignty as the soul, judges as the joints, social control as nerves, and wealth as bodily strength. For Hobbes, consensus is health; sedition is illness, civil war, and death. The metaphor of the state as a person subject to disease has long been used in American politics. However, the metaphor often takes a profoundly conservative perspective when health is seen in terms of maintaining obedience to old ways, while alternative lifestyles—and those who share these lifestyles—are treated as potential sources of infection.[13]

To the extent that migrants are believed to be in some essential way distinct from the native population, questions are likely to arise. What kind of people are they? What do they want? Why are they here? Can they be trusted? These questions can be highly destabilizing as is evident in the nativist, anti-immigrant movements that have arisen throughout American history. These battles could be seen in the early years of the republic when Anglo-Americans worried about the large number of Germans, and in the mid-nineteenth century when the Irish were targeted after they migrated because of the potato famine. Later in the century strict rules were placed on Chinese immigration, and after World War I limits were placed in some communities on speaking German in public. Debates over immigration arise each generation in various forms.

Migration and Civil Society

Migration cuts to the heart of civil society and challenges bonds of trust that unite citizens. As often happens in times of stress, rumors emerge to fill the gap, especially resting upon the disease metaphor. Three broad classes of truth claims tend to emerge about migrants as potential sources of cultural infection. One claims that they threaten moral and ethical norms, particularly sexual mores; the second claims that they produce catastrophe through disease and other means; and the third argues that they intend to usurp and overthrow the native way of life. Throughout history rumors have implied that migrants, from Jews in the diaspora to modern Latinos, are the human equivalent of germs that endanger the health of society: weakening moral purity, threatening safety, and imperiling democracy itself.

The Immoral Migrant

When immigrants arrive from vastly different backgrounds and with distinct cultural traditions, comfortable and established members of the host society, relying on stereotypes about the immigrants' countries, may quickly draw conclusions about how the immigrants might violate the stated or unstated existing social norms. In such circumstances, ignorance of these cultural traditions and an absence of trust permit wild stories to be seen as plausible. When these beliefs are tied to some measure of truth, exaggeration runs rampant, and may occur in rumors about culinary choices. Food preferences often become a stand-in for discussion of moral decline: how could someone eat something so disgusting?

PETS AS DELICACIES: FOOD PREFERENCES AS MORAL POLITICS. The widely known rumor that refugees from Southeast Asia, particularly Vietnamese, not only eat dogs and cats but actually steal pets for their repasts is of this type. These beliefs produced animosity between natives and immigrants from Stockton, California, to rural Wisconsin.[14] The recognition of different culinary traditions merged with the belief that the refugees would violate law and custom to obtain otherwise inaccessible delicacies. An account in the local newspaper, the *Stockton Record*, asserted that "Jan deNapoli claimed a $400 Siberian husky was stolen from her backyard. She said a boy later told her he had seen it eaten by Indochinese."[15] Accounts of refugees skinning and boiling cats also made the rounds. The stories were so persuasive that the city council nearly passed an ordinance criminalizing the practice. Such beliefs reveal the anxiety that strange customs and ignorance of those customs can provoke, particularly when the community is concerned about the economic and cultural effects of new migrants.

Food preferences are often visible means by which groups mark their boundaries, rejecting other groups because of their choices: tongue, chitterlings, catfish, veal, kidneys, and once even corn or tomatoes. These residents knew that their Indochinese neighbors had culinary habits different from their own (dogs are eaten in some Vietnamese restaurants and homes) and it seemed plausible to assume that any missing pet was being baked and served by Southeast Asians. Once again, the global linkage brought anxiety in its wake.

THE CATHOLIC CRISIS. While targets of rumors change over time, similar themes re-emerge. Long-time residents often feel in danger from filthy strangers, and often enough religion is taken to reveal immorality, denying our true faith, whichever it might be. Early in America's history, the group most commonly targeted was Catholics, who arrived as a result of political turmoil and famines in France and Ireland. Catholic immigrants threatened those already living in America, not only because of the traditions of their home nations, but because of their relationship to the Catholic Church, an affiliation that seemed in the eyes of many Protestants to provide an alternative political allegiance and was coupled with arcane practices and elaborate rituals, so different from the plain traditions of Protestant denominations. These Catholics were labeled Papists, and it was widely assumed that their primary affiliation was not to their new adopted nation but to the distant Pope.

As migrants grew more visible, panics arose, beginning in the 1830s. Nativist anti-Catholic propaganda spread throughout mid-nineteenth-century America, depicting Catholic priests as immoral and disloyal. Once ordained, a common argument ran, clergy were taught to lie and perjure themselves in the name of the Pope, then instructed in sin until they were masters of "impiety, immorality, falsehood, frauds in business, perjury, theft, murder, infanticide and regicide."[16] A number of books purporting to reveal hidden secrets of Catholicism included the claim that nuns in fact were little more than sex slaves for priests, who entered and left convents by way of secret passageways. The babies that were conceived were murdered at birth and concealed in secret rooms underneath convents.[17] These beliefs were not so very different than those that targeted Jews in the *Protocols of the Elders of Zion*.

In 1834, a Boston-area convent was burned by a mob after rumors circulated that it consisted of women abducted to provide free sex for priests. Two years later, Maria Monk's *Awful Disclosures of the Hotel Dieu Nunnery of Montreal* was published, claiming that nuns not only slept with priests but also ritually murdered the children after birth, on the grounds that if they died before they had a chance to sin, they would go directly to heaven. Monk's book and its sequels created such a sensation that the convent described was thoroughly searched at least twice for secret rooms containing the bodies of the murdered children.[18] With the exception of *Uncle Tom's Cabin*, the *Awful Disclosures* became the single best-selling work by a nineteenth-century American author. While Monk's stories were eventually discredited, they inspired a vast anti-Catholic literature. An imitator elaborated on her sex-and-baby-killing scenario, claiming that ritually murdered children were disposed of by being ground into sausages. "Those who bought and eat [sic] these sausages," this exposé claimed, "said they were the best sausages they ever eat."[19] Again food stands for immorality, a belief that equally applied to the Jews.

THE POLITICS OF WHITE SLAVERY. As the century developed, the assumption that immigrants were involved in abductions of young women for sexual exploitation continued. Such abductions typically occurred in spaces that were controlled by immigrants but accessible to white women. The term *white slavery* first arose in Great Britain during a moral panic concerning child prostitution, when a sensational series of articles written by the journalist W. T. Stead claimed that an underground network abducted and sold child virgins to wealthy pedophiles. His articles created a national sensation, which resulted in legislation imposing severe penalties for such traffic. No convictions were ever obtained under these laws.[20]

At the time in the United States, given our endemic racial tension, the label "white slavery" made cultural sense. The label simultaneously captured the desire for the eroticism and power that prostitution entails for clients. While some immigrants were involved in illegal activities, such as sponsoring prostitution and providing abortion, the rumors went well beyond what could be documented and reflected the anxieties of the age.[21]

Nevertheless, the controversy established rumors that such prostitution and abortion networks continued to thrive in deep secrecy. In most cases, Anglo-Saxon Americans believed that the perpetrators were part of Jewish-controlled prostitution rings and the women had been abducted for sale in brothels overseas. In fact, Jewish organizations readily conceded that there had been an increase in Jewish-controlled prostitution in European ghettos. But official investigations showed that both the procurers and the women involved were Jewish and all participated as a means of alleviating their financial hardships. Still, when a number of Jewish pimps were put on trial in Vienna in 1892 for having conspired to ship prostitutes to foreign ports as far afield as Brazil and Turkey, press coverage of the "Jewish white slave traffic" was intense and often implied that such rings were responsible for the mysterious disappearance of young non-Jewish girls. One Anti-Semitic crusader alluded to:

> Countless cases in which Christian servants employed by Jews disappear without trace, carried off to a dreadful fate in the brothels of Hungary, the Orient and South America, despite the vigilance of the legal authorities. These cases are connected with the incredible crimes committed by Jews because of their superstitions for the purpose of getting hold of Christian blood and calling to heaven for revenge.[22]

Such claims prepared the ground for a series of even more intense panics that occurred in both Great Britain and the United States in the early twentieth century, involving the abduction of young women for sexual exploitation. "All sorts of stories, sensational and wholly improbable, were repeated from mouth to mouth," one British observer noted, "of sudden disappearances, abductions and attempts to entice and allure innocent girls."[23] One of the most widespread of these held that white slavers would drug unwary girls on the street, using a sleeping potion placed in a drink or, more directly, by jabbing her with a "poisoned needle." An official Massachusetts inquiry noted that one common story involved "the administration of a narcotic drug by the use of a hypodermic needle by a procurer, who plies the needle on his victim as he passes her on the street, or as he sits beside her in the street car or in the theatre."

When such stories were investigated, the same report continued, they were "found to be a vague rumor, where one person has told another that some friend of the former (who invariably in turn referred the story further back) heard that the thing happened." Other stories, the investigators added, "were easily recognized versions of incidents in certain books or plays."[24] Some other experts, however, were inclined to say that the stories were based on some truth, due to "the extreme scantiness of women's apparel."[25]

Crusader Ernest Bell wrote in 1910, linking sex and food, those two grand generators of rumor:

> I believe that there are good grounds for the suspicion that the ice cream parlor, kept by the foreigner in the large country town, is often a recruiting station, and a feeder for the "white slave" traffic. It is certain that this is the case in the big city, and many evidences point to the conclusion that there is a kind of fellowship among these foreign proprietors of refreshment parlors which would make it entirely natural and convenient for the proprietor of a city establishment of this kind, who is entangled in the "white slave" trade, to establish relations with a man in the same business and of the same nationality in the country town. I do not mean to intimate by this that all the ice cream and fruit "saloons" having foreign-born proprietors are connected with the "white slave" traffic—but some of them are, and this fact is sufficient to cause all careful and thoughtful parents of young girls to see that they do not frequent these places.[26]

Bell's account paints a vivid, if odd, picture for contemporary eyes, but given the novelty of ice cream at the turn of the century, we can appreciate the rumor's plausibility. The production and sale of ice cream was rare until the St. Louis World's Fair of 1904, and so ice cream was still treated as an exotic delicacy, largely an Italian concoction. Before commercial freezers, it could not be stored at home, so one had to go to a "parlor" to consume it, which required crossing cultural boundaries into a potentially dangerous urban setting. Further, given the uncertain ingredients in ice cream, a dish that was not prepared by housewives, it was plausible that narcotics might be slipped into a pretty young woman's sundae.

In examining the patterns of social anxiety, often leading to the spread of rumor, historian Alan Hunt[27] suggests that rumors often refer to underlying issues that appear trivial and inconsequential. However, Hunt indicates that it may be precisely the combination of the mundane and the exotic that generates these impassioned concerns: "the triviality of such anxieties is itself significant in allowing a more deep-seated and unacknowledged anxiety to be activated without ever being directly named."[28] Hunt argues that the fear of ice cream parlors as sites of white slavery links kidnapping to nativist concerns about immigration and the fact that ice cream parlors were sites of "hetero-social conviviality." In Europe, the rumor tides flowed the other way, as stories flourished about mistreatment of Europeans by immoral Americans.

In 1971, the influential French sociologist Edgar Morin[29] examined a comparable set of rumors about kidnappings and disappearances of young French women from boutiques and dress shops in Orleans. These businesses, the rumors held, were owned by a network of Jewish shopkeepers. Female customers were injected with drugs in fitting booths, and were then sold into white slavery, sometimes transported by means of submarine. Of course, no missing persons could be found, but the sources were credible and the beliefs seemed all too plausible as they echoed the latent eroticism of traditional Jewish ritual murder stories.[30]

"WHITE SLAVERY" TODAY. We still remain concerned about "sex slavery" (no longer referred to as "white slavery") as rumor themes remain, even as their targets evolve. Today, sex slavery rings are said to lure young prostitutes from the former Soviet Union to the West and from Mexico across the border. In a controversial article in the *New York Times Magazine*, Peter Landesman echoes the fears of a century earlier:

1212-1/2 West Front Street was one of what law-enforcement officials say are dozens of active stash houses in the New York metro-
politan area—mirroring hundreds more in other major
cities...where under-age girls and young women from dozens of
countries are trafficked and held captive....Because of the porous-
ness of the US-Mexico border and the criminal networks that tra-
verse it, the towns and cities along that border have become the
main staging area in an illicit and barbaric industry, whose 'products' are women and girls....The United States has become a major
importer of sex slaves....Kevin Bales, president of Free the Slaves,
America's largest anti-slavery organization, says that the number is
at least 10,000 a year. John Miller, the State Department's director
of the Office to Monitor and Combat Trafficking in Persons, conceded: "That figure could be low. What we know is that the number
is huge." Bales estimates that there are 30,000 to 50,000 sex slaves in
captivity in the United States at any given time.[31]

A recent claim is that the Russian mafia runs white slavery outfits out
of Eastern Europe, enticing young women to work as nannies, models,
actresses, or waitresses. As many as 400,000 women have left the Ukraine
alone, a sensational 1998 report in the *New York Times* asserted, many of
them ending up in brothels in Israel, while others were allegedly auctioned
off to mafia gang members in Milan, partially stripped and standing on
blocks, just as in Southern slave markets.[32]

These "statistics" and anecdotes, depicting ethnic strangers prominently involved in the business of immorality, duplicate the rumors about
white slavery a century before. Echoing earlier anti-Semitic claims, a number of accounts circulating among right-wing nativist groups like the
National Alliance suggest that the Russian mafia is another name for Jewish-
controlled white slavery and that Israel is a central nexus in the global prostitution network.[33] "Jews like to say about the so-called 'Holocaust' of the
Second World War, 'Never again,'" a recent National Alliance editorial on
the sex-slavery topic concluded, "But by their own behavior they guarantee
that there will be."[34]

To recognize that these claims are rumor does not mean that there are
no brothels in Tel Aviv. However, the enormous and uncertain statistics and
graphic stories are meant to convince the public that attention must be
paid, often without definitive proof. Social problems are constructed by

means of graphic accounts. As the claims enter public discourse, rumor explodes as the statistics are transformed into the narrative cries of poor victims.

The Catastrophic Immigrant

We return to the concern with the diseased immigrant as constituting a threat to the health of society and its citizens. Sex and food are important, but death trumps both within the world of rumor. At the turn of the twentieth century, migrants processed at Ellis Island were confined to a quarantine hospital if authorities had any question about their mental or physical health. According to records, notations were chalked on the coats of the new arrivals—"C" for "crabs," "CT" for "trachoma," "M" for "vaginal infection," and so on.[35] Many immigrants managed to enter anyway, according to family anecdotes, by wiping off the chalk marks when inspectors were not watching. Certainly the panics caused by epidemics in Europe and Asia made government officials zealous to prevent their spread to America by scrupulously, if ineffectively, screening foreigners at the borders. But their viruses and parasites also served, and continue to serve, as metaphorical equivalents of illegal immigrants, hidden in the storehouse of the body. Can we trust that these new residents are healthy, or will they import illness? Being vigorous and healthy is taken as a condition that is essential for participating in civil society. This is particularly salient in the case of contagious illnesses, such as tuberculosis or AIDS.

TYPHOID MARY AND THE ILL AMONG US. The first of the great medical scares about immigrant workers in the United States was the concern over the infamous "Typhoid Mary," even though earlier in 1892 Russian Jews had been quarantined in a cholera scare and in 1900 Chinese were quarantined because of bubonic plague.[36] But it was a few years later that the fear took over as typhoid spread. In the summer of 1906, 11 members of a well-to-do New York City household fell ill with typhoid fever while vacationing at a Long Island summer home. Concerned that he would not be able to rent the home again, the landlord hired a private investigator who learned that similar outbreaks of disease had occurred in other homes where Mary Mallon, an Irish immigrant who had recently become the family's cook, had worked previously. Mallon was questioned, and, when she grew suspicious and belligerent, police were summoned and she was taken into custody. She was found to be a healthy carrier of the typhoid bacteria, and, as there was then no antibiotic treatment, she was forced into quarantine on an island in New York's East River.

After two years of confinement, Mallon filed a lawsuit, submitting several stool samples that tested negative for the disease, and after two more years of litigation she was released, provided that she never serve as a cook. Five years later, however, another outbreak of typhoid fever occurred at a Manhattan hospital, and it was discovered that Mallon had been working there under a pseudonym. This time authorities showed no sympathy as it seemed likely that she had deliberately continued to work in spite of knowing that she was capable of infecting others with the disease. She was confined permanently to the island, where she died 23 years later. The nickname the tabloids gave her, "Typhoid Mary," became a catch phrase for someone who wantonly exposed others to an infectious disease. It was inevitable that when cases emerged of AIDS victims who continued to engage in high-risk behavior, they became known as "AIDS Mary" or "AIDS Harry."

Rumors about disease surrounded the migration of Haitians in the early years of the AIDS epidemic. Even though we now know that the claims are not true, a common belief held that AIDS originated in Haiti or that Haiti represented a particularly large pool of infected people.[37] Haitians were seen as dangerous as homosexuals, heroin users, and hemophiliacs—one of the four Hs of AIDS transmission. Because of the early cluster of cases and the images of the impoverished and exotic island—a mysterious site of voodoo rites—the linkage of AIDS and Haiti seemed entirely plausible to many Americans.[38]

Of course, some of these claims were based on competent medical knowledge. But there were many other cases in which nonforeigners spread diseases carelessly, and in any case contamination of city water supplies with sewage was often a more important source of infection than contact with migrants. Foreigners were a convenient scapegoat for the anger that emerges after any public disaster.

THE JOHNSTOWN FLOOD AND THE BEASTLY IMMIGRANT. Immigrants have been blamed for other catastrophes besides spreading diseases. A persistent rumor blamed the origins of the disastrous Chicago Fire of 1871 on a lantern carelessly used by an Irish immigrant woman, Catherine O'Leary, while milking her cow. The official inquest found no evidence of her culpability and placed blame squarely on official incompetence. Local government gave fire companies neither the support nor the equipment necessary to fight the fire,[39] but popular memory has continued to blame Mrs. O'Leary's cow for the inferno that followed. Not only was the blaze blamed on a representative Irish immigrant, Mrs. O'Leary, but persistent rumors claimed that ethnic communities did nothing to check the fire, instead spending the entire time in a drunken orgy.

After the devastating and emblematic 1889 Johnstown Flood, a number of reporters published similar stories, claiming that migrants had both indulged in "beastly" drunkenness and in looting. One reporter noted:

> Incoming trains from Pittsburgh brought hundreds of toughs, who joined with the Slavs and Bohemians in rifling the bodies, stealing furniture, insulting women, and endeavoring to assume control of any rescuing parties that tried to seek the bodies under the bushes and in the limbs of trees. There was no one in authority, no one to take command of even a citizens' posse could it have been organized. A lawless mob seemed to control this narrow neck of land that was the only approach to the city of Johnstown. I saw persons take watches from dead men's jackets and brutally tore finger-rings from the hands of women.[40]

Striking as it is, this was by no means the most dramatic report of the flood's aftermath. Later press releases claimed that "fiendish Huns" were slicing off dead girls' fingers for their diamond rings and, in one instance, had decapitated a woman's corpse for a valuable necklace.[41]

The case of the Johnstown Flood is emblematic of how citizens often respond to disaster. For society to be ordered, bad things should not happen to good people, but if they do, these bad things should be caused by bad people. This is a core assumption by which we live our lives. If we live in a just world, we need to be confident that, although good people may be hurt, they are hurt because of malefactors.[42] We know that when something horrific happens, societies look for scapegoats, a point that was only too clear in the conspiracy stories after September 11. Sometimes the villain is a foreigner, but at other times we take a domestic group and emphasize how foreign they really are.

Historian Carl Smith, commenting on similar reactions to urban catastrophes, argues that a common response to any disaster is to blame it on any force that threatened the majority's sense of the established order. Rumors emerge after any period of disorder—whether caused by an epidemic or a natural disaster such as a fire, flood, or storm—and blame the event on the disorderly morals of an ethnic "other."[43] And so Typhoid Mary, evil ice cream parlor owners, and Vietnamese puppy snatchers are all a part of the same process. This is not a new phenomenon, but reaches back into distant history. As Adrienne Mayor has noted, in classic times rumors circulated that devastating plagues had been caused by enemies of the Greeks, who were said to have deliberately started the epidemic by trading clothing taken from dead victims.[44] Parallel accounts circulated in the 1800s about European settlers wiping out Native Americans with smallpox-infected blankets, leading to considerable hostility to white settlers.[45]

Similarly, urban disasters such as fires or floods have led to retrospective scapegoating since ancient times. In the wake of the Great Fire of Rome (64 C.E.), the emperor Nero, possibly to deflect rumors that he deliberately had the blaze set to provide space for a grander palace, blamed the followers of the new religion Christianity, a recent introduction from the distant Roman-occupied region of Judea. Many Christians were rounded up in the aftermath of the disaster, the historian Tacitus records, and "convicted not so much of the crime of setting the city afire, as of hatred against all humanity."[46]

Folklorist Carl Lindahl[47] has suggested a "David effect" for this tendency, named after the young man who was able to defeat the mighty Goliath in the Biblical Book of Samuel. After a culture's security is undercut by a devastating event, Lindahl suggests, one common reaction is to blame not a powerful entity but rather the group that is the most *powerless*.

The concept of the "catastrophic outsider" is, moreover, not even necessarily Western in nature. Dionizjusz Czubala, collecting contemporary legends in Mongolia during the early 1990s, found a similar belief that the Chinese deliberately poisoned the silk that they sent overseas to trade.[48]

An even more dramatic case in point occurred after a devastating earthquake hit central Japan on September 1, 1923, destroying nearly half of Tokyo and up to 80% of the port of Yokohama. In the wake of the devastation, second only in peacetime disasters in Japan to the seventeenth-century Meireki fire that devastated the capital Edo, a rumor spread that local Koreans planned to rise up and attack vulnerable Japanese citizens. Koreans were said to be ready to rape and kill Japanese. Thirteen years before the earthquake Japan had annexed the Korean peninsula, and many Korean laborers had immigrated to Japan, living in segregated areas where native Japanese considered them dangerous. In retrospect, no evidence can be found for the Japanese fears, but they were sufficiently plausible that vigilantes eventually killed thousands of Koreans and even several dozen Japanese men who were thought to be Koreans.[49]

Such widely known rumors and legends give moral standing to otherwise dehumanizing catastrophes by treating them as the result of a series of malign, personal acts. Epidemics and physical disasters are facilitated by a large number of factors that are, prior to the event, difficult or even impossible to detect. The common decision by the powerful to blame the powerless is a social reflex, part of the human process of coping with tragedy.

The Disloyal Migrant

If one accepts that migrants are immoral and prone to cause or capitalize on disasters, it is easy to see them as responsible for vile conspiracies. As discussed in chapter 2, the power of conspiracy rumors lies in their ability to explain large numbers of discrete facts in terms of a simple, direct explanation for a troubling reality.

Conspiracy theories associated with migrants have been present in America since our independence. The Reverend Jedediah Morse, a Boston minister, gave a series of public sermons in the 1790s, alleging that foreign groups were now at work in the United States to promote atheism and influence government policies. These groups, he asserted, belonged to the Order of the Illuminati, a Bavarian secret society that expressed sharply anticlerical views and advocated the overthrow of traditional European monarchies. A number of writers had suggested that secret Illuminati agents had fomented the French Revolution and were planning similar coups in England and the fledgling United States.

When critics challenged the minister to present concrete evidence for the alleged local Illuminati, he first pointed to an alleged group of 40 Massachusetts free-thinkers who, rumor had it, "spend the sabbath in labour and diversion, as fancy dictates; and the nights in riotous excess and promiscuous concubinage, as lust impels ... evidence that the devil is at this time gone forth, having great influence."[50] Morse next pointed to the American Society of United Irishmen, a politically radical group of Irish emigrants displaced by the 1798 rebellion, as a branch of the Illuminati.[51] In time, Rev. Morse's credibility declined, and the scare soon passed from public attention. Nevertheless, the fear of the Illuminati, a sinister group of emigrant intellectuals covertly manipulating history, lived on in tradition.

We described the importance of the famous forgery of the *Protocols of the Elders of Zion* in chapter 2 in discussing conspiracy theories relating to terrorism. But the *Protocols* also revealed a mistrust of Jewish migrants and their political machinations. In addition to the attempts to obtain political control detailed earlier, these immigrants were also claimed to promote immorality in their new home country. The tactics of these Jewish elders were said to range from secretly encouraging liberal challenges to aristocratic institutions to encouraging alcoholism and immorality among young people.[52] As the *Protocols* explained:

> It is indispensable to trouble in all countries the people's relations with their governments so as to utterly exhaust humanity with dissention, hatred, struggle, envy and even by the use of torture, by starvation, by the inoculation of diseases, by want, so that the 'goyim' see no other issue than to take refuge in our complete sovereignty."[53]

Disloyalty and immorality went hand in hand in attitudes to the Jewish diaspora. The *Protocols* were successful precisely because they so perfectly expressed the "infection" metaphor that is linked to mass immigration. While the authors realized that they were not quoting actual speeches, it is safe to assume that they took the *content* of the *Protocols* as essentially accurate—as true in effect, if not in fact—that the political and cultural world was being invaded by ethnic outsiders whose beliefs and practices were at odds with traditional religious norms and customs. Groups that considered themselves at risk readily believed that a network of outsiders was responsible for a growing sense of moral decay and malaise, and even for natural disasters.

The Infected State

Today, many Americans still consider their relationship with immigrants as that of a healthy body infected by immoral, physically dangerous, and potentially deadly agents. While we pride ourselves as being a melting-pot society (or more recently as a stewpot in the revised metaphor that embraces the value of diversity), our reaction to migrants remains ambivalent. Some rumors result from imagined racial issues; others reflect concern over an outsider culture. In our history, Americans have embraced an array of disturbing beliefs about German, Irish, Chinese, Jewish, Vietnamese, Mexican, and Arabic immigrants. Today, Swedes and Italians spread rumors about Turks and Syrians, just as Americans once spread rumors about Swedes and Italians. The basic problem is a lack of trust in the moral standing of our fellow residents, given our lack of equal status contact with them. We are uncertain—and are ready to believe the worst—about how these men and women fit into our delicately balanced civil society. The politics of plausibility that shape the ways that we understand immigrants give form to these rumors, even when the assumptions are highly questionable.

In the same April 25, 2009, talk show program quoted at the start of this chapter, conservative commentator Michael Savage dramatically synthesized all of the ways in which foreigners allegedly "sicken" America:

> ...the lying thieves in the U.S. government have nothing to say because the bottom line is more important. You cannot stop the flow of people, drugs, and whatever. After all, our commerce depends upon this flow of drugs, so you can't tell people not to go or come from Mexico. This virus has a unique combination of gene segments not seen in people or pigs before. The virus contains human virus, avian virus from North America and pig virus from North America, Europe, and Asia. No one's ever seen it before.
>
> I ask you a question: Where is the dumb moron Janet Napolitano, head of the Homeland Security Department? Why are they not looking into this as a possible terrorist attack on America? Now you say, how could this be? Because the demons in the Islamic world have been trying to modify the influenza virus for years. We've been told about this for years. Some of these scientists are very clever, and they also know because of the open borders policy with Mexico, because of the corruption in the U.S. government, it's very easy to bring an altered virus into Mexico, put it into the general population, have them march across the border. They know the U.S. government is corrupt and incapable of protecting its people. They can't stop anything because they don't want to stop anything.

The question is, what are we going to do about this? How do you protect yourself? What can you do? I'll tell you what I'm going to do, and I don't give a damn if you don't like what I'm going to say. I'm going to have no contact anywhere with an illegal alien, and that starts in the restaurants. You want intelligence? Stop eating at restaurants where they have undocumented workers in the kitchen. You're risking your life, moron.

You want to be a good liberal? Go and have some wonderful food tonight and pay no attention to the kitchen. Go ahead, idiot. Go ahead, go and eat in a restaurant now with illegal aliens all over the kitchen and you don't know if they were in Mexico yesterday or two days ago because your wonderful government doesn't give a rat's behind who's in the kitchen or whether they wiped their behind with their hands. All they care about is that the borders remain open, for obvious reasons. No, no, no, I'll start with restaurants. That's it; the door slams shut for me.[54]

The rumors that we describe in this chapter—and in the next—remind us of the importance of examining and confronting rumor in creating a just and civil society. Rumors can provide more smoke than clarity. The rumors that we tell about migrants are particularly troubling in that it takes time and effort to confront the new. Often change and diversity are mistrusted, sometimes with good cause, but often through fear. When influential media commentators equate contact with immigrants with eating excrement, contracting a deadly disease, enabling terrorist plots, fostering the trade in narcotics, and supporting a corrupt government with no desire to protect its people, the result can be the perpetration of stereotypes that make reasoned responses to social problems difficult. The rumors that we transmit about our new neighbors reveal the climate of our times, and, as this chapter has demonstrated in its historical reach, the climate has not altered as much as we suspect. Rumor sometimes can provide comfort and security when crisis emerges, but at other times it can fan the flames of mistrust. Both sets of beliefs demand attention as we strive to balance the value of tradition with preparation for change. Reading history reminds us that the current targets of rumors about immigrants are likely to be the groups who in the next generation will spread similar tales about immigrants to come.

4

"There Goes the Neighborhood"

Latino Migrants and Immigration Rumors

Have you heard the latest about those Hispanics moving into town? My friend, who is in the neighborhood crime watch organization, says there are at least four gangs operating in town. The police say crime is no worse than it was since before they moved in, but I know people are moving out like crazy. Look at Wyoming Street. And now people are afraid to go to Wal-Mart after dark because gangs are grabbing and robbing women in the parking lots. I heard there was a drive-by shooting at K-Mart, even. Everyone has a story about someone getting knifed or shot right where they live or go shopping. If we don't watch out, it won't be safe to walk outside even in the middle of the day. Something's going to have to be done.[1]

Hazleton, Pennsylvania: Land of Opportunity?

In January 2002, Excel Corporation, later renamed Cargill Meat Solutions, opened a huge meat-packing operation in Hazleton, a small city in northeastern Pennsylvania. The firm, based in Wichita, had previously opened three plants in the United States and two overseas, becoming the country's second largest supplier of pre-packaged beef and pork.[2] It openly promoted its minority hiring practices and in company brochures proudly pointed to "a large Latino population at every location."[3] At the same time, Excel purchased Taylor Meat, a local processor in the Allentown area and a heavy employer of Latinos.

Word of job opportunities created by the opening of the Hazleton plant circulated through the ranks of the Cargill employees. Suddenly the plant's opening was followed by an influx of Latinos, mainly Caribbean rather than Mexican in origin. The city planners were caught by surprise when the city's population, instead of shrinking, suddenly swelled. Estimates based on the 2000 census suggested that by mid-decade the population would fall to 22,000, but in fact it jumped to an estimated 32,000. Nearly all the new residents had Hispanic roots, mainly from the Caribbean nation of the Dominican Republic by way of New York City or New Jersey.[4]

The impact of such immigration waves on previous ethnic neighborhoods was dramatic. The same themes that we explained historically in chapter 3 were at work in this small Pennsylvania town. How did the residents, comfortable in their ethnic and religious traditions, cope with this influx? What they did, as so often occurs, is to spread rumors, revealing the willingness to accept strange beliefs as newly plausible. The rumors allow us to diagnose this town in transition as happened in past generations, where the new residents became the old-timers. The sharp dividing lines of past generations had been erased in memory to face what many residents perceived as a new threat. What was the identity of a city now shaken by immigration and by rumor?

To explore contemporary attitudes to immigrants, we focus on this small multicultural community. Hazleton is a stable community, but not a wealthy one. With an average income in 2000 of approximately $31,000, this working-class city does not compare to the national average of $43,000. Yet, despite this, Hazleton residents are proud of it having become and remained a "full-employment" city, with ample job opportunities for residents and a low unemployment rate. It has been a melting pot for several generations of European immigrants, forgetting just how hard-won that image of the melting pot had been for their forebears. But today its self-image is very much tied to core American values.

In the nineteenth century, migrants were drawn to the area by the call for cheap labor to dig anthracite coal. First Irish, then German, then a range of Eastern European "hunkies" and "polacks" settled the area. However, this mixed ethnic stock created deep divisions within the town, still visible in the city's geography. Occasionally, two churches of the same denomination are found side by side. Despite the comforting belief that these residents became unhyphenated Americans, these geographical markers reflect ancient, deeply felt prejudices, in which Irish American Catholics, for instance, resisted worshiping in the same building as more recently arrived Poles or Italians, and in which a newer generation of English-speaking Lutherans split from more traditional churches that insisted on retaining the original High-German liturgy. A common joke found in Hazleton— and in many divided American communities—holds that a local sailor was cast away on a desert island during World War II and spent his solitude constructing a detailed replica of his old neighborhood. Finally rescued, he was asked why he'd put a second Catholic church on his reconstructed home street. "Oh, that's the church I *don't* attend," he replied.

By the 1800s, it was rumored that local immigrants had been rounded up by agents from low-life and criminal elements and sent directly to Hazleton. Some worried that Irish immigrants brought with them their allegiance to the Molly Maguires, an alleged terrorist organization with historical linkages to the Irish Republican Army (IRA) through the Ancient Order of Hibernians. This collective memory of immigration provides a convenient filter by which to understand the more recent emergence of a visible Latino community in Hazleton. The city is still divided ethnically (Italian, Polish, German, Irish, and Slovak descendants each have over 10% of the population), but by 2000, 5% of the population was Hispanic, a number that increased rapidly in the next few years.[5]

Like many areas in the Rust Belt, northeastern Pennsylvania has been hit hard by the relocation of once-strong industries to the third world, seeking cheaper labor and fewer regulations. As anthracite mining grew less profitable during the mid-twentieth century, the region's economy became dependent on textile and knitting mills. In a few decades these factories began to close, first to move South and then to Latin America. Civic leaders sought to replace the lost jobs by creating industrial parks that could compete for a variety of light industries. With its stable communities, low cost of living, and access to interstate highways, Hazleton was able to survive the loss of its mining and manufacturing base. By 2003, a small industrial park expanded, with four additional locations added near interstate exchanges. This is the community to which Hispanics came to live and work.

Even if the economy had stabilized, Hazleton was losing ground. Hazleton's population, peaking at 38,000 in the mid-twentieth century, had declined steadily; it reached 23,257 in the 2000 census, with projections to shrink further. Ambitious young people had for half a century looked else-where for employment in more vibrant communities. Such people were said to have "gone to Jersey," though in fact New Jersey was only one of many markets that attracted local high-school graduates. Still, Hazleton had at least avoided becoming a ghost town like nearby coal-belt communi-ties such as Shenandoah, which grew to 25,000 by 1910, then lost 80% of its population by attrition over the next century.

As events of the next few years showed, the job opportunities that were created—low-paying factory-line or assembly positions requiring minimal education or verbal skills—made the area ideal for the next generation of migrants. As the unskilled jobs that existed were unappealing for the tech-nologically oriented children of longtime residents, the future remained uncertain.

Wyoming Street and the Wild East

Located in the heart of Hazleton's historic downtown, Wyoming Street is a well-known section of small grocery stores and shops catering to local resi-dents. When Spanish-speaking immigrants began to rent the lower-priced housing a few years back, a number of shops changed ownership to cater to this new population. These businesses included Latino groceries and restaurants and at least one *botanica*, stocking paraphernalia for Hispanic folk medicine and magic. Longtime residents soon became nervous about the growing numbers of Spanish-speaking shoppers, and rumors began to circulate about drug dealing and other criminal acts. After a *Philadelphia Inquirer* article commented that the new Latino businesses had "revital-ized" a stagnant downtown, a number of residents replied angrily. "I don't see how the city of Hazleton has been revitalized by Hispanics," one said. "There isn't one 'new' store or restaurant that appeals to me. I have stopped driving down Wyoming Street if I can help it, and all of my car doors are locked when I do. Businesses that had been there my whole life have been forced to move."[6]

White residents wondered about the background of the Hispanics they encountered. "Today, we have no idea who they are or what their background is," one said. "Are they criminals in their home country? Do they have terrorist ties? Medical issues? Mental issues?"[7] "Like Wyoming Street" quickly became a local catchword, or *metonym*, naming a complex of beliefs and stories associated with the influx of foreigners, whom white residents typically labeled "Puerto Ricans" or "Mexicans," although in fact most new residents saw themselves as Dominicans with their own national identity.

While it is easy to categorize these rumors as reflecting the ignorance of the local population, a more sympathetic approach is to recognize that they reveal an "effort after meaning." Life in Hazleton, perhaps in a state of decline, reflected a settled life for many longtime residents. As sociologist Ann Swidler[8] points out, when the settled existence of a community is disrupted, people will likely be goaded to alter their attitudes, ideologies, and cultural traditions, creating a new "toolkit" of action in which rumors are one particularly dramatic example. This leads to a variety of stories, disturbing for both residents and those who track ethnic animosity.

> [M]y great aunt…told me a story about the Puerto Ricans that live on Wyoming Street in Hazleton. She said that her friend went to drive through the street but the entire street got blocked by Puerto Ricans. She said they demanded that the driver pay five dollars in order to pass. Eventually police showed up and the crowd disappeared.[9]

Stories like this became commonplace. Similar stories have been found elsewhere when the presence of outsiders has provoked concern. Sociologists Robert Balch and Margaret Gilliam[10] found a similar story in a rural community in the state of Wyoming a generation earlier, at a time when the influx of new residents from outside had sparked persistent rumors that satanic cults were operating in the area. In what they termed "The Grapevine" rumor, local residents described how motorists who went down a lonely road were sometimes harassed by hooded cult members, who tried to block them from driving away by forming a "human grapevine" across the road. The emergence of a grapevine in Hazleton not only expresses concern over the presence of large groups of immigrants in a previously safe neighborhood but also reflects doubt that local authorities can buffer the threat. Authorities did rescue the person eventually, but the message was that the local police, overwhelmed by the influx of Hispanics, could not respond quickly.

The Violent Migrant: Rumor and Collective Response

Rumors circulate in the larger society after traumatic events such as terrorist attacks and natural disasters, but they also are sparked by triggering events on the local scale, such as odd happenings or violent crimes. For instance, when a young Dominican immigrant was shot dead in a daylight fracas in downtown Hazleton, rumors quickly spread that a number of dangerous Latino gangs had begun operating in town.

Surely a bloody murder in the midst of a previously secure neighborhood provokes an intense need to explain the significance of the event. Rumors provide this information, and also assess why the agencies responsible for providing security have not done their job. Despite its economic strains, Hazleton was—and still is—a city with a comfortingly low crime rate, half the national average.[11] Yet, at the same moment that rumor reveals an uncertain trust in institutions and the quality of the information that they provide, it reveals trust in the knowledge of fellow citizens. Put another way, people in one's social network are treated as credible sources. Rumor reveals trust in one's neighbors and co-workers at the moment that it questions trust in institutions. Trust may unite one group while dividing the larger community of which the group is a part.

From 1999 to 2003, there had been only two reported murders. However, after a second murder followed the first, in which a longtime resident was shot by two Latinos,[12] a wave of protest spread through the city. Spearheaded by Mayor Lou Barletta, proudly admitting his immigrant ancestry, citizens proposed to the Hazleton City Council an Illegal Immigration Relief Act. This introduced tough new fines for landlords renting rooms to undocumented Latinos, as well as license revocation for any business that hired them. It also established English as the official language of the city and removed Spanish translations from its official paperwork.

Mayor Barletta found himself nationally celebrated because of Hazleton's tough new law. He told the press that he had received over 1,500 e-mail responses to the media coverage, most of it staunchly favorable. Certainly this was the case on a public reaction board set up by the *Philadelphia Inquirer*, which ran a feature story after the act was passed by the city council.[13] Many comments were bluntly critical of Latinos, both legal and illegal. Most residents strongly supported the mayor's initiative, hoping that such acts would help, in one native's words, "restore Hazleton to the peaceful, clean community it was in my youth."[14] Images of dirt and disorder were common in the popular imagination, as they had been when other ethnic groups were targeted. But immigrants were outraged at the tough rhetoric of the new act. "Latinos found out about this city and came here looking for a better life for their families, to live the American dream we all want to live," a Latino community leader responded, adding, "Downtown was abandoned. Latinos have revived it."[15]

The passage of the ordinance in June 2006 led to a hot and predictable debate in which some residents and onlookers from other regions aired stereotypes that they had heard about Latino migrants. "AMERICANS have more of a right to a better life in their own country than some foreign invaders whether they are legal or not!" one reader exclaimed, concluding, "GET OUT OF HAZLETON! GET OUT OF AMERICA!"[16] Another wrote, "Our way of life and social structure is being eroded by aliens coming here and turning it into the hole they left. I say it's time to keep our Country our Country, send them back."[17] Most residents avoided and rejected such fiery language, but communicated through rumor, claiming that after all, these things were *true*.

Rumors spread images of the newcomers not just as potentially dangerous individuals, but as members of criminal organizations. While few residents of Hazleton considered the Latinos in their midst to be terrorists, many worried that the desire to commit crime was a prime motive for Latino migration. It has been a stable belief that immigrants are criminals, sometimes forced to leave their home countries by local authorities. A college student reported a common rumor in this vein:

> A majority of the Latinos are criminals from big cities. They found Hazleton [Pennsylvania] because of fliers about cheap housing and work. These fliers were posted in the early nineties in cities like Philadelphia, Pittsburgh, and New York City. This was new territory, so they say the criminals jumped at the opportunity.[18]

This rumor had been communicated for several years before a progressive mayor was defeated for reelection in the 1990s after rumors spread that billboards throughout New Jersey encouraged Hispanics to move to town. One of the older Catholic churches, whose belfry is a prominent landmark, was nicknamed "Taco Bell." The priests were said to encourage the Mexican migrant workers, to whom they had provided charity during the migrants' seasonal visits to the Hazleton area, to settle permanently in town.

Drug dealing had been a notorious problem in northeastern Pennsylvania even before Latinos arrived in large numbers: in 2002–2003, Hazleton police, using wiretaps, apprehended a major cocaine-distributing ring in the area. Connected to a drug source on the Caribbean island of St. Lucia, the ring included a few participants with Latino names, but the majority of those charged, including the ringleader, had common Hazleton-area surnames like Fisher, Lawson, Vetter, and Allegretto.[19]

Nevertheless, as the Latino presence became more visible, city officials blamed them for a supposed rise in drug-related crime. A note was allegedly found at the site of the first murder saying "DDP 4 Life," an allusion to a New York City–based gang, "Dominicans Don't Play." Some observers interpreted nearby graffiti reflecting gang symbols and names. Finally, when the perpetrator was arraigned, he was photographed allegedly flashing "a gang symbol" as he left the court.[20]

Officials produced a PowerPoint presentation, shown to local organizations, suggesting that as many as 10 gangs might be operating in the town, among them the DDP, the Crips, and the Trinitarios, which Hazleton authorities openly termed a Dominican "terror organization." The main evidence for their presence, however, was not a documented spike in criminal acts, but photographs of graffiti spray-painted on the walls of buildings and in playgrounds. Officials were unsure whether these were left by the first waves of gang members marking off turf or were acts of ostension by wannabes seeking to inspire fear.[21] Nevertheless, rumors soon were ubiquitous that gang activity was both common and frightening. A very common element was that their intitiation rites involved committing a violent act against a non-Latino resident. One student reported, "it was rumored that proposed members of the Bloods [the name of another gang said to be active in the area] would go to people's doors asking for the time and when the person who had answered the door would lift their wrist to look at their watch, the Blood member would slit that person's wrist and run off."[22]

A year later, a local student reported consensus among her family's friends that "illegal Hispanic immigrants bring with them terrible violence [and] gang related crimes, and these two factors lead to the harm and death to unsuspecting innocent American citizens." Supporting this belief, an e-mail had circulated at both her parents' workplaces, warning them about such gangs' initiation processes. The student continued:

> Supposedly, to be initiated into this gang, the rookie members must drive around town without their lights on, waiting for a considerate driver to flash their lights at them to tell them to put their lights on. Once this happens, the gang member follows the considerate driver until he can find a place to drive them off the road and shoot them dead. After this, he/she is then a member of this deadly

clan. The e-mail sent around at work places is possibly an example of an urban legend, but also is a popular rumor because of these gangs' increased activity in Hazleton, and illegal Hispanics' membership in these gangs.[23]

These kinds of "gang initiation" were hardly new to the region: as early as the 1960s, ethnic gangs were said to carry out initiations by castrating a young boy in a public restroom, and stories of "slasher" rites like those described above were widespread by the late 1970s. The "Lights Out" initiation was the focus of a nationwide rumor-panic in the fall of 1993.[24] Hence Mayor Barletta and his supporters built on a long-standing foundation of belief about secret cults or gangs, which were assumed to be, like Al Qaeda, foreign based and anti-American in their intentions. He did not consider these fears to be based on flimsy rumor, but on hard fact. And, increasingly, so did most residents of the area. One student observed, "Late at night if you drive through the city there are gangs everywhere. You can't even go to the mall without seeing them or hearing them. They feel the need to talk very loudly as they go through.... They wouldn't move out out of the way for people or anything."[25] Both in rhetoric and the criteria of plausibility, the new "gang" rumors were similar to other panics that had affected the same area in recent years, though this time the face of the threat was a new one.

Showdown: Rumors as Scripts for Violence

The wide circulation of hostile rumors creates an atmosphere in which individuals can feel themselves justified in carrying out acts of violence against randomly chosen representatives of the "boogiemen." During a 1987 panic in the Hazleton area, many students in one of the local high schools became convinced that a group of "weirdo" classmates were planning to commit a mass killing at the spring prom. An intense official investigation followed, during which the "weirdos'" school and public library records were examined to see if they had been reading books on Satanism, and the principal received an anonymous tip that some of the group had been seen at a cult meeting in Allentown. While no evidence of evil intentions emerged, the principal remarked, with seeming satisfaction, that in the end a group of students had accosted them in the street and "busted ass," ending the crisis.[26]

The same potential for violence emerged once again in the area in the neighboring small town of Shenandoah, this time in response to the "illegal immigrant" crisis, fueled by the rumors discussed previously about immigrants "taking over." On July 12, 2008, a group of teenagers returning from a Polish American fire company block party spotted a Latino youth, Luis Ramirez, walking with a 15-year-old Anglo girl. Angered by the sight, the group of youths told the girl, "Get your Mexican boyfriend out of here," then began shouting ethnic slurs at him: "This is Shenandoah!" "This is America!" "Go back to Mexico!" A brawl ensued, with the five locals, all members of the high school football team, taking on Ramirez, who lashed out at those who mocked him. In the end, Ramirez was knocked to the pavement and then kicked in the head. He suffered severe brain damage and died two days later without recovering consciousness. As the group dispersed, one shouted back at the girl the injured man had been accompanying, "You [expletive] bitch! You tell your [expletive] Mexican friends to get the [expletive] out of Shenandoah or you're going to be laying [expletive] next to him!"[27]

The affair led to a detailed investigation, during which it was determined that Ramirez was in fact an undocumented immigrant who had been living with the daughter of a local Anglo resident and with whom he had had two children. (The girl with whom he was walking was his girlfriend's younger sister.) The members of the mob who had beaten him were identified and charged. Two agreed to cooperate with authorities: one, a juvenile, issued an apology for his actions in court and was sentenced to 90 days in a treatment center, while another pled guilty to a federal charge of violating Ramirez's civil rights and agreed to testify against the others. The two central figures were charged with third-degree murder and ethnic intimidation and tried in Shenandoah late in April 2009. In the verdict, handed down on May 1, the jury acquitted the two youths of all serious charges, finding them guilty only of simple assault and alcohol offenses. Members of the community celebrated, cheering in the courtroom and driving through the town streets honking car horns.[28]

To be fair, the brawl took place in a confused moment, with all the participants impaired by drinking, and testimony was unclear as to who had delivered the blows and kicks that led to the immigrant's death. All agreed that Ramirez had participated in the fight, so he was not a passive victim. Nevertheless, David Neiwert, a freelance journalist concerned with "hate talk," called the death a "classic bias crime," incited by and accompanied with explicit racially charged insults. It is not surprising that the residents of Shenandoah expressed resentment at being portrayed as intolerant in the national press: after all, a highlight of their summer season is a "Parade of Nations," in which representatives of every ethnic group who immigrated to the area are given a place in a public procession displaying ethnic dress and music.

But Neiwert found many similar situations in investigating other areas, including contemporary Germany that had experienced an abrupt change in ethnic population. In such cases, he found that residents desire to remain aligned with the neighbors they already know, in the face of newcomers seen as threats, and so they choose to look away or not notice when an explicitly bigoted remark is aired. "After all, there is a mantra common to all rural communities," Neiwert concluded. "This is a nice town. People are nice to each other. If someone wants to be a racist, well, most people won't encourage them, but they won't speak out against it, either."[29] His insight is supported by Shenandoah citizens who shared their reactions with local reporters, passing over the anti-Latino slurs and the rumors that stood behind them in silence. "I think there was no evidence and I think the jury made the right decision," one said the morning afterward. "They are good kids who had too much to drink and were involved in an altercation. Unfortunately someone passed away because of it. Guys fight. Guys fight in other towns."[30] In other words, the result was unfortunate, but nothing unusual happened here, certainly nothing worth punishing "good kids" for doing.

In the end, the event reminds us of the lynching incidents that occurred in the American South a century ago, often provoked by groups of whites seeing a black person in the company of a young white girl. The permeation of the area with anti-Latino beliefs and stories about the intentions of these new residents made the attack easy to initiate and simple to justify. Ultimately, rumor is not just talk, not simply a claim that can be assessed as true or not. It is a set of ideas that satisfies a social need and can be used as a basis for action. In this case, the action was deadly.

Who to Believe?

Improvising the Future

As often happens in cases of uncertainty, coupled with the threat of community displacement, neighbors gather to make sense of the disturbing changes to their established life, improvising news and sharing their standards of morality with those to whom they feel close. Students of rumor have repeatedly pointed out that oral performances are *emergent* events in which one person not only transmits information or warnings about well-known events but also seeks the advice and approval of others.[31] This was the position of long-standing local residents. These rumor sessions permit groups to address social concerns by gossiping about alleged actual events in ways that they could not comfortably do through attacking other groups directly.

No one wishes to be called a racist or bigot, certainly not in a community explicitly and proudly built on immigration. By emphasizing that their statements are simply *fact*, these residents could gain personal distance from beliefs that would otherwise be taken as reflecting prejudice.[32] Speakers took the role of reporter, spreading the news, but not vouching for its moral implications. For instance, rather than asserting that some ethnic or racial group is particularly prone to criminal behavior, the narrator describes a horrific crime. If this leads to the conclusion that the targeted group is wicked, so be it. This process of sense making highlights how members of a community justify their own claims, relying not only on the assumed plausibility of the claim but also on their own credibility.

Credible Sources

We have emphasized that people rely on their friends, neighbors, strangers, Web sites, and various forms of media to improvise news and to determine what to believe. But to this point, we have focused more on the politics of plausibility, rather than the politics of credibility. But credibility is crucial in a world of talk, particularly when we look to tight-knit communities, and it is not just that people are or are not trustworthy, but through their narration, they create an aura of credibility. People need to set the stage so that others are primed to believe them. We don't believe everything we hear, and we do not believe everyone we hear. We do believe stories that are told well and told dramatically and then are justified. Examining rumor diffusion in a small city allows us to capture some of the ways that sources proclaim their credibility, attempting to convince others that what they are saying should be considered seriously, not merely dismissed out of hand. Consider a case in point:

A local student, challenged to think about rumor, shared a story that she had heard in her community and believed completely. On a discussion forum, she wrote:

A mother and a daughter of about two years old were at a grocery store. The mother left her cart (with the child in it) and returned a second later to find that her child was gone. She told this to management and they locked all the exits. They searched the store for her and she was found about fifteen minutes later in the bathroom. She didn't have any cuts or anything, but some of her hair was shaved off to make her look like a boy. I suppose the criminal would do this so he could escape with her. A witness then told the manager that the kidnapper was a Hispanic guy who looked to be in his 20s.[33]

This is a local variant of a widely known contemporary legend, titled "The Attempted Abduction," that has circulated in the United States since at least 1980.[34] The content is considered plausible by many as there have been some highly publicized cases in which children were abducted from malls or grocery stores. Since that time, a number of chains have instituted specific drills, such as Wal-Mart's "Code Adam," to handle cases of missing children and to deter kidnappers. In a dangerous world, the claim seems plausible, but should we believe these gothic stories? Does the source know of what she speaks? In practice, the evaluation of information is linked to the performance of its source, as the circumstances of communication affect the extent to which informant credibility is judged to be crucial. One evaluates the narrator, as well as what is narrated, and narrators often discover that their reputations are linked to their storylines.

Admittedly on some occasions, such as in the immediate aftermath of a disaster or in times of political upheaval, demands for knowledge swamp the characteristics or the character of a narrator. After the assassination of President Kennedy, people questioned strangers on the street as to what happened; the same happened after September 11. But these are exceptional cases in which the demand for immediate news overwhelms all other considerations. In most cases, such as the account of the kidnapped child, evaluating the source of the material is central to the politics of credibility. As French sociologist Jean-Bruno Renard[35] revealed in his study of rumors that alleged that stickers were being sold that were laced with LSD, the presence of an authoritative (or authoritative-sounding) name in photocopied texts often proved influential in how widely the flier circulated. Mere assertions that "Cumberland County Police say" or "According to Dr. Smith" were sufficient grounds for many participants to consider the claims well founded and worth sharing.

Credibility is produced by *interaction strategies*—that is, how individuals present themselves—as well as by institutional position. In other words, speakers must *perform credibility*, either for themselves or for their (alleged) source, through impression management or through trading on status markers that derive from the source's social position. The credibility that derives from one's position is readily appreciated as one's social location is recognized in such deference forms as "Dr." or "Officer." The status that results from these positions is directly tied to the speaker, even recognizing that different audiences may perceive institutional status in light of their own cultural assumptions of how much trust to give, say, a doctor, politician, or community activist.

By contrast, credibility that emerges during the presentation of a rumor must be demonstrated by the speaker through what social scientists refer to as *impression management*—presenting one's self to others in a manner to garner respect and trust.[36] The speaker must convince an audience that he or she is a reputable and responsible person, someone whose account can be trusted. As people are often "married" to the information they spread, they attempt to avoid the label of liar, deceiver, or fool. Though many take some care in what they share, at times speakers fail to check closely into the truth of their statements. When uncertain information is being transmitted, a narrator may place rhetorical distance between himself or herself and the story, asking for confirmation or emphasizing that he or she heard it from another.

A narrator with a reputation as trustworthy and candid finds that this public self rubs off on what is shared. Some individuals by virtue of their position within an information network are believed to have legitimate access to facts, becoming "honest brokers" in their reportage. Although this doesn't always apply, it reflects our expectations. The awarding of authoritativeness is linked to our perception of the speaker's connection to "truth" and to our assumption of his or her willingness to provide that truth with disinterest.

Justifying a "Kidnapping"

We return to how the earlier kidnapping story was presented. The text is typical of many discussed by folklorists: a simple recitation of a narrative. However, in context, rumors (and their lengthier cousins, legends) are never presented in this way, because of the need to generate credibility. The student's preface to the story, which we deliberately omitted in presenting it previously, is just as important as the story itself:

I heard this legend from my mom one time when I was talking to her about work that day. I work at Wal-Mart, and there had been a child found crying near the corner of the store. An employee asked the child what was wrong and he said he'd lost his mommy. Within ten minutes, he was reunited with his mom. My mom then told me this story that she had heard from my aunt.... [the text follows].[37]

The student begins by saying that the narrative to follow is a "legend," a term that shows that she is aware that its literal truth may be judged as being unreliable by others. (As a result of a greater awareness of rumors and legends in part because of the presence of books and Web sites that aim at debunking stories, many performances begin with statements such as "This is *not* one of those urban legends but...," which of course concedes exactly the same thing.) Announcing that a story is either one that circulates widely or a variant of those that do removes the narrator from direct responsibility for the story's accuracy. Yet, if the narrator had considered the story entirely incredible, the student could have gone directly to the text of the legend, presenting it simply "for laughs."[38]

Instead, she opens by setting the story as a genuine instance of a child at risk. The narrator, who was present when the child was found and returned to his mother, emerges as someone who is well aware of what can happen in a large store. Audiences typically give considerable weight to truth claims from individuals who are perceived to be in a position to know. Government spokespersons are often granted this assumption of closeness, particularly with regard to their statements of fact, as opposed to statements of motivation. For instance, as citizens, we may doubt the president's press secretary in describing *why* the president acted, whereas it would be odd to question *whether* the president acted. By virtue of his government position, the press secretary has the authority to know. These people have the knowledge and the position to be credible reporters, and audiences often treat this information as fact, releasing it from the demands of personal evaluation. However, when (as often occurs) government spokespersons are seen as having hidden motivations, linked to a desire for deception, these claims are sharply questioned.

Audiences routinely decide whether a speaker is likely to have acquired information from trustworthy sources, and then judge the degree to which they will accept or act on the information in light of how it was obtained. Perhaps surprisingly, personal gossip often carries greater weight as truth than do broad claims from friends about the larger social world. These narrators are deemed more likely to know about their own personal lives than about more distant institutions. A narrator's assertion of having heard information from the media or from one's friends, often an essential part of truth claims, is a strategy to bolster trustworthiness, given one's distance from the reported events. So, when the student turns from the account of the lost child that occurred in her own store to the more controversial "legend" that occurred in an unnamed and generic "grocery store," she does so by attributing it to her mother, who in turn heard it from her sister, two family members that she knows and trusts.

Many narrators include their own statements about the assumed motivation of those who told them. The student concluded her account of the kidnapping narrative by announcing:

> I would think that the message of this legend is to always have an eye on your kids because there are crazy people out there who would look for an opportunity to commit a crime. I think it suggests that people are not as precautionary as they should be. For all the things that are reported on the news, people need to see that it can actually happen to them.[39]

The goal of this story extends beyond the ethnic threat implied by the reference to a "Hispanic guy," but also addresses a danger closer to home, the unwary or neglectful parent who gives a stranger the chance to endanger children. Her expressed motivation fits the authority of the opening: mothers mean well for their offspring, and the narrator's own experience as a store employee proves that children do get separated from careless parents. She becomes a credible witness because of her position at the store, even if she had no firsthand knowledge of the kidnapping. The narrative itself may not be true, but it is similar to personal experiences shared by the narrator and audience, as well as exposure to "all the things that are reported on the news," including high-profile cases of child abduction and murder.

Trust and Rumor in Changing Communities

At this point we expand our discussion from Hazleton to numerous other places facing social change through widespread immigration. As we described in discussing rumors of terrorism, for a society to survive and flourish, mutual trust must exist. Part of this stems from the need for predictability and part from a desire for moral clarity.[40] Put another way, trust is a defense against uncertainty and vulnerability.[41] A community that lacks trust requires high levels of coercion to prevent social breakdown. A place in which rumors circulate both derives from and contributes to the social organization of trust. In one sense, the presence of rumor reveals weakened trust in institutions. Those who disseminate such claims argue—implicitly or explicitly—that the information from authoritative sources is either incomplete or inaccurate. In such circumstances, institutions are perceived to have collapsed; they are perceived as deceptive, incompetent, and/or immoral. The facts "out there" must be learned by alternate means, because they cannot be learned directly.

As we have emphasized, the same rumor types appear repeatedly in slightly varying forms over years, decades, and sometimes centuries. Rumor taps into basic human beliefs and fears. The concerns about the proper boundaries of a community and about those strangers outside the borders wishing to enter are central to these apprehensions. Although we might wish to conceive of ourselves as accepting all humanity, such is rarely the case. The citizens of Hazleton, good and kind people as they surely are, have the same fears that have existed throughout recorded history when migration shook a culture that was imagined to be stable.

As expected in examining contemporary rumors about immigration, we find variations on those themes raised in chapter 3. Today, as at the time of "Typhoid Mary," members of the public see migrants as a potentially catastrophic "infection" of America and nativists ask that government expel them, restoring America to its imagined purity. The Chinese of the nineteenth century were treated not so differently from Haitians in the 1980s. Most dramatically, given the means by which they arrived in America, the attempts to repatriate blacks to Africa represent the same process, backed as it was by a set of noxious racial rumors. The result is to place these outsiders into an ethnic basement and to ignore the historical lessons learned from previous generations of migrants.

A dramatic set of rumors speaks to the process through which these strangers arrived, unbidden and unwanted. Despite the intention of the American government to control the border and to limit the number of undocumented migrants, the common perception is that the borders are porous, and that millions of migrants have entered, blending in with their fellow immigrants to supply a job market thirsting for low-paid laborers. But how? Rumors abound that describe deceptive strategies of entry by land, sea, and even air.

In 2003, an Internet message claimed that a 135-pound woman was discovered hidden behind the dashboard of a car. As reported on Snopes.com, "A U.S. Customs Primary Inspector at a border crossing asked the driver of [a] Suburban for vehicle registration. Suddenly, a hand came out of the glove compartment, producing the requested document, which the driver showed the inspector."[42] Surely this comic episode is fictionalized, but according to *U.S. Customs Today*,[43] the smuggling of "human contraband" is increasingly common. In another instance, a man hid himself inside a minivan seat. As in so many cases of rumors, we cannot know whether the claim derives from an actual attempt or whether the attempt was made because a rumor was heard and a desperate immigrant subsequently decided to try it. Folklorists describe the process by which people enact the rumors that they have heard as *ostension*.[44] The story may not be valid when first told, but because it is told, it subsequently becomes true as it is acted out.

A more sinister set of stereotypes is added when the smuggling of terrorists into the country is considered. According to a news release by DEBKAfile, a security-oriented Web site, evidence suggests that Al Qaeda and other terrorist organizations are using ship containers to smuggle operatives into the country. On October 18, 2001, soon after the September 11 attacks, DEBKA reported that dock inspectors in Italy had found a suspected terrorist inside a cargo container that had been "converted into a luxurious suite," complete with a bed, a kitchen, food, water, and a cell phone. The stowaway reportedly had passports and security permits that would allow him access to sensitive areas of three American airports.[45] Perhaps the story is false,[46] but it fits many concerned Americans' perception that our international borders are poorly defended and a constant source of danger.

Ethnic Competition and the Rumor Mill

But what happens once those immigrants arrive? Not content to remain in poverty, most strive to succeed. Sociologists studying the development of ethnic communities in industrial cities in the early twentieth century found patterns that were to be repeated in Hazleton. William I. Thomas and Florian Znaniecki in their classic study *The Polish Peasant in Europe and America* discovered that the establishment of a Polish American community involved the displacement of previously settled ethnic cultures. Ethnic group rivalry—and prejudice—often is based on patterns of realistic group competition for resources. This pattern was duplicated repeatedly throughout the twentieth century and into the twenty-first. However, what is considered to be economic competition is transformed through the magic of rumor into moral complaint.

Ironically, the rumors and beliefs about the moral character of immigrants that we discussed in chapter 3 were spread again by the grandchildren of those immigrants. The first arrivals search for places where real estate values are low, allowing moderately prosperous entrepreneurs to buy properties to rent to poorer migrants or to open small businesses catering to the diaspora's needs in their native language. If these first moves succeed, Thomas and Znaniecki suggest, "territorial concentration begins at once," a process in which "the original population of the district is slowly but ceaselessly driven away" to non-Polish neighborhoods.[47]

In Hazleton, local families that were displaced or surrounded by Spanish-speaking neighbors responded with fear and anger, just as in earlier times, when Irish or German neighborhoods were displaced by Polish or Italian populations. Surely those who were displaced worry about their material future, but this was transformed into a battle over patriotism and virtue. Local residents worried about whether these new immigrants truly cared for their adopted country, pointing to the display of symbols of their homeland. "Some [Latino] students refuse to stand for the Pledge of Allegiance," a citizen complained, continuing, "Some of the few businesses they have opened fly the Mexican flag…no sign of the American flag."[48]

Gang Rumors and the Fate of Community

It was not only in Hazleton, but nationally that many rumors and panics were sparked by the presence of Latino gangs. Many of these rumors have targeted one particular group, MS-13 (Mara Salvatrucha-13), said to be the most secretive and violent gang currently operating. MS-13 is a predominantly Salvadorian gang, whose name translates into "street-tough Salvadorians." Gang members include many Latinos and now even some African Americans. Some claim that there may be 10,000 members in the United States and many times that number in Central America. The number 13 supposedly stands for the 13 rules that gang members must follow. "There are entire towns down here now that are overrun by the MS-13 gang," one citizen responded in the *Philadelphia Inquirer* online comments forum on the immigrant tensions in Hazleton. "The least they do is paint their gang sign over every inch of a building."[49]

In recent years the media have publicized accounts of gruesome murders committed in other localities, allegedly by Latino gang members targeting other Latinos believed to be police informants. Sometimes members of the jury feel at risk. In one such case, a commentator noted, "The courtroom that the trial was heard in was packed with gang members who would sit and stare menacingly at the jury. A reporter asked one of the gang members why so many attended. He said, 'We just want to make sure we don't forget who was there [on the jury].' "[50] There is no question that the drug trade involves frequent and brutal violence, but the disproportionate media coverage of malicious Latino gangs creates a stereotype that consistently outstrips the reality.

Similar claims have been circulated through the media. A special on MS-13, termed "The World's Most Dangerous Gang" and produced on the National Geographic Channel, gave alleged interpretations of "gang" graffiti. It claimed that "Hand signals suggesting the devil's horns are often waved," sometimes in complicated patterns to transmit messages understood only by other gang members.[51] By 2005, the federal Department of Homeland Security had named MS-13 "the fastest-growing gang in the country" and claimed that its cells were important in smuggling illegal immigrants. Some Homeland Security officials even expressed a belief that MS-13 and Al Qaeda were linked.[52]

Concern over the laxity of border patrolling in Arizona led to the organization of the Minuteman Project, a volunteer civilian group pledged to protect America from the "tens of millions of invading illegal aliens who are devouring and plundering our nation." Shortly after armed Minutemen began to carry out vigils along the Arizona/Mexico border in March 2005, rumors circulated via the Internet that MS-13 gang bosses had given orders for their followers in Phoenix and Los Angeles to attack the vigilantes. These rumors were reported as fact in the conservative *Washington Times*,[53] and an observer at one of the Minuteman compounds recorded that on the evening of April 4, "a credible threat" was received "that armed MS-13 gang members were about to lead a charge of hundreds of Mexicans 'over the wire' and against the Minuteman posts." The vigilantes donned body armor and prepared for the assault, but it, like other warnings passed within the organization, never materialized.[54]

Although the Al Qaeda/Latino gang connection was never documented, it remains plausible in the minds of many who advocate a stronger approach to illegal immigration. A manifesto posted on the Web site of the North Carolina–based PAC Americans for Legal Immigration argued that such "illegals" should be tried and imprisoned in this country rather than being deported. As there is no evidence that they will be prosecuted in Mexico, the writer said, "deportation will result in an unstoppable revolving door of violent crime in America." Latino gangs, especially MS-13, the argument continues, "must be crushed with the full force of American law enforcement. The gang mentality is the terrorist mentality and cannot be allowed to flourish."[55] The spread of MS-13 rumors on talk radio contributed to the defeat of immigration reform in 2007.

Certainly MS-13 rumors have produced the same kind of collective action on the part of vigilantes that rumors of home-grown teenaged satanic cults with their own cryptic graffiti and hand signals did in the 1980s and 1990s, when they were a prominent source of concern.[56] Similar claims that "cults" were just about to commit school massacres or other acts of violence led to similar shows of vigilantism, which did not completely dissipate but remained, paradoxically, as a memory of pride, a sign that collective acts by the majority can defeat even frightening threats. When rumor panics occur, the failure of boogiemen to appear, whether Satanists, serial killers, or gang members, does not destroy the beliefs on which the panics are based, but only postpones the day of reckoning.

Migrants as Unamerican Freeloaders

We have previously described rumors describing the dangers of immigrants, violent or diseased, but others focus on how these newcomers unfairly milk the system and how the system encourages them do so. Even apparently peaceable migrants are tainted by the belief that they are freeloaders. These narratives include a widely known body of rumors suggesting that immigrants gain free access to social services provided by an overly indulgent government.

One of the most prevalent rumors about immigrants is that while they benefit from government-provided services such as welfare and public education, they are exempt from paying taxes. "Today they [migrants] come…buy a home today and apply for welfare tomorrow!" one Hazleton resident complained. "They have overburdened the school district, the police force, the clinics. They pay no taxes."[57]

In the *New Yorker*, William Finnegan, recounting the travails of Somali migrants in Lewiston, Maine, noted the same beliefs: "Everyone had heard rumors: that the Somalis were getting free cars and vast sums of welfare money and preferment in public housing, and that they would soon bankrupt the town."[58] The rumor became so widespread that Pennsylvania Republican Congressman Todd Platts felt called upon to deny it on his congressional Web site, although he reported that immigrants, like American citizens, are eligible under some circumstances for interest-free business loans from the Small Business Administration.[59]

Illegal immigrants do not, of course, file income-tax returns, but this does not mean that they are exempt from taxes. Rather, it means that the money their employers routinely deduct from their paychecks goes into government accounts that the immigrant has no means of tapping. The Social Security Administration recently estimated that as much as 10% of its current surplus income came from payroll taxes collected from illegal immigrants, providing the system with a free $7 billion that will be paid in benefits to American citizens.[60]

Still, rumors and legends claim the opposite: that migrants do not pay the Social Security tax but collect benefits anyhow. "If they get citizenship," one Hazleton resident fretted, "they can bring their parents, grandparents, etc. here, and these folks will be eligible to receive YOUR Social Security money even though they haven't paid a dime into the system."[61] "It seems to me that they have a network of advocates who coach them on how to milk the system every step of the way," another suggested.[62]

The urban legend Web site Snopes.com found numerous claims that "The U.S. government grants a seven-year tax holiday to certain favored groups of immigrants and provides them with free housing, new cars, and clothing allowances as well."[63] According to the Web site, the rumor dates back into the 1960s shortly after immigration reform, when Americans had to confront the presence of new residents. This rumor, often suggesting that American citizens were suffering economically, revealed a profound resentment while suggesting that it was plausible that our government and its agencies would willingly provide preferential treatment.

As Barbara Mikkelson[64] emphasizes, these rumors often target particular ethnic groups, typically designating the one that is most recently visible and troubling in the narrator's region. When immigrants are newly prominent and seem to be thriving, a backlash is likely. As Mikkelson points out, Cubans in Miami are targeted as are Arabs in Detroit. Just as Somalis were the focus in Maine, in many communities Asians are said to be receiving tax breaks, free clothing, and new cars.[65]

Within this body of rumors, privileged immigrants are said to be eligible for a five- or seven-year income-tax holiday, or in other versions from paying sales taxes. One variant has the government providing a tax holiday, a new car, a house, and an allowance for purchasing shoes! In some rumors the tax holiday is said to be transferable to other members of the immigrant's family, permitting a relative to run a business, keeping it tax free for an additional seven years.[66]

This category of rumor was found in Australia in 1986, where it focused on Vietnamese migrants who were said to receive a tax break and a new car. In England, this rumor is known as "The Secret Furniture Store." According to Snopes.com, here's how the rumor goes:

> Immigrants to the UK know only two words of English: "Social Security." Upon their arrival at the port of entry, immigrants utter these words to the immigration officer on duty, causing a special social worker to be summoned. The immigrants are then taken by the social worker to a secret warehouse, where they are allowed to choose color televisions, living room sets, beds, stoves, and whatever they need. Everything they pick out is loaded onto a truck for delivery to their new home. The immigrants are also given keys to a new municipal dwelling, along with registration books for welfare benefits for all the family.[67]

These rumors as presented on the Internet seem like literary creations, rewritten from oral presentations, but they remain part of face-to-face communication among frustrated citizens. An account of a right-wing radio talk show hosted by BBC London notes that callers claimed that luxury flats were being constructed for immigrants in an otherwise dilapidated housing project, followed by the conclusion, "too many immigrants come in—that's the cause of our housing problem."[68] Another conservative radio talk show, this time out of a station in Cork, Ireland, had callers repeatedly claim that immigrants were given free cars by the Irish government, along with "money for children's birthday parties." In the wake of this program, a conservative Irish politician claimed that "spongers, wasters, and conmen" had taken the country hostage and called for an end to immigration. "The majority of them are here for economic reasons," he said, "while the tax-payer is paying for it all."[69]

In the United States, the rumor about the five- or seven-year tax break is widely known, but refers more often to tax breaks for business than to personal income taxes. Consider the following Internet posts: "It [tax breaks] appears to be true because all of the hotels in my area are run by Indians driving Lexus' and barely speaking English"; "I think I heard some-thing about middle east people getting like a 7 year tax break when they come here"; "I think any (or particular) immigrant groups that come into the U.S. and start a business get a 5 or 7 year fed tax break, either greatly reduced or pay no taxes at all. Sometimes it can continue by changing fam-ily members as the owner and such"; or "I know several immigrants who own a shrimping business. They got a 5 year tax break."[70]

Admittedly, new business owners who are *legal* immigrants can use government benefits to reduce their taxes and even receive "tax-free" loans, just like native-born and naturalized Americans. But the belief that immi-grants have a five- or seven-year tax-free holiday is not true, however plau-sible it may seem to those who feel oppressed by their own mounting tax bills. In any case, the perception is widespread that the tax burden is unequally distributed and that migrants, sometimes assisted by sharp advi-sors, are getting a "free ride" at the expense of the average citizen. "Why should they be allowed to stay, and with benefits that many legal citizens do not even have?" one citizen demanded, concluding, "No way, ship them the hell[71] back to where they came from. Sorry, the melting pot is closed."[72]

Improvising Immigrants and Crackdown Rumors

Although we have focused in this chapter on how mainstream American cul-ture has responded to immigrants, rumor is found in all communities. Immigrants reside in a world of uncertainty and ambiguity, and it is not sur-prising that they, too, share rumors that help explain what might happen to them. Migrants search after meaning under ambiguous conditions in which institutional trust is barely present, trying to discover where the truth lies.

Although the prevailing image of immigrant communities envisions them as shadowy and criminal, in general, the world of immigrants—documented and undocumented alike—is much more stable and tradi-tional. They may have illegally jumped the queue and violated immigration procedures, but most are hardworking and law abiding. Given their problematic legal status and lack of political clout, there is considerable benefit to be gained by local politicians by announcing a get-tough policy, then following up with highly visible raids and deportations.

These attacks can be effective forms of symbolic politics in precisely the same ways that prostitution raids are: dramatic and soon forgotten, since neither problem can be solved by an occasional raid. Given American immigration policy, many immigrants—particularly Latinos—share rumors, often incorrect but politically perceptive, about raids to be conducted by the Immigration and Customs Enforcement (ICE). In these accounts, the ICE is always waiting to pounce in a human game of cat and mouse, often to respond to popular demands to "crack down" on illegal residents. These rumors, spread among the powerless, target the government as a source of threat, perhaps similar to some of the conspiracy rumors that we discussed in chapter 2. The concern here, too, is what is going to happen next, and, in the form of improvised news, the community searches for relevant clues.

Occasionally, a rumor spreads that the INS is planning a crackdown or raid, and, to be safe, undocumented workers hide until the danger has passed. Certainly these men and women live in uncertain and unstable circumstances and the information about their immigration status is crucial for their well-being. As a result, they are prone to believe the worst. These features—importance and ambiguity—provide the basis for the rapid spread of rumor. Consider three examples from Seattle, Aspen, and Houston:

> The last time Adelina Garcia saw her four friends was at a Christmas party in their apartment complex in Lacey [Washington]. When next she heard from them, they were telephoning from Mexico to report they'd been picked up by immigration authorities less than a month ago and summarily deported.... "Now, we're scared to go out shopping to buy things—everybody is worried," Garcia says. "When we have to go, we wait until after it gets dark."...Within the far-reaching immigrant grapevine, the men's deportations give life to persistent rumors that began a month ago about regionwide roundups—rumors that are keeping immigrants away from church services, summer-school classes, English classes, and health clinics. Now there's concern that fear may keep many away from the Hispanic Seafair Organization Festival at Seward Park today.[73]

A large number of Latino immigrants did not show up for work at local temp agencies Monday, the apparent fallout from a rumor about widespread immigration raids in the valley. "Some guys came in in the morning and said they didn't want to work, or called me and said they heard about immigration checkpoints in El Jebel," said Claudia Miranda, office manager for Mountain Temps in Carbondale. "People were actually refusing to come to work today, and many people stayed home."[74]

One day after city and community officials denounced a rumor of raids on illegal immigrants, some are still in doubt. The rumor began last week and prompted some undocumented people to leave their homes, and not even show up at work.... Lina Benitez... says she lives in fear, scared she could be deported at any time. "The people are fearful of going to the store to shop, to school or to work," she says. "For fear of being detained." For some, that fear is too real to ignore despite the truth.[75]

Other rumors have targeted Oakland, California,[76] and Shelton, Washington.[77] Such claims seem entirely plausible in the context of the life-worlds of these workers and the politics of their communities.

Given that debate has been intense about changes in American immigration policy, confusion is not surprising, and this confusion feeds rumors. When in early 2004 President Bush floated ideas on immigration reform, those musings were taken by many within the immigrant community as a new reality, triggering a wave of misunderstandings. Many immigrants believed that these presidential suggestions had become law.[78] It remains to be seen whether changes in approach to illegal immigration of the Obama administration—which claims to focus their attention on the employers of the immigrants—will alter the rumors and, if so, in what way. Illegal immigrants will remain targeted, but not directly. Under this new policy, being gainfully employed will become more difficult.

With the defeat of immigration reform in Congress in 2007 and no current prospects for reform, rumors that address the concerns of immigrants continue to be spread, addressing fears that the communities believe are plausible. The desperation of many men and women decreases their critical ability,[79] creating a willingness to believe whatever fearful assertion has the greatest impact on their lives—better to believe a rumor and be safe than to be skeptical and deported. At the same moment that American citizens share rumors that they use to understand the plans, actions, and intentions of illegal residents, these residents respond with rumors that help them cope with the uncertainty of their lives.

Making Sense of the Stranger

As we described in chapter 3, the presence of immigrants has long raised questions about how we should think about our nation. Who really belongs? It is understandable that when cultures come into contact there will be a period of adjustment. Often in time hostility becomes cooperation, and so it is likely to be again as the confusions of the new become routine realities.

Anyone who has traveled recognizes the confusion that arises from new ways of doing things. Customs that we take for granted at home turn into complex uncertainties abroad. The problem for an immigrant is far more difficult than for the casual tourist. Immigrants' choices are ambiguous and clouded, and people in their communities on whom they rely may be equally puzzled. Wrong decisions can have severe, unforeseen repercussions.

The position of the immigrant is a classic instance of an effort after meaning—the need to acquire knowledge in the face of ambiguity— precisely as described by rumor scholars Gordon Allport and Leo Postman in their classic *The Psychology of Rumor*.[80] Information for the immigrant is critical, yet uncertain, leading to the proliferation of rumor.

With rapid and wide-scale immigration, the status quo is altered without the consent of the governed. Citizens fear that, in the words of one anxious citizen, "We are getting the lowest of the low," and that the honest, devout, and law-abiding will suffer. Those cultural, economic, and political virtues that bolster social trust are threatened. Citizens may fear for their position in the status hierarchy, particularly those Americans who feel economically marginal and distressed. On occasion, these fears are well founded: Latino gangs such as MS-13 do exist and have committed real criminal acts, just as some Italian, Chinese, Jewish, and Polish immigrants once used robbery, prostitution, and organized crime to survive. Still, the fears often outrun the realities and ignore the lessons learned from previous generations of immigrants as they fought discrimination and bigotry. And those who tolerate bigoted rumors risk creating an atmosphere that may flare into dangerous violence and repeat some of the most shameful moments in our country's past.

The string of rumors that have emerged since the passage of the 1965 Immigration Act testifies to the fact that political reality influences rumor diffusion. The changes that were brought about by the new immigration policy were real, and the changes within American communities were sufficiently dramatic to call for interpretations and explanations among longtime residents. The beliefs and stories that became prominent are those that spoke to the values, customs, hopes, and fears of the rumor public. As immigrants alter the face of America, these changes generate rumor, shaping relations of trust and the contours of civil society.

Towns like Hazleton, Pennsylvania, have found themselves in the center of this maelstrom of change without their own consent. Rumors are one means by which neighbors seek order, often in a rough and thorny fashion. Once the new migrants become established and influential, attacks subside. We wish to believe that this is a result of people learning to know and accept each other, but perhaps the truth is less optimistic: the people displaced by an ethnic shift simply move somewhere else, as in the "white flight" to the suburbs in response to black migration. Or, as Neiwert suggests, the aggrieved simply find it more difficult to organize against outsiders when they gain enough social power to ensure their safety.[81] Either way, nothing really changes, and, perhaps, as we noted in chapter 3, after a generation or two, the children of immigrants show the same bigotry toward the next arrivals as was shown to them.

5

Tourist Troubles

The Travels of Global Rumor

> It's unlikely that a certain Senator's wife will be wearing to any more public functions a medallion her husband picked up for her on an air junket to Hong Kong. She was very proud of it for quite a while—until the evening, in fact, that a Chinese Nationalist diplomat, over to address the U.N., informed her gravely that the literal translation of the Chinese characters on the medallion read, "Licensed prostitute, City of Shanghai."[1]

With international travel increasingly common throughout the developed world, the contacts between the first and third worlds are not only between migrants and citizens but also between tourists and locals. Inevitably, when cultures meet, some degree of disorientation occurs among members of both groups, resulting in tension that sparks narrative.

Understandably, nations that rely on tourist income have zealously created and maintained quasi-authentic traditions with which to attract visitors and sell indigenous foods and crafts, even at the cost of local cynicism. The economic and social effect of these strategies is so great that there are now journals and academic programs devoted to "tourism studies," examining, among other things, how history is fabricated in order to exploit or capitalize on tourist naïveté.

Many tourists who visit Ireland are drawn to Blarney Castle in a village near Cork and told solemnly that part of the sacred

Stone of Scone is built into its parapets. To gain its supernatural "gift of gab," tourists are told that they should kiss the block during their visit. In reality, this is not an easy task, as visitors must lower themselves through an opening in the parapet as a guide holds their legs firmly to keep them from dropping 90 feet below, until their lips are level with the magical stone. While the belief is told to visitors with great solemnity, the residents of Blarney are bemused by tourists' willingness to engage in this risky but comic ritual. One native of Blarney admitted on an Internet message board:

> My grandfather told me that in the old days they used to whiz on the Blarney stone and then laugh at the tourists in the morning. It doesn't happen now though—it is secured and they disinfect it regularly.[2] Interesting note, many people who think they kissed the Blarney stone actually didn't. You have to lay on your back and tilt your head back—a lot of tourists end up kissing the stone located above the real Blarney stone. We are too polite to tell them.[3]

These claims, like the myth of the stone itself, may fall in the category of rumor, legend (a more solidified and traditional form of rumor narrative, applicable to many of the stories in this chapter), or joke. The difference may be less salient than it appears, since all three genres allow tellers and listeners to address tension through a dramatic narrative. The confrontation with tourist strangers is so compelling that unsettling claims are made, spread, and, many times, accepted even if the original story is understood facetiously. Certainly jokes about ethnic others, whether tourists or natives, have existed for centuries, alongside both authentic and apocryphal stories about naïve foreigners and contaminating migrants.

In this chapter, we explore these claims, analyzing the conflicts and breaches in trust occasioned by tourism and travel. Just as recent immigrants are baffled and confused by ways of doing things that we take for granted, American tourists risk being embarrassed or even harmed by being oblivious to cultural differences while traveling. In a culture that we know well, we trust our strategies of understanding people and acting appropriately. But when abroad, people and tasks may not be what they seem.

Sweaters and Tattoos

We begin with a classic story, a variant of which opened the chapter, presented *con brio* by poet John Ciardi in the pages of *Saturday Review*:

> The lady had visited Chinatown and had there spotted some Chinese writing so pleasing to her eye that she whipped out a Polaroid, photographed it, and went home to block out the characters on a larger scale as a decorative motif across the breast of an otherwise plain but definitely high-style sweater she then knitted. The total effect of the sweater…was described as "dramatic" until, at the party there always is, someone (the friend of a friend) who had been brought up in China as the son of a missionary and who had studied Chinese, took one look and let out a guffaw that always comes. The characters, in their well-designed row across the designer's well-designed breast, read: "This dish cheap but unmistakably good."[4]

Ciardi's essay underlines the boundary between humor and rumor. Many rumors in a world that treasures self-described "urban legends" as entertaining but clearly apocryphal stories present humorous factoids as truth claims. It is unclear how many of those in the audience take the claim as serious as opposed to giggling at a silly story, but it remains significant that these stories, unlike those presented explicitly as jokes, are represented as events that could *potentially* have occurred in real life. Therefore, it is instructive to explore the gray boundary between seriously presented truth claims and statements meant to be seen as humorous.

Narratives for Real or for Laughs

Much material in this chapter straddles the line between rumor and humor, and the narratives may be used for both purposes: to raise a laugh while still suggesting caution in one's travels. Often humor, seemingly innocuous, can convey profound concerns and anxieties, similar to rumor. Whereas rumor proposes an actual event, humor transforms actual events into fantasy. Through amusement, the tension between the world as we find it and the world as it should be is announced through the mistakes and hidden beliefs of the targets of the jokes.

The line between joke and rumor has always been smudged, in part because humor has been one of the more effective strategies used by narrators. Folklorist Gillian Bennett[5] points to a sharp rhetorical difference between narratives that were being represented as literal truth and those being told for laughs, that is, simply as an entertaining story. She noted several strategies that made rumor and legend, whether oral or written, operate more like jokes than truth claims: reference to the account as a story; vagueness about persons, place, and time; omission of orientation and concluding moral; and the presence of a punch line.

Ciardi's narrative reflects that smudged line and could be taken as either fiction or fact, but the phrase "the party there always is" serves as a verbal wink to a sophisticated audience, indicating that he doubts the tale. What the story does and does not include proves significant. Unlike strongly held truth claims, the story does not identify the protagonist as more than a generic "lady" and presents no reasons, at the beginning or end, for accepting it as a genuine experience. But it does include a number of literary embellishments—"an otherwise plain but definitely high-style sweater"—and the humorous repetition in the "well-designed row across the designer's well-designed breast." Finally, the story ends with a guffaw-inducing punch line, not with a discussion of what the story signifies for the teller and listener in real life. Ciardi's account is a literary confection, not a serious warning about the dangers of cultural tourism. Nevertheless, his audience would implicitly realize that the narrative is part of a larger tradition in which Americans reveal ignorance of other cultures by wearing objects, clothes, or even tattoos with unintentionally amusing meanings.

The narrative core of Ciardi's story is actually over 150 years old. In 1855, Nathaniel Hawthorne, then serving as a U.S. consul in Liverpool, alluded in his private notebook to a "funny story" he had heard about the wife of a former American ambassador. She had bought a shawl in a London shop and then wore it proudly on many social occasions. However, "She had not taken care to remove the ticket from the shawl," the story went, "so that she exhibited herself to the eyes of the metropolis with this label—'PERFECTLY CHASTE 15/S'—certainly a moderate valuation of perfect chastity."[6] Not only the wool was chaste, but so was the lady—and, at 15 shillings, cheap as well. The form of the variant he recorded, with its identification as a story and clear punch line, indicates that he treated it as humor rather than fact. Later entries, however, show that Hawthorne repeatedly encountered many similar "queer stories (doubtless, in many cases, fabulous)" concerning the social gaffes made by the wives of American diplomats. In one case, he noted with some irritation, an English host "had the face to tell [such a] foolish story for truth, and as indicating the mistakes into which Americans are liable to fall."[7] Clearly tension between humor and rumor existed in narrative even then.

Mishaps of the Oriental Imagination

Contemporary stories, particularly those detailing American mishaps with Chinese culture, have continued to spread, often alleging to be genuine truth claims but actually circulating in conduits devoted to jokes and other forms of humor. A second version of Ciardi's tale was posted as a "true story" on a Web site devoted to humor among engineers who write computer code:

> Like a lot of Unicode engineers, Jim would occasionally take his wife with him on his foreign travels. On their last trip to China, his wife became enamored of calligraphy and Chinese characters. In fact, at one point while having lunch in a simple Chinese restaurant, she noticed an especially beautiful rendering of a few characters on a handwritten luncheon menu. She discreetly tucked the menu in her purse. Being an avid knitter and skilled at designing intricate patterns, within a few months she had produced a stunning white sweater with the same Chinese symbols hand-stitched down the front. She received compliments galore whenever she wore it. She was also quite excited to wear it to the next Unicode event. The sweater seemed to attract a lot of interest and many more compliments. She knew the Unicode experts would really appreciate her attention to the styling of the Chinese characters. After dinner another Unicode engineer came up to Jim's wife and asked where she got the symbols. He then wanted to know if she knew what they meant. "I'm afraid to ask, but tell me anyway," she said. Even she had to laugh when he told her their meaning. "This is a cheap dish—but good."[8]

Here the Unicode engineers transformed a generic text, adding details that link it to their local culture.

The theme of such narratives becomes exaggerated when individuals choose to have Chinese characters tattooed—a greater commitment than purchasing a gift with an embarrassing inscription or customizing clothing with such a symbol. Chinese does not have an alphabet based on consonants, vowels, or syllables, but uses pictograms to represent entire words.[9] To spell a person's name or corporate product requires searching for a string of words in Chinese that sounds like the Western name, or the reverse, spelling out the Chinese syllables phonetically in Western characters. The range of amusing errors that can result from this practice is endless, ranging from Chinese restaurant names such as "Fu King" or "Yung Hao" to the many alleged linguistic blunders made by American corporations in attempting to market products in China. Both Coca-Cola and Pepsi-Cola have been targets of widely circulated lists of failed advertising campaigns in which product names or slogans allegedly had embarrassing meanings to Chinese consumers. The name Coca-Cola, for instance, became "Bite the wax tadpole" or "Female horse stuffed with wax," depending on the dialect.[10] Pepsi's attempt to render its sales pitch of the 1960s, "Come alive! You're in the Pepsi generation," was garbled into Chinese in a form that meant something like "Pepsi brings your ancestors back from the grave."[11] The mistakes can go both ways. A widely distributed photograph, for instance, showed a Beijing street sign that was intended to lead Western tourists to an "Ethnic Culture Center"; instead, it directed them to a "Racist Park."[12]

There may be some truth to each of these claims, as the difficulty of translating English into Chinese and vice versa has led to many genuinely amusing errors. Nevertheless, the circulation of these bloopers on self-proclaimed Internet joke lists suggests that they circulate more as humorous items than as serious warnings. One Web site is "dedicated to the misuse of Chinese characters in Western culture,"[13] and displays a range of tattooing errors emblazoned on the bodies of young Americans. One woman remarked that when she attempted to have the Chinese letter "L" tattooed on her ankle, the word "hand" was substituted. She noted ruefully, "In the end I decided to keep the tattoo as a reminder to myself of the consequences of making a hasty decision that will be a permanent part of your life."[14]

Other accounts are similarly amusing, each told as a personal experience anecdote: "A friend of mine [in] Israel…got a tattoo there, thinking that it said 'party girl.' Within Israel she never ran into any Chinese that could tell her what it really meant. When she came to Canada she found out it meant prostitute,"[15] and "When I was on vacation, a lady came up to me with a Chinese tattoo and asked me what it said. I was very reluctant to tell her (and eventually lied to her), since the tattoo had the traditional writing for the word 'chun' (stupid)."[16] One tattoo parlor was said to include among the stock designs offered (and, it is said, used) one in Chinese that read, "I'm so stupid that I don't know what this means."[17]

Perhaps the most dramatic example was a "news story" that was published by a British newspaper, *Metro*, in June 2002:

> A teenager who paid £90 to have his arm tattooed with Chinese characters got a shock when he learned the message read: "At the end of the day, this is an ugly boy." Hairdresser Lee Becks thought he had Mandarin for "Love, honour and obey" etched into his skin. The 18-year-old found out he had been tricked when he saw the effect it had on a woman serving in a Chinese take-away.... "The young woman blushed and was very reluctant to translate for me. Then she admitted what it really said." A "totally mortified" Mr. Becks went back to the tattoo parlour in Southend the next day—only to find it had closed....Mr. Becks plans to spend £600 to have the tattoo removed by laser.[18]

Although this alternative translation is presented as serious and treated as such in Internet discussions, the story has the air of a hoax. The difference between the intended message and the actual one is too great and the fact that the tattoo parlor had conveniently just closed too coincidental, but in the world of rumor anything is possible. A related version, clearly humorous, subsequently appeared in September 2002 on "Souf Oaklin fo' Life!!!" a Pittsburgh-area satirical Web site, which captures the anxiety evident in the attempts to embrace the strange and exotic.

> Pitt junior Brandon Smith wanted a tattoo that proclaimed his manliness, so he decided to get the Chinese characters for "strength" and "honor" on his chest. After 20 minutes under the needle of local tattoo artist Andy Sakai, he emerged with the symbol for "small penis" embedded in his flesh....Sakai, an award-winning tattoo artist,[19] was tired of seeing sacred Japanese words, symbols of his heritage, inked on random white people....Any time a customer came to Sakai's home studio wanting Japanese tattooed on them, he modified it into a profane word or phrase. "I think I'm helping my fellow man by labeling all the stupid people in the world," he explained. "It's not a crime, it's a public service."[20]

While this is clever satire, published on a humorous Web site, following the tradition of *The Onion*, the national humor newspaper, what makes it more significant is the fact that many readers believed it and discussed it as a serious news article on several Web sites. Some readers felt that these students got what they deserved and others felt that the tattoo artist was malicious. The controversy suggests the important role of trust—and its breach—in cross-cultural relations. Customers want to reveal their cultural sophistication by having an exotic symbol etched on their body, but this decision relies on trusting the Asian artist who may see the request as offensive. Because of ethnic animosity, the trust may be misplaced.

Pets: Endangered or Dangerous?

As is apparent, rumors, even when they seem innocuous, are responsive to the political world around them. In the guise of being amusing stories, they address fundamental issues of concern. The laughs that they garner are often prickly and rueful, as in a complex of humorous stories concerning cross-cultural encounters between tourists and pets. Funny, certainly, but what is the message that stands behind them? Why are these stories so often spread and why do many people see them as filled with essential truth? At their core, such accounts reveal how little we know about foreign lands and how devastating our misjudgments can be, and, so, implicitly these stories—jokes and rumors both—warn us to be on guard.

In one series, the tourists bring a cherished pet on vacation. Through a misunderstanding, the animal is cooked and served to its owners. In a second, the tourists find a mysterious but dangerous pet to which they become attached. Both began as facetious stories—more humor than rumor—and circulated as self-proclaimed urban legends. Yet each developed grimmer variants. These double-layered stories suggest that when we strip away the merriment, powerful anxieties remain a common theme of the close examination of rumor and jokes. It is precisely because rumor and humor appear to mean so little—mental chewing gum perhaps—that they can smuggle so much sensitive, unspoken material into conversation.

The first rumor apparently derives from a news item circulated by Reuters in 1971, crediting a Swiss newspaper as its source. According to this account, a couple from Zurich visited Hong Kong, taking their pet poodle with them. When they went to a local restaurant, they ordered a meal, and asked the waiter to give their dog something to eat. "The waiter had trouble understanding the couple," the Reuters story noted, but eventually took the dog away with him. Some time later, the waiter returned, carrying a dish covered with a fancy silver lid. The couple lifted it and found that the chef had assumed that the poodle was to be cooked as their main course. Folklorist Jan Harold Brunvand found numerous variations circulating in the 1980s, many of which showed unusual attention to the description of the cooked poodle, which was, variously, served "under glass, on a bed of rice, with its own jeweled collar in its mouth, and...with an apple in its mouth and parsley springs stuck in its ears."[21]

The story was widely circulated and sometimes was said to have occurred at a local restaurant run by recent immigrants. However, it is difficult to demonstrate that it was ever presented as fact, even if it reveals through the guise of humor the same cross-cultural distance and mistrust found elsewhere. Brunvand identifies it as "an outrageously silly urban legend," and Barbara Mikkelson notes that it appeared in a wide variety of anthologies of such narratives, often accompanied by comic illustrations or even adapted to comic-book format. In such cases, it might have incorporated the genuine concerns, mentioned previously, that such cultural strangers were capable of abducting and eating neighborhood pets, a theme that, as we described, sometimes emerges in rumors about immigrants—often Chinese or Vietnamese.[22]

More often the victims are naïve visitors, and the misunderstanding of the waiter is a consequence of the outsiders' ignorance. The poodle in the most widely collected version symbolizes that the couple is wealthy and implies that they hire domestic help to perform menial chores. The core motif—the accidental cooking of the pet—precedes a humorous urban legend that appeared a few years later, in which a wealthy couple, temporarily deprived of domestic help, attempt to give their poodle a bath. In the end, they dry the pet off by placing it in the microwave, with fatal results.[23]

In Western culture, pets are sometimes treated as family members with a status akin to children. This tendency suggested to Brunvand that the microwaved pet story might have derived from an older, grimmer legend complex that was current in Latin America as early as 1949[24] and resurfaced in the United States and in Europe during the early 1970s. In this story, a baby is cooked by a domestic servant or babysitter. Here the babysitter is not a foreigner but a psychotic or drug-addled teenager, but in even the earliest recorded versions the child is given the same gourmet treatment as the poodle. In the 1949 Argentinian version, the horrified parents find their baby "on a large platter, roasted and garnished with potatoes." In the 1970s American versions, this scene is often further ornamented:

> The mother rushed into the kitchen. There she found the table set for two with her best china and crystal. The lights were out and there were lit candles on the table. In the oven was their baby.... [The sitter] said, "Look, I fixed a special meal for you."[25]

The Latino version clearly was accepted as being a plausible story. Psychoanalyst Marie Langer noted that she found the story everywhere among servants and other working-class informants, "accepted as truth by people generally capable of critical judgment."[26] However, the tasty elaborations found in the more recent versions suggest that the story was found more and more to be an opportunity for "sick humor." Other Internet postings follow this tendency by providing suggestions for the best way to cook and serve fetus, scrambled with barbecue sauce.[27]

This narrative re-emerged in 1995 with a Chinese connection. Several religious newsletters and Web sites circulated an article, claiming to be from the *Eastern Express*, a short-lived (but genuine) English-language publication in Hong Kong. This magazine was said to have found evidence that Chinese hospitals routinely sold aborted fetuses to people who then cooked and ate them for their alleged health benefits. This news story, like the 1971 Reuters tale, made much ado about the preparation of the ghastly dish. "Usually, I washed the fetuses clean, and added ginger, orange peel, and pork to make soup," a Hong Kong gourmand was quoted as saying. "After taking it for a while, I felt a lot better and my asthma disappeared. I used to take placenta, but it was not so helpful."[28]

This article reads much like an *Onion*-style hoax, and in its original context it may well have been such. (In fact, while the *Eastern Express* was a real newspaper and the reporter credited was an actual Western journalist then working in Hong Kong, we could not determine if the article ever did in fact appear in that publication on the credited date.) Nevertheless, it was not taken as a joke by many North American readers, particularly among religious antiabortion groups, who quoted and circulated the piece widely during the spring of 1995. The article generated so much attention among the Religious Right that Congressman Frank Wolf (R-VA) called for the federal government to revoke China's "most favored" trade status if the reports proved to be genuine.[29] The move to investigate the matter gathered steam when Senator Jesse Helms (R-NC), chair of the Foreign Relations Committee, called for hearings on the matter, but the controversy cooled when the Chinese government denied the story and solid evidence to support it proved elusive.

Nevertheless, the story, which echoed the debate on the use of fetal stem cells, refused to die. In 2001, a series of e-mails forwarded visual files that purported to show babies and fetuses being made into gourmet dishes. The most commonly forwarded images showed a large Asian male with a plate containing what appear to be body parts of a dismembered baby, including a large doll-like head with eyes. In one he is bringing a piece of ribs to his mouth with a tiny arm and hand attached. The text accompanying the photographs asserted that roasted and barbecued fetuses had become a gourmet dish in Taiwan. Investigation determined that these two photographs were in fact part of a montage of photographs, titled "Eating People," concocted by Zhu Yu, a Beijing conceptual artist. In other performances, Zhu had himself filmed while eating what he said were cooked human brains and insisted to interviewers that he actually had committed cannibalism "for art's sake." Others, observing that the blackened "body parts" in the photos look more like pieces of a cut-apart hollow plastic doll, suggested that the whole affair was a tongue-in-cheek performance inspired by the 1995 rumor.[30]

In this case, the belief that people care so little about human life that they are willing to sanction abortion inspired an ongoing complex of hoaxes, truth claims, official investigations, and possibly a few actual public enactments. These rumors gain credibility when linked to the culinary preferences of distant cultures. Americans' deep-seated ignorance of Chinese culture began as a "silly urban legend" and developed into an accusation of cannibalism, as it resonates with deep-seated moral and political concerns. The story was plausible in that it fit the concerns that some Americans, often religious conservatives, had with China's population policies, sharply limiting family size and promoting abortion. These foolish stories dealt with very sensitive subjects. The targets were not to be outdone, and the stories were answered by Chinese artists who perpetuated and extended the affair, perhaps to satirize Americans' misunderstandings of Chinese culture. That these stories and images spread across continents indicates the extent to which rumor and satire are global commodities.

Hugs for Puppies?

"The Mexican Pet," another pet-based joke/rumor complex, was widely circulated after emerging in the 1980s and still is spread today. This story also has a political component, a critique of naïve Americans who are ignorant of the dangers of illegal immigration. We must strip away the frothy, jokey covering to reveal concerns that address the political debates of the day. Within rumor one often discovers a vigorous—and even tough-minded—political dialogue. The narrative describes naïve tourists returning from Mexico with a small, cute pet, typically sneaking the animal through American customs.[31] Many early texts tended to be highly developed as literary tales rather than as literal truth claims. One 1983 newspaper account reads:

> A couple who lives somewhere in the vast plains of the state of North Dakota recently quit those endless horizons for a time to vacation in Mexico. It is believed that they stayed in the city of Oaxaca, far in the southern reaches of that country. In their hostel, they summoned a dinner from room service and, having dined, placed the dishes outside their door to be fetched away. Some time later, on emerging from their room, they found those dishes still awaiting. But attending to the remnants of the repast was a tiny dog. A Chihuahua, they discerned immediately…was nervously nibbling away at their table scraps. Though it made to escape at the sight of them, the little animal found itself swept up into the woman's arms and into the hearts of both the travelers. It was so small, so obviously fearful and disquieted, that they stroked and petted it and calmed it with their soothing words and manner.… As with all things good, the idyll drew to a close and the vacationers faced a dilemma. The law proscribed transporting their beloved friend across the border. Yet, they could not bear to part with it.… Praying that no yips or barks betray their mission, the woman secreted the quivering, precious bundle deep in a large purse.… Back home in North Dakota, the pair romped and frolicked with the new addition to their household.… Mindful that it had borne no tags when they discovered it, and eager to ensure the well-being of their friend, they took it to a veterinary clinic for immunizations. They said they would return on the morrow. Within hours, a vet called them on the telephone. "Are you certain," he said, "that you want to

keep this animal?" Of, course, of course, they replied. What could prompt him to raise such a question? "Because," he said, "this is not a Chihuahua. This is not a dog. This is a Mexican water rat."[32]

This version has the earmarks of an anecdote: a vague context, lack of evaluation, highly elaborated diction ("attending to the remnants of the repast"), and a dramatic punch line. Moreover, the fact that the husband and wife are tourists is crucial to the story. While the North Dakota locale is hyperbolized ("the vast plains of North Dakota"), the detail aptly contrasts mundane safety and exotic danger. These tourists are late-twentieth-century innocents abroad, and the text places most of its emphasis on characterizing the couple as both provincial and naïvely sentimental. They instinctively bond with the wee animal, stroking, petting, calming, soothing, and finally romping and frolicking with it. They avoid government regulations out of foolish humanitarianism. Their pity defeats their sense. The tourists are aware that their acts are illegal, but conspire to deceive the authorities by smuggling the animal out in a womblike purse.

Other versions have the wife placing the animal directly next to her body, carrying it under her coat or sweater, and further identifying the pet as a substitute baby, who is "reborn" in safe and secure America.[33] This excessive affection for the unfamiliar animal, of course, sets up the punch line that exposes the couple's ignorance.

The Mexican Pet and Immigration Policy

From the start, "The Mexican Pet" presented a much bleaker image. Brunvand reports that he began hearing this story around 1983. Why 1983? During this time, the problem of undocumented aliens was receiving extended attention in the United States, as is again the case today. If nothing else, the Mexican pet is an undocumented alien. It is a stand-in for those workers who naïve Americans believe they need, but who can turn deadly in ways discussed in chapter 4. Those members of Hispanic gangs described previously might have appeared to be innocent schoolchildren when they first arrived. Here the rumor warns: don't believe what you see. Cute foreigners are fundamentally different from cute Americans. The metaphor of the dog/rat is a powerful one in allowing narrators to proclaim the concern without being tagged as bigoted. Here is a "real case" of tragedy brought on by sympathy. When one reads such stories with their metaphors, one can almost believe that rumor is poetry.

In many texts, the rat is a dangerous, contaminating scavenger—a homeless animal that survives on its wits, providing a vivid image of the new wave of immigrants in the popular imagination. In Brunvand's defining text, after which his popular book *The Mexican Pet* was titled, the animal begins oozing mucus around its eyes and foaming at the mouth: a loathsome if memorable image of stranger danger. The veterinarian's assessment is more brutal than the journalistic one quoted earlier: "First of all…it's a Mexican sewer rat. And second, it's dying."[34] Another variant, which now seems to be the dominant one in Web-based versions, gives the last line as "Second, it has rabies," emphasizing the threat to the homeland. In many texts, the rat attacks other family pets, or even the couple's children. Brunvand records one text in which the vet simply grabs the pet and kills it on the spot by breaking its neck, before delivering the punch line. While the animal may have a deceptive, harmless appearance, its true nature is horrifying and hazardous.

Further, the analogy between "stray" animals and illegal immigrants is a common one among critics of the current situation. An anonymous Web-posted editorial commented:

> I don't *hate* illegal immigrants. I don't *hate* pit bulls, either. But if a stray pit bull wandered into my yard…one that was undocumented (does it have rabies? Parvo? Does it have a new, exotic disease that my dog has no immunity to? Will it attack? Will it have puppies that will have puppies that will have puppies? Will it ever go away?), I'd have to take a rational, pro-active approach to the threat this stray dog may have on the safety of what's mine.… I'd either call the doggie police (animal control) to have it removed, confined, observed and possibly exterminated, or, if I felt that my dog or my family were in immediate danger from this uninvited dog I'd be inclined to shoot it. Or put a few bowls of anti freeze out in its favorite loitering spots.[35]

Texts began to circulate in Western Europe at the same time and for parallel reasons. A related version of this tale was spread in France in the mid-1980s at the time that Jean-Marie Le Pen and his nativist National Front began emphasizing the problems allegedly caused by African and Middle Eastern immigration into France. In 1986, according to folklorist

Véronique Campion-Vincent,[36] a common story was spread of a young couple who is touched by a very small, sweet dog who followed them around affectionately during a holiday in West Africa. They return to France hiding the dog, but after a few days the newcomer slits their cat's throat and is identified by a vet as "a big, ill rat." Again, the punch line provides a dramatic warning not to become attached to innocent-appearing foreigners. Like many contemporary rumors about social change, the text is fundamentally conservative, revealing the perception of dangers of naïve globalism. Those cute little third-world pets are really vicious wild beasts, infected with dreaded diseases, themes that connect to those rumors about migrants. While these animals are unexceptional in the streets of Mexico City, Lagos, Bangkok, Sao Paulo, or Mumbai, they—like foreign workers[37]—have no place in "advanced" societies.

While the American versions first emphasized Mexico, as globalization increased the locations of these rumors expanded. Consider the following American text about Haitian rats:

> My mother said she heard this from a friend who said it happened to some friends of hers. Seems this couple was fishing in their boat off the Florida coast when they saw what looked like a small dog frantically swimming around in the ocean. So, as most people would, they went and fished it out and fed it food and the dog ate out of their hands. So they wrapped it in a blanket and took it home. The next morning the family wakes up to find bloody pieces of the family cat [and the dog] snarling and popping its teeth at anyone who comes near. When they call the animal control officer and start to describe what has happened, he tells them, "Get out of the house and wait till I get there with the sheriff." Assumedly they shot the dog, but the animal control officer tells them that their dog is not a dog at all, but a forty-pound Haitian rat which don't look like rats at all, and are noted for their size and ferocity.[38]

A variation of this story places the boat off the coast of Washington and turns the dog into a Chinese water rat. A third does away with the tourist motif and has the dangerous animal, like contemporary illegal immigrants, simply show up at the port of entry. "This story was told to my husband by one of the truck drivers at work," this variant begins, using the formula that suggests that the events actually happened. "It is supposed to be true," the narrator insists, "but then someone told him that he found it on the Internet. I have not been able to confirm it." The wife of the truck driver has a job on the Boston docks, the variant goes, where her co-workers had gotten used to feeding a stray dog. She agreed to adopt it, coaxed it into her car, cleaned it, and let the newcomer sleep with her on the bed. "The next day," this text continues:

> She came home from work and found the dog had eaten her cat. The only thing left of the cat was the skull. There was no blood anywhere. She called the veterinarian who told her to bring the dog right in. He could not do anything for the cat, but the bones from the cat could do injury to the dog. She brought the dog right in and was in the waiting room when the nurse asked her to step into one of the rooms immediately!! When she got in the room the Vet asked her where she got the dog and she told her it was a stray she found where she works near the docks in Boston. The vet told her he had to kill it immediately—that it was not a dog, but a 40-pound Cambodian rat that came in from one of the ships in the harbor. The rat was so big that it looked liked a small dog with a little snub tail.[39]

These stories do what good stories always do, provide salient details that demonstrate their veracity (naming the place or type of animal). They convince audiences in their specifics that the events might have happened and that, as connected to the debate on immigration, they fit into a politics of plausibility. However, the concern with cross-national migration is by no means limited to the United States, and other citizens of other developed nations were attuned to these concerns as well. When people share anxieties, stories can easily jump across national boundaries to be found in Germany, New Zealand, or Canada with their own confirming details.

As a result, similar stories about cross-cultural contact are collected outside the United States. In 1998, a dispute was reported from New Zealand when a story similar to "The Cambodian Rat" emerged and circulated widely. A government quarantine officer told the *Christchurch Press* that he felt obliged to investigate, since rabies is not present in that country and considerable care is taken not to allow the disease to enter. "But so far it has been driving us mad," he admitted. "We have not been able to catch up with anybody who has actually been involved in this. Everyone has heard the rumour." The animal was variously described as a Korean freezer rat or a Taiwanese rat.[40]

A similar account apparently appeared in a newspaper in the Ukraine and was republished in the *Columbus Dispatch:*

> A newspaper in Kiev, *Vseukrainskiye Vedomosti* (*All-Ukraine Gazette*) reported a tale of mistaken identity that endangered a child and left its parents "thunderstruck." Victor R. returned from an unnamed foreign destination with what he thought was a bull-terrier puppy for his wife and son. At first, the animal ate normally and did not demand much attention. But the paper said that on the sixth day the parents were awakened by the screams of their 3-year-old whose ear was being chewed off by the animal. The child was treated for minor wounds, and a veterinarian informed the parents that their pet was actually a rare species of Pakistani rat, which in its early stage of development resembles a bull-terrier puppy.[41]

Even in the former Soviet Union, contact with the developing world—and its denizens—is perceived to be dangerous.

Hospitality Hazards

Dangers of contamination exist in milder forms even when the "aliens" remain at home. A common legend during the early 1990s was set in an exclusive hotel, typically in the Caribbean (Jamaica, Bahamas, St. Maarten, or the Virgin Islands) or Central America (Mexico, Costa Rica), and occasionally even romantic Europe (Rome, Paris, or the French Riviera).[42] The earliest recorded text was posted on a Web site devoted to debunking contemporary legends:

> I heard this story twice in the past six months, and I'm convinced that it is the stuff of urban folklore. In both cases, the events described definitely happened to persons known to the story-teller....It seems that this couple go to some island resort for a vacation, and one day while they are out of their room, it is burgled. (Groan, not this story again...right??) They are relieved of their traveler's checks and cash, but, because they have the AmEx...checks, they happily continue their vacation. Upon returning home, they have their many rolls of film developed. In

the midst of one of the rolls are found photos of someone's exposed derriere, cheeks parted, with one (possibly more?) of the vacationers' toothbrushes inserted, business end in, of course, into the bunghole presumably belonging to one of the burglars. The first time I heard this story I gacked, the second time, it began to dawn on me that this fell into the category of folklore. Right. Am I right? Or did these two parties happen to fall victim to the same clever perpetrator?[43]

This presentation reveals an uneasy ambivalence: the narrator begins by stating that he is convinced that it is just an urban legend, yet his motive for posting it is precisely to be reassured. The ending, "Right. Am I right?" poignantly demonstrates that he is torn between thinking this story is funny and thinking that it is horrid. Two other accounts show similar ambivalence: one narrator says he heard it as "news" but comments "it feels like an urban legend." Another refers to a friend who "swears it must be true" and solicits "a stack of reports…to demonstrate that it qualifies for legend status."[44] News and contemporary legend have an uncertain boundary.

However, the story soon was accepted into the canon of well-known urban legends, as evident in a variant a year later:

Some American tourists were staying in a nice Jamaican hotel. One day they were out of their room and the room was burglarized. The thieves took everything except the camera and the personal bathroom items. The Americans stayed and finished their vacation, still making use of whatever the thieves left behind, including the toothbrushes. When they got home and got the film developed there was a picture of a large Jamaican man, with no pants on, bent over with a toothbrush sticking out his…Well, let's just say that you would be pretty darn sorry if that was your toothbrush![45]

Many of these legends have a racial component as the thieves are local black men or Hispanics. However, tellers who prefer to avoid such racially problematic descriptions set the story in seemingly less foreign vacation spots, such as this version set in Paris, still exotic, but less racially problematic:

This nice American family of four goes to Paris, France on vacation. They check into a hotel and go sightseeing and all the other touristy things. A few days into their (until then) pleasant, normal vacation, they go for lunch at a café. They return to find that their hotel room has been broken into. Fortunately, it seems to have been a rather surgical strike and very few of their possessions are stolen or even out of place. Two displacements, however, strike the family as odd: their four toothbrushes are strewn around the sink, and their camera is set out in the open on one of the beds. The hotel management is apologetic and blames the bellboy. The bellboy, who had seemed so nice, if unnervingly suave to the family upon their arrival, had just quit his job on the morning of the break-in. The Americans get the missing portion of their American Express Travelers' Cheques refunded, check into a new hotel, wind up the tail end of their trip, and head back to America....In America they develop the pictures in the camera. Half are of the family in front of the Eiffel Tower, but the other half of the pictures in the roll feature various views of the bellboy, smiling deliriously, with the four family toothbrushes stuck up his bootie.[46]

As noted, race need not always be a central feature of this tale of international immorality. More important is the exotic location and the strangeness of the customs and the people. While thefts at home are also violations—and sometimes thieves defecate in the home that they had violated[47]—a theft when one is traveling is a fearful violation, and, when accompanied by the degrading affront, suggests a statement about one's role as a tourist. But when race is directly or implicitly involved, as it is in most versions of the rumor, the tellers reveal their racial (and class) anxieties.

The next version—from Germany—makes race explicit, particularly as the rumor is set in Africa. It tells of a Swissair flight attendant who was allowed a stopover in Africa. When she returned to her hotel room unexpectedly to retrieve something she had forgotten, she "saw the black hotel boy brushing his teeth with her toothbrush," or, in a more pointed variant, "scrubbing the rim of the washbasin with her toothbrush."[48]

As the story spread, its form was shaped to provide a potent (and disgusting) warning about the dangers of life in exotic locals. The central theme—the perverse dangers of paradise—also became one of the central themes in the next legend complex, one of the most pervasive and disturbing of the past decade, far from the light humor of the earlier accounts in the chapter.

Welcome to the World of AIDS

Vacations can spark romance. The rules that constrain behavior are lifted when one is away from those who exert moral control. This is, in an exaggerated form, the motivating principle behind the "Girls Gone Wild" videos, exercises in cinematography that depend on the institution of spring break, a liminal moment. Partners found on holiday come from backgrounds very different from one's own, and as such they are a source of danger. Do we really know them, and can we trust their attentions and affections?

As HIV became increasingly prevalent in the 1980s, the stories about the virus traded on the question of how well one knew one's lover. It's bad enough to pick up a partner at a local bar, but a greater anxiety arises from foreign trysts. The most extensive account of these stories that spread widely during the period from the late 1980s into the mid-1990s is that provided by Diane Goldstein in her analysis of AIDS-related folklore in Newfoundland. Goldstein emphasizes that it is the distant, exotic locale—either the Caribbean or Florida for these stolid Newfoundlanders—that escalates the danger. One version from a young Newfoundland student reveals the dimensions of the story:

> This girl needed a break and decided to go to Florida for a month or two holiday, I think. While she was there she met a man who seemed to be...the man of her dreams. He had money, he treated her like gold, and he gave her everything she wanted. She fell in love with him and...during her last night there they slept together. The next day he brought her to the airport for her return to St. John's [Newfoundland]. He gave her a small gift-wrapped box and told her not to open it until she got home. They...said goodbye and she left, hoping that someday they would be married and the gift would be an [engagement] ring. The suspense was killing her and...she decided to open the gift on the plane. It was a small coffin with a piece of paper saying "Welcome to the World of AIDS."[49]

Similar accounts from the United States focus on vacations in Central America or the Caribbean. In these stories of romantic risk, chaste young women fall in love in a world whose moral boundaries are uncertain. The following text, couched in a literary style and posted on a Web site devoted to "all the funny e-mails that get forwarded around the internet," shows the simple oral version recorded by Goldstein transformed into a sensuous morality tale:

A woman from Seattle named Mary decided to escape the rainy winter months and spend a few weeks in Aruba. Her travel agent booked her a suite in a deluxe resort hotel on a gorgeous private beach. 30 min. after she checked in, Mary was lounging on the beach enjoying the attentions of a very handsome cabana boy. The cabana boy set up a large beach umbrella for her, brought her fresh towels and refreshing drinks from the bar and even rubbed sunscreen on her back and shoulders. Mary relished the luxury of having a personal attendant. Then one evening, as she was about to go to bed, there was a knock at her door. It was the cabana boy with a bottle of Dom Perignon and a bowl of strawberries. Mary invited him in and they spent the night together having sex; in fact, they spent every night of Mary's vacation together. On the morning of her departure, Mary almost wept at the thought of leaving her handsome young lover. After they had said their good-byes, a woman from the front desk took Mary aside. "Excuse my intrusion, miss," she said. "But have you been intimate with that man?" "How dare you stick your nose in my business! Where's the hotel manager?" Mary exclaimed. "I know I have offended you, miss. Do whatever you must. But take my advice as well: When you return home, go to your doctor and have a blood test. That boy has AIDS and he does not care if he infects anyone else." Mary was shocked and terrified. Back in Seattle, her doctor gave her the bad news: she was indeed infected with HIV. Mary spent days locked in her apartment weeping. But then she became angry. Since the boy in Aruba was doing all he could to infect unsuspecting women, she would seduce every man she could. That night Mary went to a hotel bar and picked up a businessman. The next morning, when the man woke up, he found that Mary was gone. But in the bathroom, scrawled across the mirror in blood red lipstick was the message, "Welcome to the world of AIDS!"[50]

The tagline of this version is the same as the domestic rumor about a man picking up a woman at a bar for a one-night stand in his hotel room and finding that she wrote—in lipstick—"Welcome to the World of AIDS" on the bathroom mirror.[51] However, rather than emphasizing sexual irresponsibility, this text stresses the danger of leaving one's home community.

The stories are sufficiently plausible that they are sometimes printed as news accounts, such as:

A British AIDS counselor warned that infected playboys at Spanish resorts had formed a cult devoted to giving the disease to vacationing girls. He said that in two cases British girls, after a holiday affair in Spain, were given little farewell gifts to carry with them on the plane home. The packages contained a small wooden coffin inscribed with "Welcome to the death club. Now you've got AIDS." The two girls are said to be undergoing three months of testing to see if they have in fact caught the disease.[52]

Like so many other rumors, this is a story of trust, searching for security in a world that is hazy and dark. Through rumor, communities discuss with whom and under what conditions we should fall in love. These stories, conservative—or at least stressing traditional morality—as rumor often is, argue that we need to know the background of those with whom we develop intimate connections. People can be appealing in person, but what is their back story? Who are they? Murderers, rapists, and the infected often have a bright smile, a toned body, and a smooth tongue. But until they can be vouched for by friends and neighbors, their seductions could be evilly intended. Love and romance, these stories assert, need to begin at home. Community is treated as the proper location of sex, love, and commitment.

The resort, populated by strangers looking for thrills and excitement, is filled with threats of the most intimate kind. The story, allegedly about sex, is also profoundly about trust. Who is this new person, so slick and cool, who wishes to enter my life? Reject sweet nothings, but believe the knowing moral evaluations of one's neighbors.

These versions take behavior that is both cruel and bizarre and transform it into a morality play that emphasizes how close-knit, established social networks provide a bulwark against danger. The strength of community provides security, and as the scene of a story becomes more exotic it becomes easier to believe, despite its surface implausibility. Courtship begins at home.

Tourist Troubles

As Americans travel on a global circuit, stories that depend on misunderstandings and mishaps have a ready audience. We remain uncertain about the rules and hazards that follow from our visits. Given a lack of knowledge, much belief falls along a continuum of plausibility, revealing the assumptions that we draw upon when we separate ourselves from our community. Tourism combines both approaching and avoiding. Globalization brings people and their cultures closer but simultaneously makes our differences all the more visible and troubling. Our dilemma derives from an attempt to fit foreign spaces into a sheltered social and cultural template. In realizing that these cozy templates do not fully fit, we often emphasize the differences by means of spreading rumors.

In some instances our own poor judgment puts ourselves and our family in mortal danger, as in the case of "The Mexican Pet." In other instances, as in stories that depict the danger of romance abroad, the danger results from the actions of others. We believe that we can read our foreign experiences, only to discover to our dismay that such a soothing belief is deceptive. Even as we travel, we manage to erase the central and consequential differences to which we should attend, leading us into the troubles depicted by rumor. This has to do with a conflict of identity between us and them, where identity is tied to traditional ways of doing things. Who we are is indelibly tied to our standards of behavior; who they are is tied to their actions as well. If we act in different ways abroad, we may decide that we have become different people, perhaps becoming strangers to ourselves.

One additional feature makes this set of stories distinct from many of the others we discuss. While the emotional tone of these globalization rumors varies widely, many of them are told to amuse. While this cannot be said of the AIDS stories with which we conclude, horrific for sure, many others, such as those accounts about language errors, are jokes, in practice if not in fact.

This inherent variety reveals something important about rumors. They are emotionally pliable, and need not fall into any tight, neat category. Some rumors insist on their truth value, while others, like many in this chapter, are not much concerned with whether they are accepted as fact. They serve various emotional purposes, even while their goal as talk is to bolster community belonging and question cultural differences.

The emotional versatility of rumors challenges the belief that they are always spread by credulous, naïve people, easily taken in or uncaring of the truth. Rumor tellers are not always suckers for the bizarre or bogus. Some stories are spread for the sheer joy of the telling or in wondering whether a part of the story might possibly be true. Take the case of those stickers that children used to lick to place into scrapbooks. Some rumors claimed that drug groups imbued them with LSD, a rumor that caught the attention of French marketing researcher Jean-Noël Kapferer.[53] Kapferer discovered that strength of belief in its truthfulness was not closely linked to one's willingness to transmit it. In fact, his survey showed that people who considered it "doubtful" were twice as likely to pass it on to others than those who "wholly believed" it.[54] The explanation, Kapferer reasoned, was that people hearing the rumor sought the views of their circle of friends before reaching a firm opinion. "This is the way that public opinion is formed," Kapferer concluded, "based on exchanges between individuals."[55] In rumors of war or crisis, we might not have this luxury, but certainly this applies to rumors of travel.

We might better consider rumor not so much an *answer* than a *question*, a socially acceptable opportunity to raise a sensitive or engaging issue, encouraging others to share what they know. Rumor is not so much a statement that is true or false, or even believed or disbelieved, but one about which groups of people can legitimately *debate*. In practice, truth claims are often not passed on as declarative statements—"This *happened*"—but rather as questions—"*Did* this happen?"

Yet, even as we debate these issues—sometimes sharing jokes and humorous anecdotes—a message is present. Tourists may be foolish, but in some measure they represent others in their home culture. People wish to expand their horizons, but we worry about what we are getting ourselves into when we veer from the beaten path. In our laughter, we reveal insecurity over these novel and temporary environments. As has often been recognized, playful conversation can be as political as serious talk. In each case, we discuss the boundaries of our world. In establishing trust, jokes matter as much as devout moralizing.

6

The Menace of International Trade

Eighty years ago, in January 1930, Americans were transfixed by the possibility of an incipient pandemic: psittacosis—or parrot fever. In December, a Maryland couple had purchased a parrot from a Baltimore pet shop. Soon the bird sickened and eventually died, and shortly afterward its owners became dangerously—and mysteriously—ill. This real, although uncommon, disease was spread by parrots and other exotic birds; at the time there was no known treatment. Many Americans purchased parrots as glamorous pets, particularly from Argentina, where the epidemic was thought to have begun. In response to frightening media accounts, many birds were killed, a U.S. admiral ordered sailors to cast their pets into the sea, and President Herbert Hoover took time from confronting the Great Depression to consider an executive order banning the importation of parrots. In time, the disease proved far less devastating than expected (and the original victims recovered), and the scare passed from public memory. Yet, as Harvard historian Jill Lepore noted: "As the story grew, it took on certain familiar—and, as it turned out, durable—features that borrow as much from pulp fiction as from public health: super scientists fight super bugs in race to defeat foreign menace invading American homes, beneath the very Christmas tree."[1] The Science Service in their *Science Newsletter* reported on an article published in the prestigious *Journal of the American Medical Association*, noting that parrot fever should remind us that "it is no longer possible for any person or nation to live in isolation."[2] Certainly not in a global economy.

Nothing better exemplifies the dangers of globalization—as they are perceived—than stories that reveal threats from foreign imports, particularly those that have their origins or are manufactured in the developing nations. At one time, not so long ago, periphery nations—the third world—sent natural resources to core nations—the first world—and received manufactured products in exchange. Today, manufacturing jobs are rapidly flowing from the United States and Western Europe to these periphery regions. At first, manufacturing spread to the Little Tigers of Asia (Hong Kong, South Korea, Singapore, and Taiwan) and now it has spread to other Asian, South American, Caribbean, Eastern European, Middle Eastern, and even African nations. China is becoming a major source of both manufactured and agricultural goods, a basis for increasing concern and rumors in the West.

The American trade deficit, which in 2006 reached a record $763 billion before moderating in the wake of the worldwide economic crisis,[3] testifies both to the craving that Americans have for inexpensive products and the growth of manufacturing in the third world. Such a startling deficit not only worries many but also increases the sense of threat that unchecked trade can produce, particularly when some of the nations maintain lax regulation of the products exported. Documented defects in the quality of Chinese products—pet food, seafood, children's toys, cosmetics, and medicines—suggest that not all the claims are fanciful, and anyone of a certain age can recall when the label "Made in Japan" also symbolized poor quality. However, the fact that these products were foreign and produced by nonwhites surely contributed, albeit irrationally, to the sense of discomfort. Documented claims about Chinese products are matched by fanciful claims, such as concerns about carcinogenic chopsticks and candy canes.[4]

At the same time that our economy was threatened, our workers were harmed. Given the wage structures and environmental rules of industrializing nations, it is difficult for advanced nations to compete when consumers search for discounted goods. As our purchases are increasingly manufactured in developing nations, there is fertile ground in which rumors can take root.

In this chapter, we examine how the threat of globalization is expressed through mercantile folklore. We describe claims that address the importation of manufactured goods from overseas, the perils of the importation of raw materials, and even the contamination of Corona beer, a claim that underlines threats to the United States from Mexico, our largest third-world trading partner.

Once again, rumor is a barometer of popular concerns. When the manufacturing base of a nation appears to disintegrate, rumor is there to shore it up by suggesting that cheap products may be dangerous. Of course, this chapter also reveals the limits of rumor as persuasion. While rumors can cause people to reflect for a moment, they cannot impact the structural changes in the world economy. In terms of warning Americans about dangerous products from abroad, rumor—for better or worse—fights a rear-guard action, worrying citizens about forces that are very difficult for them to alter.

Department Store Snakes and Spiders in Yuccas

Some rumors live on. They may disappear for a while, but they regularly re-emerge. Those that reveal this pattern are labeled "diving rumors." Like a skilled diver, these rumors appear, then plunge beneath the surface, only to reappear. People tire of stories once they know them, and move to other narratives. These rumors then are in remission until enough people have forgotten them and are readily available when a new trigger emerges that captures a similar theme.

Among these classic rumors is the claim that a department store shopper is bitten by an insect or snake sewn into the lining of imported clothing or carpets, or otherwise hidden in an imported manufactured product. This text has been collected for over 40 years, and if it is not as widely spread as it once was at the beginning of the concern over international trade, it still appears with regularity. This rumor complex is known generically as "The Department Store Snake" or "The Snake in the Blanket."[5]

In 1975, Fine collected a version from a Boston college student who wrote:

> [This] was a strange, true story about a woman being bit by a snake. The woman was taken to Norwood [Massachusetts] Hospital because of the bite on her arm. It was diagnosed as a snake bite and it wasn't understood how she got it. She was asked to report her doings during the day and she reported that she had tried on coats

at Sears. The coats she tried on were then searched and in one coat was found a snake on the sleeve lining. This coat was made in Taiwan and somehow the snake got in the lining of the coat.

The account contains most of the main themes of this rumor with the threat hidden in a warm, safe product. During this period, most of the texts reported an Asian source for the snake. More recent versions change the origin of the snake and the store involved. Taiwan, seen as too "Western," is replaced by countries like Guatemala and Bangladesh, and Sears has been replaced by Wal-Mart, Target, or other discount superstores, but the fundamental structure of the account remains constant. Another variant suggests that snake eggs have been laid in the folds of an electric blanket. When the blanket is turned on, the heat hatches the eggs.[6]

The rumor continues unabated today. Folklorist Paul Smith[7] provides a typical version:

> Several summers ago a housewife in New York suffered a very unfortunate accident while out shopping. It transpired that she had gone into a large department store to look for a wicker clothes-basket with a lid. As she looked through the baskets she kept putting her hand inside the lid and running her fingers round the rim to check that they did not have any loose canes that would snag the clothes as they were pushed in and pulled out. When going through this procedure, all of a sudden she gave a cry and fell to the floor. She was immediately rushed to hospital but was found dead on arrival. On examination it was discovered that she had died as a result of a snake bite. When the baskets were checked they found a large and deadly poisonous snake in the bottom of the one she was seen to examine last. It was concluded that the snake had arrived in America having been shipped in the basket from the Far East.

Folklorist Jan Harold Brunvand[8] suggested a quarter century ago that by the early 1980s, "The Department Store Snake" legend no longer had the potency that it had a decade previously. But in 1991, the *Omaha World-Herald*[9] reported a similar account, naming the Burlington Coat Factory Outlet:

> An Omaha woman suddenly became deathly sick. Doctors trying to determine what the cause might be asked her to trace her

whereabouts that day. The woman remembered that she had tried on coats at a store. The coats were checked. Young poisonous snakes were found in the collar of a coat the woman had tried on. One had bitten her. The coat was imported from a country where a snake had laid eggs in the fur. The eggs had hatched some time after the coat had been shipped to the store, and the young snakes were still in the fur.

Elsewhere in the article the reporter reveals that these coats were imported from South America or the Far East.

A current example found on the folklore Web site About.com has similar themes:

Apparently a woman entered the emergency room one day with an inflamed neck, which was an allergic reaction from a snake bite. The woman had no idea where she had received the bite and could only recall feeling a sharp pain in her neck when she wore her new winter coat the previous day. Well, they checked out her coat, which was made in some South American country, and found a snake sewn inside the lining. The snake may have been trapped in the coat, but it had managed to bite the woman through the material.[10]

Rumor is most effective when there is one specific target shared in all the stories' variants. By the 1990s, many of these texts targeted coats sold at the national discount chain Burlington Coat Factory, reflecting the association of legends with the largest or most prominent company in a market segment. Fine suggests that this connection between a dominant corporation and a powerful rumor makes sense in that when narrators attempt to communicate a memorable story, they select those firms of which audiences will first think. As a result, the story comes to have an increased plausibility in that these are the companies that will first come to mind. Fine labeled this process the "Goliath effect," recognizing that, given our fears of conspiracy, bigness connects to a plausible claim that the corporation may be engaging in nefarious or uncaring activities.[11] In the case of Burlington Coat Factory, spokespersons admit that they are "constantly" asked about the story, but claim that there has never been a case to which the rumor might refer.

The truth might be disconcerting to some consumers. Ric Bramble, a corporate spokesperson, noted, "We buy coats from vendors. If a snake is in there, it's got to sit in a distribution center for a few months before it's sent to the stores. Are you going to tell me, it survived all that time up a sleeve?"[12] Bramble's candor may not be the ideal marketing strategy, but it is refreshing, reminding consumers that their supposedly "brand-new" coats have in fact been sitting in a cold warehouse. It is a relief to know that, had there been a live snake in the coat when it left the third-world clothing mill, it would surely be dead by now. Nevertheless, the truth of the "brand-new" coat's international travels highlights an essential fact: consumers simply don't know who made the product they are touching and under what conditions, a concern that gives potency to the antisweatshop movement. Despite the new target, the text maintains the fundamental features of earlier versions and continues to serve to warn consumers.

Brunvand claims that "The Department Store Snake" rumor was newly minted in late 1968 or early 1969. However, there are related versions from the 1930s in England in which an upper-class lady receives a fur coat from India as a gift and is bitten by a snake,[13] clearly a precursor of the contemporary account that is more directly linked to consumerism. The only proof that the account of department store snakes derives from the late 1960s is the absence of texts from before that period and then suddenly a large number collected at the end of the 1960s, when folklorists happened to begin looking for rumors and contemporary legends about the dangers of modern society, sensitized to the issue by the ferment of the period that questioned the basis of then-current social life, politics, and culture. Even if the story was not created in the late 1960s, one might conclude that its popularity was amplified by the fact that the Vietnam War was in full force, which meant that Asian dangers were highly salient to Americans. Vietnam was not then a manufacturing nation, but it may have been easy for Americans to associate menace with Asian products.

However, we should not conclude too readily that the existence of the war in Vietnam explains the whole of this warning about the dangers of global manufacturing. Perhaps the war biased Americans against Asian cultures, but if the narratives were only about the effects of the war, the text would likely speak more directly to these issues—or at least the metaphorical connection would be salient. A rumor about dangers of the import-export market seems thin gruel from which to critique a deadly and losing war. To understand why people spread narratives, the internal details must be explored for consistency and the external validity must also be explored. That is, as we noted in discussing the rumor of "The Mexican Pet" in chapter 5, the explanation must connect to some political or social strains evident at the time.[14]

As in many rumor complexes, "The Department Store Snake" texts reveal considerable variation. In the early versions, the imported object was from Asia—particularly the arc from Japan and the Philippines to India, Pakistan, and Iran. More recently, South and Central American nations have been added to the story as manufacturing has expanded, with some countries such as Japan and Taiwan dropped as those are now seen as industrialized and "Western" and others, such as Iran, eliminated because of the absence of trade with the United States. Significantly, the danger transmitted in the rumors is *not* as one might expect from nations that are profoundly impoverished, but precisely from those trading partners that pose fundamental economic challenges to America.[15] Rather than suggesting that these stories reflect the "basic cultural mistrust of the mysterious East,"[16] as they were once described, the primary mistrust appears to be economic, not cultural.

These snakes are not from nations that are primary exporters of raw materials, but from those nations from which we now import manufactured goods. The goods are products that once were made in the United States but now are manufactured abroad because of lower labor costs and, significantly, lax safety and environmental conditions. Furthermore, these products (blankets, carpets, rugs, blouses, and winter coats) are "warm" and "soft,"[17] symbolic contrasts to the poisonous fangs hidden within. An early informant made the moral explicit by advising, "Don't buy Japanese goods." Some narrators have claimed to have altered their buying habits as a result.[18] The vendors from whom these manufactured items are purchased are typically large American department stores, often discount big-box stores, such as K-Mart or Wal-Mart. An irony is evident: American corporations provide the distribution system for products that originate elsewhere, and our manufacturing sector and job base are weakened as a consequence. Significantly, in those versions in which consumers pursue justice through the courts, the *American* store is sued, not the anonymous foreign firm that manufactured the product.

The past half century has witnessed a steady erosion of American manufacturing power, as the growth of factories throughout Asia, Latin America, and the Caribbean demonstrate. By the late 1980s, many manufactured products were produced on the Pacific rim: motorcycles, clothing, steel, textiles, and television sets. This area of the world still remains the source of much American clothing, machinery, and electronics. The beginning of this process was evident by the late 1960s,[19] which coincides with the rise of

"The Department Store Snake" narrative. Unlike mercantile legends about raw materials, which will be discussed, these texts build on a fear of foreign competition and the suspicion that large American stores are willing to put their customers at risk to make a profit. This belief dramatically underlines the steady change in the American economy from being production based to one based on distribution and services. These stories are still heard and believed but, as we no longer see ourselves as primarily a manufacturing nation, are no longer as culturally salient as they once were, suggesting that the fight against foreign manufactured goods has been won—by them. With our long exposure to foreign goods and the fact that we have taken such manufacturing for granted, the rumor may be edging toward the end of its life cycle.

Prickly Dangers: Bringing Exotics Home

A now common story involves the importation of raw produce in the form of yucca trees or cacti into the United States and Western Europe. In this story, deadly spiders are reportedly found in the plant. This claim reinforces the underlying dangers of purchasing items from distant nations. The risks of contact with foreigners, the story warns, are considerable. Brunvand[20] reports a text from England about yuccas from Africa, Véronique Campion-Vincent[21] found that "The Spiders in the Yucca" story was widely known in France in 1986, and Bengt af Klintberg[22] collected texts in Sweden and Finland about yuccas and cacti imported from Central America.

The following American text from Kalamazoo, Michigan, is narrated as a firsthand story, reported by a spouse of the victim's coworker:

> We [she and her husband] purchased a cactus from Frank's Nursery and Crafts.[23] When we took it home, I noticed that it seemed to move on its own. My husband said it was all in my imagination. The next day he decided that it was indeed moving. We called Frank's and they said that it couldn't move on its own. A while later, they called back and said to get out of the house at once. People from Frank's arrived and said that the motion was caused by a tarantula having babies inside the plant.[24]

In this version, the purchaser is not injured by the spider; still, it does require experts to set things right. The presence of experts reveals that the danger is real, not something that can be handled by the consumer, and in this sense the moving cactus suggests the rumor of "The Mexican Pet," which required the knowledge of the veterinarian.

In 1990, columnist Brian O'Neill of the *Pittsburgh Press* reported a variant that claimed that the cactus was purchased from the high-profile Swedish home-design store IKEA (the legend had previously been widely known in Sweden):

> A woman bought a cactus out there at the Swedish furniture store in Robinson, and after she brought it home, her little boy said, "Mommy, the plant waved at me." She didn't believe him, of course, but then she looked at it and, sure enough, the plant was swaying. So Mom called the Phipps Conservatory. "Get it out of your house!" The guy on the phone said. "And call the police." When the police arrived, they sliced the plant open, only to find...TARANTULAS.[25]

O'Neill recounted that another version had the customer set the cactus on fire. The rumor plagued IKEA stores in other regions (and also Marks and Spencer stores in England). In fact, tarantulas do not lay their eggs in cacti nor do their egg sacs explode, and there are no documented cases of cacti filled with spiders.

By 1993, the belief had obtained such currency that the *New York Times* felt it necessary to debunk the story by consulting experts at the Desert Museum in Tucson and at the University of New Mexico, who claimed it was "almost certainly" false.[26] On the surface, these spider legends parallel the rumors about department store snakes, but they reflect different psycho-economic dynamics. In "The Department Store Snake," the focus is on the store rather than the product. The kernel of that story includes a woman going into a store, touching or trying on an item, being bitten, and (sometimes) suing the store. By contrast, with the yucca legend, the raw material is the focus. It is a story about the exotic wild being transported into the domestic world. The kernel of the yucca narrative is the plant, the snake/spider, the call to an expert (a local botanical garden, mail-order company, grocery store, or florist), and the dramatic response. Yet, in fact, the precise origin of the plant is not really important: the danger is from the otherness of an unknown and exotic locale rather than from economic competition. The central theme is the conflict between the dangerous wilderness and the tamed urban environment. In this sense, these yucca narratives remind us of the tourist stories, described in chapter 5, where the wild and the naïve meet. Americans confront the rest of the world on their terms (that is, in light of the dangers of nature) and on our terms (that is, in terms of economic competition). In both cases, of the natural and of the economic, rumors suggest that we can easily be harmed.

The Forbidden Fruit of Foreignness

"The Department Store Snake" narrative describes the dangers of the world economy as derived from manufactured goods produced by economically competitive countries, even if the threat is really from the wild. "The Spider in the Yucca," on the other hand, focuses on the dangers of the natural world—"Nature red in tooth and claw"—not mere economic competition. But some legends manage to capture both dangers using raw products as part of the core narrative. The tarantula, spider, or snake hiding in a bunch of fruit is such as example; it is spread in both Europe[27] and the United States. Swedish folklorist Bengt af Klintberg[28] collected the following text in Stockholm:

> My wife came home last week from work and told me about a woman, a friend of a friend, who had been out driving with her family. The two children were sitting in the back seat. The kids became hungry, and she gave each of them a banana. All of a sudden one of the kids says: "Mum, the banana bit me!" The parents didn't pay any special attention to it. After a while, however, upon turning around, the mother found one of the kids lying there unconscious. They hurried to the hospital, but the doctors could not save the child, who died some hours later. One of the doctors told them that three or four similar accidents had happened before. There seemed to be some poisonous snake that laid eggs in bananas, which hatched into the peels.

A recent story on the Internet recounted that "My neighbor just told me that the deadliest spider in the world has recently been introduced to our county and can be brought home when you buy bananas. Evidently people are bit on the fingers as they peel the banana and expose the spider and their fingers rot off."[29]

This set of rumors is especially challenging to discuss as there is some truth to them, although the death toll is fanciful. Snakes and especially spiders do in fact hitchhike around the world by hiding inside big bunches of bananas or boxes of grape clusters. But even if such rumors are based on a substantial body of verifiable fact, the contexts in which they are reported and discussed reveal the troubling meanings consumers find in them. A fact may be simply a fact, but when it is endlessly discussed, we must pay attention to which underlying fears are being fueled by the fact.

The banana has been the subject of particular attention in rumors from the beginnings of its import into Western markets. While it has been associated with tropical settings since colonial times, having been introduced into Central America from Africa during the Spanish settlement, it was not grown in exportable quantities until around 1900. While many varieties of banana were used as starchy cooked vegetables, shippers became aware that certain sweeter varieties could be harvested in a rock-hard green state and then consumed raw weeks or months later after the fruit slowly ripened during shipment. Consumers were slow to accept the fruit as safe, however; cookbooks from the early twentieth century, before bananas were ripened artificially by exposing them to ethylene,[30] recommended that they be baked or fried rather than simply peeled and consumed raw.

In 1895, a team of doctors published a book with the frightening title *The Relation of Food to Health and Premature Death*. This book specifically implicated green bananas in bringing on acute attacks of deadly cholera. Even when ripened through storage, the doctors said, such fruits were "not suitable to be eaten raw" and should in all cases be cooked until soft or else avoided altogether.[31] "Popular and quasi-scientific opinion has it that the banana is difficult to digest," a popular health handbook said as late as 1935. The truth is, this source asserted, when harvested in an unripe state, its "green starch" remained inedible, even when kept until they were apparently ripe. "They are much like green apples, green peaches, etc.," readers were told, "and may result in trouble when eaten."[32] Ironically, given American attitudes toward Chinese products and foods, the Chinese have similar worries about bananas. In spring 2007, Chinese consumers were frightened by rumors that suggested that bananas from the southern Chinese island of Hainan could spread the SARS virus, following earlier rumors that these same bananas might cause cancer.[33]

The innocuous act of peeling and eating a banana was thus seen as a risky proposition through much of the early twentieth century (and in

China, today). A common joke in the 1940s, based on serious rumor, told of two girls who bought bananas for the first time while on a train trip. One peeled hers and took the first bite, at which point the train entered a tunnel. "Have you started your banana yet?" she asked the other. When she replied no, the first adds, "Well, don't [...] It makes you go blind."[34] Cultural historian Marina Warner says, "the laughter it inspires" (like much of the humor in rumors and legends) "reverberates around its paradoxical potency and defends against the threatening associations that it sets stirring."[35] The fact that bananas were seen as exotic, foreign, and unknown—like the ice cream treats that we described in chapter 4—makes these rumors plausible to their audiences. Until the fruits became integrated into domestic food cultures, anything was possible. Even if by the 1940s bananas were not seen as dangerous in the United States, the memory lingered and they were still good for a laugh, which played off the older concerns. Add to this the phallic imagery of the banana, and the joke may have had several layers: nativist and sexual.

Immigrants and the Dangers of Fruit

The importation of bananas was handled by "native" harvesters and dock loaders in exotic countries in Africa or Central America and transported into the care of a rapidly developing network of grocery wholesalers in the United States. Early in the century the wholesalers were often ethnic immigrants, largely Mediterranean in origin, and so "The Spider in the Fruit" rumor reflects a bias against these immigrants. Rumor always manages to incorporate concerns of the population—such as with the exotic and the foreign—into the storyline. Not only is the fruit deadly but also its handlers are dangerous.

As historian Hasia Diner has documented, Italian immigrants, used to a culture based on limited amounts of available food, were particularly concerned with establishing local groceries, reliable sources for food, in American cities. Italian Americans quickly organized complex culinary networks of food distribution for supplying fellow immigrants with pasta and other foods identified as "old country." As these ventures evolved, they also began to provide fresh fruits and vegetables to a mass market. The wholesalers implemented the organizational strategies they had learned in Italy to establish large-scale agricultural enterprises, moving products from truck farms surrounding major urban centers to low-cost pushcarts and fruit stands.[36] As a result, Italian Americans who achieved management positions in these fruit-and-vegetable networks rose quickly in economic and political status. The Del Monte Corporation was one of several Italian-dominated consortia of fresh produce wholesalers that emerged in the 1880s and within a few years became dominant suppliers of foodstuffs to cities. Food, Hasia Diner concludes, was for immigrants no longer a "badge of class subjugation" but rather "a step up from poverty."[37]

The novelty and tropical origins of the banana, for all the protection that the peel provided to insulate the flesh of the fruit from the touch of foreigners, quickly became a focus for a wide range of contemporary legends. That bananas could be linked with both Italian food culture and anti-Italian prejudice reveals how rumor can simultaneously convey surprising positive and negative messages.

A Hidden Menace

The most dramatic legends asserted that the fruit itself was not only dangerous to eat but also, like "The Spider in the Yucca" rumors, the hiding place for a deadly menace. Poisonous spiders, especially tarantulas, would hide inside bunches of bananas and fatally bite people who reached in to remove a single fruit. By 1910, these legends were so prevalent that the popular investigative journalist Samuel Hopkins Adams included them in a debunking article presenting a whole series of apocryphal stories about snakes, spiders, and centipedes.[38] He admitted that tarantulas might "frequently drop out of banana bunches from South or Central America, to the discomfiture of the unsuspecting grocer." But he was more skeptical of a St. Louis news account, headlined "IN TWO WEEKS Three Men Have Died from Bites of Tarantulas," and claiming that "the victims were banana handlers in the wholesale fruit district." An "exhaustive inquiry," particularly among area immigrant fruit dealers, could not verify the story. Adams concluded, "The report was a pure fake."

Nevertheless, the legend remained active throughout the century. In Davenport, Iowa, the same story turned up about fruit handlers in New Orleans, though this time the insect was a black widow spider.[39] Growing up in New York in the late 1950s, Fine heard stories about people fatally bitten by tarantulas hiding in bunches of bananas. In 1957, popular singer Harry Belafonte made a hit recording of a Caribbean work song that included these words:

A beautiful bunch o' ripe banana
Daylight come and me wan' go home
Hide the deadly black tarantula
Daylight come and me wan' go home[40]

Although rumor is often treated as a synonym for error or deception, this is not always the case. Not all rumors are false; rumors are simply not proven at the time that they are transmitted and when the teller lacks the credibility to make a certain claim. While some rumors are wild and doubtful to skeptics, others reflect exaggerations of actual occurrences. In the case of rumors about insects and fruit, there is some measure of truth. In fact, tarantulas and other species of spider have in fact been found in bunches of bananas, although, contrary to the rumors, no serious injuries have resulted. A story posted to a news reaction site discussing a real incident recounted:

> This story reminded me of something that happened to my grand-mother when she was a young, newly married woman in the 1920s. She had purchased a large bunch of bananas within the last day or so. She was sitting in her living room reading a book, when she saw something moving out of the corner of her eye. There, crawling up the living room wall, was a huge tarantula. As the story goes, she literally threw the book at the spider. [...] This event supposedly happened fairly frequently in days past.[41]

Even now, real spiders continue to emerge from bananas: in June 2005, BBC News reported that a man "collapsed in pain" at a Sainsbury supermarket and was taken to the hospital after being bitten by a "giant crab spider" as he handled a bunch of bananas, imported from the African nation of Cameroon. "I picked up a couple of bananas," the victim told press, "and felt something sharp like a needle. It was the size of a 50p piece." Sainsbury, a leading British grocery chain, described the event as an "extremely rare occurrence," and the victim, Mr. Travenen, was released from the hospital without permanent injury.[42] Experts assured the public that the crab spider, one of many species nicknamed "banana spiders," had regularly been found in imported produce but that its bite, while "locally painful," was essentially harmless.[43]

It is possible that in some of the rumor variations of this story, the spider was introduced into the produce as a joke or as an attempt to extort money from the store: attempts to present narratives by literally enacting them is, as we have previously noted, a form of what folklorists term "ostension," the acting out of a rumor or legend.[44] However, it is not necessary to presume this, as spiders, even black widows, do in fact emerge from store-bought produce on an occasional basis.[45] Of course, other kinds of vermin, such as beetles, weevils, and slugs, are likewise accidentally transported into markets in lettuce, green beans, onions, and the like, and unlucky shoppers carry them home. These incidents, though equally real and unsettling, are not newsworthy, and so they tend not to generate nationally distributed press releases or discussions on Internet reaction boards the way that stories of spiders do. The *poisonous spider*—and many see all spiders as potentially deadly—hiding in a bunch or cluster of fruit is newsworthy, and thus comes to local or national attention.

Using Fruit Rumors

Just as we discussed how rumors of terrorism can be used to make political points that the narrator believes are important, the same is true of mercantile rumors. They can support a desire for more pesticides or even attempts to crack down on ethnic groups. Through a close look at how these incidents are discussed, underlying attitudes become clear.

After three separate cases were reported in the Boston area in 2003, grocers and representatives of the table grape industry contended that the increasing presence of spiders was the result of increased restrictions on the use of pesticides in the California growing fields. These restrictions resulted from a nationwide boycott on table grapes, called by United Farm Workers (UFW) leader Cesar Chavez, protesting, among other things, the health hazards faced by Latino migrant pickers entering fields that had been sprayed with insecticides. The boycott culminated in 1969 with a series of new contracts between the UFW and leading growers, promising to curtail the use of pesticides shortly before harvest. The reduction in chemicals was good for the migrants, but also good for insect pests, the increase in which, according to growers, attracted deadly spiders to the harvested fruit.[46] The presence of the poisonous pest in consumers' market baskets was said to be a direct consequence of activism intended to benefit the immigrant worker, even though it placed grocery patrons and their young children at some small risk. The persistence of this rumor surely reflects a subtle bias against immigrant workers, implying that their immediate physical well-being is less important than that of the American public, as well as suggesting the interest of growers in increasing their use of pesticides.

The spider's presence in the rumor also symbolically expresses the fruit's "uncleanness" because of its contact with ethnic others. After a case in which a black widow was found by a mother in Halifax, Nova Scotia, while washing a bunch of grapes for her 3-year-old, a long-haul trucker sent the following ungrammatical note to the newspaper's response column, connecting the event to his perception of imported goods and, by extension, immigrant dockworkers:

> [A]fter unloading produce, fruit that i picked up in the southern US or ships that brought it in from overseas, to US ports i see spiders, snakes, etc in traILER A LOT,,,, and on an other note, if you seen what is done this stuff you eat,, you would not eat it, i seen dock workers urinating on tomatoes,, banana,s produce being stored in warehouses that filthy and smell of cat pee, i seen [...] ships thaT bring in banana.s so dirty,, i would [not] even go with 100 feet of them[.][47]

Apparently spontaneous and strongly felt comments such as these emphasize that the subtext of legends and rumors in this category is that products from foreign lands are handled by persons stereotypically seen as unclean and immoral. The purchase of an exotic product implies the danger of coming into contact with "vermin," whether arachnid or human.

"The Snake in the Greens" rumor provides an instructive contrast. Brunvand first heard of the story from an Atlanta correspondent:

> My wife, who works as a therapist at the Emory University Hospital, learned of a woman shopping for collard (or mustard or whatever) greens at the DeKalb Farmers' Market, felt a sharp prick in her finger as she dug around in the greens, became ill, went out to her car, was found there dead by her husband. Later a baby rattler was found in the greens. Everything was hushed up by the market, of course, for fear of losing business...Within a few days the same thing was reported at other Atlanta markets, and soon after that a woman "died" at a supermarket down in Savannah.[48]

Sociologist Dan Miller[49] reported a similar rumor soon after from a low-income black area of Dayton, Ohio, where it was alleged that "a poor old woman had died after being bitten by a poisonous snake in the produce section of a supermarket commonly patronized by west Dayton residents." A characteristic account went as follows:

> [W]hile commuting to work, I observed a woman get on the bus and sit next to another woman—an acquaintance. After exchanging greetings one of the women initiated a conversation by asking the other if she had "heard the news about the poor old woman who had been bitten by a snake at Kroger's." This statement was quickly followed by "and they didn't do a thing about it." The other woman had heard the story and replied, "Yes, ain't that the way it is?" They continued their conversation, moving from topic to topic but maintaining a general focus on their demeaning experiences in supermarkets, at the mall, and with the local utility company.[50]

Inevitably, Miller noted, variations of this rumor were embedded in a general discussion concerning "the traditional relationship between whites and blacks and of their dehumanizing dependency on large corporations that often are unresponsive to their problems."[51]

Seen only in terms of a text removed from its social setting, at first it seems similar to "The Department Store Snake" or "The Spider in the Bananas/Grapes." However, when we examine it in its social context, we see the rumor is quite different in significance. It is never important where the greens originated, only that the white-owned firms "hushed up" the incident "for fear of losing business," or simply "didn't do a thing about it." Here the venomous snake is not seen as the fault of dirty foreigners or well-meaning activists doing migrant workers a favor, but simply of the callousness of wealthy American business owners. In other words, big business is the culprit in this racial narrative.

Hoaxes and Internet Gullibility

It is little wonder that the banana and the hitchhiking spider both became vehicles for acts of "Internet terrorism" in the form of widely distributed hoaxed memos. These examples are quite different from the rumors and legends discussed elsewhere, as they circulate as complex documents that are forwarded from computer to computer, much as similar hoaxes or parodies were previously passed on as office photocopy lore or "faxlore."[52] While they contain more information than the often brief and allusive texts such as the ones Miller overheard, they also are more difficult to assess. Are they legends, traditional narratives that are really and truly debated by communities, or rumors that express plausible possibilities? Or are they burlesques, *antilegends* in fact, not taken seriously by the audiences for which they were intended and serving only as an exposé of the gullibility of some readers?[53] However we define them, it is clear that they comment on rumor elements that the hoaxer knows are prevalent, and that their widespread distribution is at least a partial vindication of their plausibility.

Virtual Bananas

An early Internet rumor was a memo that first appeared in January 2000,[54] asserting that "several shipments of bananas from Costa Rica have been infected with necrotizing fasciitis, otherwise known as flesh-eating bacteria." The disease "has decimated the monkey population in Costa Rica," the memo continued, and now scientists had learned that the germ can be transmitted on "the skin of fruits in the region, most notably the banana, which is Costa Rica's largest export." Readers were advised not to purchase bananas for at least three weeks and to seek medical attention if they had eaten a banana in the previous days and developed "a fever followed by a skin infection."

The memo purported to come from the "Manheim Research Institute," which, as almost every person who forwarded it in its emergent days noted, did not exist. Nevertheless, authorities were quick to counter it: Tim Debus, vice president of the International Banana Association, saw it as a form of "Internet terrorism" and expressed concern that sales of Costa Rican bananas might actually plummet.[55] The Centers for Disease Control and Prevention (CDC) also quickly issued a statement that "The usual route of transmission for these bacteria is from person to person. Sometimes, they can be transmitted in foods, but this would be an unlikely cause for necrotizing fasciitis. The Food and Drug Administration (FDA) and CDC agree that the bacteria cannot survive long on the surface of a banana."[56] However, the CDC's statement stopped short of categorically denying the claim. Significantly, a CDC spokesman conceded to a blogger that "theoretically, it's possible,"[57] and the spread and discussion of the memo continued.

The source of this hoax was never determined, so the motivations of its creator cannot be assessed with any certainty. An interesting coda to the memo suggests that one concern of the author was government conspiracy:

The FDA has been reluctant to issue a countrywide warning because of fear of a nationwide panic. They have secretly admitted that they feel upwards of 15,000 Americans will be affected by this but that these are "acceptable numbers." Please forward this to as many of the people you care about as possible as we do not feel 15,000 people is an acceptable number.

The idea that this rumor reveals a conspiracy to keep the danger secret is itself a common motif in contemporary legend, one that suggests that the danger is not, in fact, the ethnic other (in this case, Costa Rican "monkeys" rather than human Latinos), but rather the "evil elites" who increasingly are seen as controlling our corporations and our government.[58] The danger is also linked to international trade, revealing the dangers of globalization that seem plausible to many Americans. The description of "flesh-eating bacteria" does resemble in many ways the aftereffects of real poisonous spider bites, where a wasting necrosis—or simply skin or tissue death—often develops around the site of the bite. But the legend contains too many implausible elements to generate thoughtful belief; in fact, its most dramatic effect may be that it did, for a time, distract banana importers and government officials from their regular jobs, just as real terrorists sometimes find that the threat of an attack is as disabling as an actual incident.

Spiders in the John

A second hoax, also tied to international contact, though not to global trade as such, is that of "The Spider in the Restroom." Although this text is not a mercantile rumor as such, it addresses similar fears. This memo appeared on the Internet in August 1999.[59] It began by citing an article in "the *Journal of the United Medical Association (JUMA)*" stating that a medical mystery behind three Chicago-area deaths had been solved. Investigators found that they each had dined at a restaurant called "Big Chappies" at "Blare Airport." By this point, careful readers would have picked up the indications of a hoax: there is a well-known *Journal of the **American** Medical Association*, but there is no *JUMA*; in fact, both it and "chappies" are well-known urban slang phrases referring to the buttocks.[60] Further, there is no Blare Airport in Chicago, but rather O'Hare.

The anal humor continued as the pseudomedical explanation revealed that all the victims had sat on a particular toilet infested with "the South American Blush Spider (*Arachnius glutens*),"[61] where they were bitten on their buttocks. A coda added that "The Civilian Aeronautics Board (CAB)" had inspected flights from South America and discovered nests of these spiders on four different planes. "So please, before you use a public toilet," the memo ended, "lift the seat to check for spiders. It can save your life!"[62]

Our routine use of public toilets has become fraught with risk, as suggested by the many facilities that provide free seat covers to prevent accidental contamination from body fluids left by previous users. A persistent rumor among adolescents for decades has been that one could contract an STD by sitting on a toilet seat where an infected person has recently masturbated and left some of his semen on the surface. This belief might, further, be related to older folklore about black widow spiders, which in earlier times were said to live under the wooden frames in outhouses and bite men who sat down on them. A recent article of the (real) *Journal of the American Academy of Nurse Practitioners* explains:

> During the 1800s, the most frequent site of the black widow spider bite in male patients was the penis. A typical bite scenario occurred when a man used an outdoor privy (outhouse). The black widow likes to nest and spin her web beneath the toilet seat. When her web is touched with an object (in this case a man's penis or scrotum), the spider senses that insect prey has landed on her web. She then rushes to the site and bites the object vigorously, much the same way she would a large insect.[63]

In fact, so frequently reported were spider bites on the penis that many people, such as one of folklorist Vance Randolph's Ozark informants, suspected that many people used it as a polite excuse to be treated for the more common but "unmentionable" condition of gonorrhea.[64]

Spiders Debunked

So it was that the contemporary "Spider in the Restroom" story contained some plausible elements among the many tokens of its status as satire. However, in late September 1999, two entomologists at University of California, Riverside, Richard Vetter and P. Kirk Visscher, became aware of the story and established a Web site that attempted to debunk the hoax. In its first two weeks, the Web page received nearly 50,000 hits. They were able to trace the hoax back to its author, Steven Heard, employed by the travel industry in northern California. He asserted that he had only sent the story to a "few friends" (actually 30 friends and relatives) and had no idea that it would spread around the country. Some of his contacts were kept in the dark, while others, informed that it was a hoax, were requested not to reveal it unless specifically questioned. Later, however, he claimed that the story was "partially a test to see if I could make it work, and partly to teach people not to be so gullible."[65]

Heard's experiment evidently succeeded better than he could have imagined: the story produced fear among many arachnophobes, allegedly causing some to lose sleep and almost to change travel plans. We know that at least two authorities were so convinced that they were willing to spread the rumor using their names and affiliations. But while Heard's hoax might decrease the amount of trust that some place in the claims of our fellow citizens, limiting the communalism of civil society, for those who were quickly able to spot the signs of a joke it was enjoyable proof of how gullible and easily manipulated their fellow citizens could be.

Unfortunately, rumors are easier to start than to stop, and the spiders continued to weave their webs. By 2002, the story had appeared again, but now the scene became Jacksonville, Florida. The restaurant was the Olive Garden, the flight was from India, and the spider was the two-striped Telamonia, *Telamonia dimidiata*. Unlike the South American blush spider, this creature is an actual jumping spider from India, Bhutan, and Sumatra, although it is apparently harmless. But like the earlier rumor, we can assume that this story, building on the earlier hoax, is a deliberate fraud.[66] A more recent version places the deaths in "South Wilkes-Barre, Pennsylvania," and the location is "Hart's Family Restaurant."[67] No doubt mischievous individuals will continue to spread the story in the years ahead, each time emphasizing the dangers from the most mundane aspects of everyday life.

Although some have argued that these rumors reveal the *lack* of trust in everyday life, they actually reveal an excess of trust in what constitutes plausible information. Dr. Jennifer Taylor, a clinical psychologist at McLean Hospital outside of Boston, suggests that the prevalence of rumors demonstrates that "people don't know how to evaluate what is possible from what's totally outlandish."[68] If information appears to come from an expert, audiences are likely to consider it plausible, as the source is credible, no matter how preposterous the content.

The Mexican Beer Connection

For the United States, Mexico is the portal to the third world. We are sandwiched between Mexico and Canada and have cordial, if prickly, relations with both. However, our images of our neighbors diverge markedly. Ask yourself if you believe that American customs at the Canadian border should be run like those at the Mexican border. Can you imagine that young men might have attempted to avoid the Vietnam-era draft by fleeing to Mexico? Do you worry that young Canadians are trying to sneak into the United States to pick fruit? Without doubt, how most Americans think about Mexicans and Canadians is dramatically different.[69]

For many non-Latino Americans, Canada is America North, while Mexico is rarely considered America South. Numerous factors produce this cognitive divergence: race, language, culture, wealth, prejudice, and historical circumstance. The differences are dramatic and powerful. Many Americans see Mexico as an underdeveloped nation, an exotic location suffused with violence, crime, gangs, and poverty, and recently, particularly in the aftermath of NAFTA, as an emerging economic rival.[70] These themes are evident in an archetypal threat from Mexico as reflected in the world of rumor: the fear of urine in Corona beer, although the rumor of "The Mexican Pet," as described in chapter 5, also fits within the same tradition.

Corona Extra beer is brewed by the Mexico City–based Modelo brewery and has for decades been a favored brand in that country. Its emergence into the American market was sudden and explosive: its success was engineered by Carlos Alvarez, a Mexican national who worked as the Modelo export director. In 1981, Alvarez experimented with marketing Corona Extra in the United States. Initial sales were so encouraging that in 1986, Alvarez came across the border to start a beverage distribution company in San Antonio, Texas, named the Gambrinus Company. Gaining distribution rights for the beer in Texas and the East Coast, Gambrinus quickly built the brand into the best-selling beer from the third world in the United States.

In 1987, Corona Extra had passed Canada's Molson beer as the number two import beer and was threatening to dethrone the Dutch beer Heineken, for decades America's favored foreign beer.[71] At this time, Corona was selling nearly three times as much as the second and third most popular third-world beers combined.[72] However, the explosive growth of Corona's popularity came to an abrupt halt when rumors began to spread that the drink was contaminated.

The rumor, which was typically presented as a declarative statement and often spread without much of an accompanying narrative, claimed Mexican workers urinate into bottles shipped to the United States, giving the beer its distinctive bright yellow color and copious foam. Those spreading the rumor alleged that the information had been validated on a TV news show, variously identified as *60 Minutes, 20/20,* or *Nightline.*[73] This claim appears to have emerged in 1986 or 1987 in California and was traced back to a competing beer wholesaler named Luce and Sons in Reno, Nevada, which was subsequently sued for $3 million by Corona's importer, Barton Beers. In an out-of-court settlement, Luce and Sons, which sold other imported beers such as Heineken, but not Corona, declared publicly that Corona was "free of any contamination."[74] However it began, the rumor diffused rapidly, and by 1987 was known in Boise, Phoenix, Seattle, Minneapolis, Milwaukee, and Chicago. At that time Corona's importer went public, denying the rumor in news accounts and placing ads, as well as having their executives appear on talk shows.[75] Nevertheless, sales plummeted as media denials simply spread the rumor to audiences that had not heard it through gossip.

Corona and the Goliath Effect

As Fine[76] argued in describing the "Goliath effect," Corona beer, given its prominence, was a natural target for corporate rumors. It fills a particular market niche, appealing to a young, adventurous, but fickle audience looking for new options (it was sometimes called the "yuppie cocktail"), rather than to older, brand-loyal beer drinkers. During the time the rumor was at its peak, Corona Extra was the fastest-growing imported beer, having increased its sales by 170% in 1986. For a time in 1987, the demand outpaced the supply of the beer.[77] But many consumers considered it a fad, and beer companies have been traditional targets of rumor, as tales about the political preferences of the owners of Coors, Stroh's, and Anheuser-Busch attest. The rumors about Coors are particularly widespread, as some drinkers falsely consider the company, which had been politically conservative, to be linked to far-right hate groups. Other rumors spread about beer companies' allegedly favorable attitudes toward gun control. Thus, it was inevitable that, as a novelty and a brand leader, Corona Extra would attract corporate rumors. The economic motives of rival distributors were clearly a factor, and while we should be skeptical that Luce and Sons actually began the rumor, their salespeople may have spread it with gusto.

The question now emerges: why did *this* rumor attach itself to Corona Extra, rather than one more familiar to beer companies, such as the belief that Coors was linked to neo-Nazis or the Klan? It appears that Corona Extra was linked more to fears of immigration than corporate politics: its distributor was himself Mexican, and purchase of the brand obviously favors the Mexican economy over American-owned businesses (although, to be fair, the U.S. brand leader Anheuser-Busch now is a part owner of the Modelo brewery). The plausibility of the story is enhanced by the brand's appearance: a bright yellow beer distributed in a clear bottle, which produces an unusual amount of foam when poured, looking to many like urine being expelled into a toilet.[78] Although Gambrinus produced a beer-testing company's certification that the product was free from foreign substances,[79] one can well imagine that, once the suggestion was made, some American beer drinkers could not avoid the suspicion that the bottle they were drinking might have been contaminated, perhaps by a Mexican worker in an act of sabotage.

But what might be the worker's motive for doing so? We recall the long-haul trucker's comment, quoted earlier, that dock workers were prone to urinate on fresh produce like bananas and tomatoes, simply because they and the environment in which they work are dirty. From this perspective, someone who believes that Mexican workers are deeply immoral and angry over their working conditions would have no trouble believing that they would relieve themselves in the Mexican bottling plant where Corona beer is bottled, the urine inevitably leaking into the vats of the brew as it is bottled for export. This interpretation would be all the more symbolic for people familiar with the belief that consuming beer produces copious urination, a well-known theme in barroom lore. Add that the American distributor was itself founded by Mexicans and you have, for suspicious minds, ample grounds for passing up the brand in favor of an all-American brew.

Moreover, underlying these facts is the reality that many U.S. citizens found it plausible that Mexican workers might be deliberately motivated to commit such an act of sabotage. America's Latin neighbors, particularly Mexico, are steadily replacing the nations of the Far East as far as our fears of competition, as the heated debate over the economic effects of NAFTA indicates.

Piss and Power

A well-known belief in many world cultures holds that one can gain a psychological advantage over another by secretly placing urine (or other bodily fluids, including spit, menstrual blood, or semen) into something that he or she eats or drinks. One form of this belief was collected by Harry Hyatt as part of his voluminous fieldwork on African American magical folklore during the 1930s. When a man wants to keep a woman faithful to him and ensure that she not flirt with other men, Hyatt's informant explained, "He takes and gives her his urine to drink unbeknownst to her, like in beer or wine, and she won't even look at another man, won't have any nature towards any other man. That urine keeps her mine [mind] on that one man..."[80]

Another reflection of the same belief is the nineteenth-century rumor that Chinese immigrants, who often worked as cooks for work crews in the American West, secretly urinated in the pots of coffee that they served Anglos, in order to gain a similar control over them. The belief inspired a widespread children's rhyme, often recited as part of a prank where a naïve classmate is made to mime taking a drink from a glass. Then the game leader giggles and says, "Me Chinese, Me play joke, Me put pee pee in your Coke!"[81] From this perspective, the rumor has yet another dimension: the mysterious way in which a beer from Mexico, widely treated as a low-status third-world country, became a high-status beverage in the United States, and in a matter of a few years, not over decades as with Corona's competitors. The rumor combines the danger of the tropics with the immorality associated with Latinos through relying upon a well-honed history of racial prejudice. With public concern over illnesses from bodily fluids, this rumor reflects the fear of sexual diseases and lack of proper hygiene. And, just as the snake and the banana have both symbolized the male sex organ in bawdy folklore since the early 1900s, so, too, the urine in bottled beer could be a slightly more acceptable replacement for semen, the archetypal body fluid that spreads AIDS, among other STDs.

As we saw in the case of "The Mexican Pet," *a Mexican connection* exists in American folklore—a connection associated with our fear of Mexican immigrants in the United States, our belief in the Mexican lack of hygiene, and our fear of Mexico's economic competition. Many global rumors are, in some way, linked to our southern neighbors. Mexico represents the image of the third world in our midst: neighbors who remain strangers. The success of Mexican ventures in the United States remains problematic, as it does for the Asian ventures mentioned in "The Snake in the Blanket" variants.

Gambrinus struggled for several years to recoup the market it had lost through the rumor. Through a series of shrewd business deals, executives managed to reduce the price of the brand to a level that focus groups said was fair for a "Mexican" beer, eliminating the elitist image of the brand. In addition, they maintained the advertising emphasis on the "vacation" theme, presenting Corona Extra as an opportunity to engage in culinary tourism and imaginatively visit, not a grimy Mexico City brewery with employees relieving themselves in corners, but a pristine vacation beach on a tropical shore. Sales rebounded in the mid-1990s, and in 1997 Corona Extra finally surpassed Heineken to become America's top imported beer. Current statistics show that the brand is now Mexico's number one exported beer and, indeed, the fifth best-selling brand worldwide.[82] The custom of placing a lime slice in an opened bottle caught on for American consumers, and even though a second rumor emerged that this practice was originally started by locals to kill the fly eggs that were usually found under the cap,[83] this time sales were not affected. Corona Beer, like the Mexican immigrants who introduced it to Americans, now seems a permanent part of the country's landscape. Perhaps this is a reflection that over time products that had been seen as exotic are considered mundane, much as we noted with the decline in the prevalence of rumors about the department store snake.

A World of Change

We live in a shrinking world. We rely on each other's labor more than ever, but we often do not feel comforted by this economic interdependence. These connections tug at the strings of nationalism and undermine the sense of control that dominant societies treasure. Hegemony can no longer be taken for granted in a globalized world of free and open trade and in a world in which industrial technologies are readily exported and enthusiastically adopted abroad. If the middle third of the twentieth century witnessed the rise of American industrial and political dominance, the final third reflected the cracking of that ascendancy. As the reality of this disintegration filters down to the general population, warnings emerge through the power of rumor. The world has become decentered with threats to those who benefited from their dominance.

As noted, unlike nations of Europe, we have no well-established nativist parties protesting against cultural decay. Rather, the complexity of our feelings is displayed within our folklore. The concern emerges via rumor that hidden within the world economy are dangers: spiders, germs, disease, and unwanted immigrants. Such rumors suggest that foreigners represent a hidden invasion of one part of the world by another. First-world citizens worry that third-world problems may soon become first-world problems.

The second theme—reflected in the Corona beer rumor and "The Department Store Snake" legend—is that the material advantages of the first world are steadily and rapidly flowing to the third world. The economic base of all segments of the world is beginning to look increasingly similar, or so our fears suggest. Further, we contribute to our own demise by distributing products from overseas in competition with our own manufactured goods. Are we poisoning ourselves in the name of profits?

These two intersecting themes—fear of contamination and fear of competition—demonstrate that we come to terms with the world economy through mercantile rumors. As the economy shifts, so does our social psychology, and so do our narratives.

7

Global Trafficking in Bodies

The newspaper headline was almost too graphic to be believed: "Gang of Clowns Stole My Baby," trumpeted a São Paulo tabloid. According to the newspaper, slum dwellers had reported that two men dressed as clowns, along with a woman costumed as a ballerina, had prowled the Brazilian shanties looking for unattended children and luring them into a van. There the children were killed and their vital organs surgically removed. To add insult to injury, the kidnappers left the bodies at the family home with a note of thanks and the equivalent of $80. This story was consistent with another tale of parents who had their child exhumed after dying in the hospital. The autopsy revealed that the eyes were missing and the body stuffed with sawdust.[1] Oh, the horror!

Most of the rumors discussed throughout the book reveal how Americans see—and fear—the rest of the world. In contrast, this chapter reminds us that rumors are found wherever circumstances are ambiguous, issues are important, and critical ability is low. In the process, some rumors acquire enormous symbolic value and powerful political potency; they capture basic themes about how people and groups believe the world operates, changing over time to adapt to shifting mores and standards of what is plausible. This is certainly true of claims of trafficking in the vital essences of the human body, a subject of rumor since ancient times.

Long before organs could be transplanted, blood was the bodily fluid in demand. Aristocratic vampires or members of secret societies or religious outsiders, often Jews, abducted ordinary people, particularly children, so that their blood could be used to restore or maintain the health of the wealthy and powerful or to engage in arcane rituals. Now, because of the relatively easy and safe availability of blood, these stories are less common.

Instead, rumors focus on a startling recent triumph of medicine: the surgical ability to transplant body parts. A half century ago this might have seemed like the stuff of science fiction—more Doctor Frankenstein than managed health care. Today, eyes, hearts, lungs, kidneys, livers, and even faces are successfully transplanted. Transplant operations are increasingly routine, even though necessary body parts remain in short supply. While the most successful transplants are those from close relations, surgeons are able to transplant the organs of strangers, using drugs to prevent organ rejection. Nevertheless, because of long-standing cultural taboos, this new technique has created powerful social tensions, as anthropologist Donald Joralemon has observed. We resist the potential violation of our body, either by the "invasion" (however necessary) of a stranger's body part or the removal of one of our essential organs for use by another. Just as our body's immune system serves as a defense against physical affronts, Joralemon argues that the social system responds automatically with repugnance when faced with the idea of unchecked organ harvesting.[2] Perhaps we should avoid treating society as analogous to a body, but it is true that individuals often are offended and shocked by such violations.

In response, rumors have depicted the threat to ordinary persons whose body parts might prove useful to an unscrupulous stranger. These rumors, unfortunately, are not merely the product of overheated imaginations but depend on real and dismaying trends that are the consequences of globalization.

In this chapter, we look first at the rumors that became prevalent in industrialized countries; like rumors reviewed in previous chapters, they depict unwary tourists victimized in unfamiliar surroundings. We then turn from these widespread stories to a much greater and more disturbing range of rumors told by the residents of impoverished nations. For third-world residents, the danger is not tourism but the tourist, the wealthy stranger who invades their neighborhood for ambiguous and potentially unscrupulous reasons. Claims of body-part thefts arose in the mid-1980s, often linked to the publicity given to the international adoption of children. As in so many cases of rumor, the fact that a particular story lacks evidence does not mean that the claims are entirely false. The absence of evidence does not by itself demonstrate that such crimes are impossible. There is enough discouraging truth in accounts of international organ transfers that one would be naïve to suggest that kidnapping for this purpose is impossible. While some proclaim that stories of murdered children are the work of politically motivated hate-mongers,[3] one might more prudently conceive these stories as plausibility markers. They serve to indicate what people consider to be possible in the hard and challenging world in which they live, and, as discussed in chapter 2, they remind us of how natural and "obvious" beliefs in elite conspiracies often are.

Like the rumors discussed earlier in this chapter, these claims are too good to be false; unlike those stories that attach themselves to wealthy people who feel they have control over their lives, these are believed by the underclass and powerless. Such men and women have good reason for suspicion. People who feel themselves oppressed by forces—political or economic—that are outside of their control construct beliefs, supporting them with the specific events described by rumor, that explain the sad and unjust conditions of their lives. Returning to our previous discussion of conspiracies, these elite conspiracy theories can produce anger, resistance, resignation, or even some comfort in feeling that the root of their oppression is now clear.

Body-Part Thefts and Tourism

Our world has a much greater demand for organs than supply, so the economy of transplants is skewed. This prompts inevitable questions about the just distribution of body parts. From where do such organs originate? Who should have first access? Should there be an international market in organs? Should we rely only on formal nongovernmental organizations (NGOs) to transfer organs? Since selling one's organs in an open market is generally deemed improper, organs are treated as gifts. However, given that transplant donations often involve life-and-death decisions, the desire to obtain an organ quickly is powerfully motivated.

Many rumors suggest that organs are stolen—cut from a victim's body— and sold on the black market. This makes sense in light of our understanding of the desperation of recipients and the amount of money involved.

Most rumors focus on kidney transplants, as these transplants are relatively common and successful, and as donors can survive the loss of a kidney.

Early versions of a rumor in the United States, first found in the late winter of 1991, suggested that kidney theft was the outcome of a sexual liaison with a stranger—a one-night stand—as in these two accounts:

A group of young men…went to New York City for a weekend of fun. One of them was attracted to a woman he met in a bar, and told his buddies he was going to spend the night at her place and would get in touch with them later. They didn't hear from him until late the next day when he phoned to say "I think I'm in such-and-such a hotel in room number so-and-so, but something's wrong with me and you'd better come and get me." When the friends arrived at the hotel room they found their friend in bed and the sheets splattered with blood. He was very weak. When they tried to help him out of bed, they discovered a fresh surgical closure on his back and still more blood, so they rushed him to a hospital. There it was discovered that the man had had one of his kidneys removed, and they concluded that he had been drugged so his kidney could be taken for sale on the black market for human organs.[4]

This guy went out last Saturday night to a party. He was having a good time, had a couple of beers and some girl seemed to like him and invited him to go to another party. He quickly agreed and decided to go along with her. She took him to a party in some apartment and they continued to drink and even got involved with some other drugs (unknown which). The next thing he knew, he woke up completely naked in a bathtub filled with ice. He was still feeling the effects of the drugs, but looked around to see he was alone. He looked down at his chest, which had "CALL 911 OR YOU WILL DIE" written on it in lipstick. He saw a phone was on a stand next to the tub, so he picked it up and dialed. He explained to the EMS operator what the situation was and that he didn't know where he was, what he took, or why he was really calling. She advised him to get out of the tub. He did, and she asked him to look himself over in the mirror. He did, and appeared normal, so she told him to check his back. He did, only to find two 9 inch slits on his lower back. She told him to get back in the tub immediately, and they sent a rescue team over. Apparently, after being examined, he found out more of what had happened. His kidneys were stolen. They are worth 10,000 dollars each on the black market. (I was unaware this even existed). Several guesses are in order: The second party was a sham, the people involved had to be at least medical students, and it was not just recreational drugs he was given. Regardless, he is currently in the hospital on life support, awaiting a spare kidney.[5]

Layers of trust found in routine social encounters may be misplaced in passion and in the night's darkness. In this sense, these kidney theft rumors are cousins of the "Welcome to the World of AIDS" rumors described in chapter 5. The organ-theft rumors critique gender roles, revealing male anxiety that they may be the victims in sexual encounters.[6] The rumor presents an encounter that seems all too similar to rape with genders switched.[7] Further, the casual nature of the sexual encounter suggests a lack of responsibility on the victim's part, so that whether male or female, the victim deserves to be punished. Folklorist Elissa Henken[8] has collected other variants in which women were the victims of the organ theft, generally as a result of no worse a decision than attending a party.

Although many rumors are set in American cities (particularly in exotic tourist destinations such as Miami or Las Vegas), variants parallel the tourist rumors recounted previously. In one instance, described by Dutch folklorist Peter Burger, a tourist from the Netherlands visiting Tunisia was the victim of the kidney heist, and in a version from folklorist Mark Moravec, the tourist was an Australian visitor to Los Angeles.[9] Another account suggests that the kidney heist occurred on a visit to Mexico by singer Linda Ronstadt's brother.[10] Swedish legend scholar Bengt af Klintberg, noting this theme of travel in the variants he collected, labeled this story as "The Wandering Kidney."[11] The following text makes a border crossing explicit:

> I live in San Diego, a very large American city with a pronounced military presence. Downtown Tijuana, Mexico, lies a mere 30 minutes away, and is a prime partying hub for well-paid soldiers who are under the legal drinking age. A friend of mine heard from her boss on a naval base the harrowing tale of the sailor from that very base who got slipped a bad drink in TJ and woke up missing both

kidneys. This version included the usual bathtub full of ice, and "Call 9-1-1" scrawled in lipstick on the mirror.[12]

Mexico is not the only country implicated in "The Wandering Kidney" rumor. Other countries appear in the story where affluent people come in contact with those from less-developed lands, trading on the plausibility of the tourism stories described in chapter 5. Consider an account collected from a student at the University of California at Berkeley:

> This guy is jogging on the beach. It's in the Caribbean. I can't remember if it's Bermuda or what. So he's on vacation and he's jogging.... Basically he's mugged. They use chloroform, the whole thing. He wakes up in the bushes, and he feels some pain. He finds stitches in his back. So he goes to the hospital, and his kidney is gone. Otherwise, he's in perfect health, but he's missing a kidney.... It is like a rape. It's about fear of intense violation. Theft of the most intimate thing you have.[13]

Other instances depict a couple from Sweden who vacation in Brazil where a young child approached them, asking them to sign a petition to oppose cutting down the rainforest. The petition was actually a consent form that allowed their kidneys to be used for transplantation. Another version about an Irish couple vacationing in Rio de Janeiro comments on the vast disparity between the rich and poor neighborhoods. The husband vanishes and, despite efforts by the police and the embassy, cannot be located in the usual tourist spots. Much later, he's discovered wandering the street "in a dazed state," whereupon it's found that one of his kidneys has been surgically removed.[14]

A different variant describes a woman on an Indian vacation in Goa. She was taken with stomach pains, described as appendicitis. She learned after her hospital stay that one of her kidneys had been removed, but her appendix remained.[15] Other accounts depict tourists from Germany who vacation in Turkey and Austrians who vacation on Italy's Adriatic coast, as well as numerous Italian texts presenting the danger of tourists from the north of Italy traveling to Sicily. Many rumors assert the existence of a vigorous and widespread "organ mafia."[16]

These stories combine the *gender threat* found in AIDS rumors with the *absence of trust* of tourist adventures. Many of the rumors that we discussed in chapter 5, addressing immorality, dealt with women being infected by men. These tales turn the tables. Here, after sexual intimacy, it is often the man who discovers that he has been betrayed. These accounts remind us that in a sexually active society, we may know relatively little of those whom we bed. This uncertainty leads to anxiety, which is expressed in the form of rumor, and reminds us that it "really could happen." To express the fears directly might make the teller seem frightened—and in this case lacking in masculine swagger—but told as an actual occurrence, the point can be made. This is especially true in discussing sex away from home where our partners are strangers, both socially and culturally. Residents in these exotic locales are said to embrace different moral standards. Unlike the texts to which we now turn, these narratives warning of cultural danger are similar to other rumors from developed nations that we have analyzed previously.

Children and the Kidnap Van

Rumors about the theft of body parts are not new. The first mention of the motif apparently appears in the encyclopedic *Natural History* (xxvi.2) by the Roman author Pliny the Elder, which records the belief that whenever any of the Egyptian pharaohs contracted leprosy, he would have his servants kidnap and slaughter a group of common people and then bathe in their warm blood in golden bathtubs specially made for the purpose. A similar rumor dogged the Hungarian aristocrat Elizabeth Báthory (1560–1614) to her death: when political enemies resented her skill in governing her estate alone after her husband's death, they used the blood libel to turn her subjects against her, claiming that she had ordered hundreds of commoners abducted and murdered for her pleasure. In one commonly recorded version, she bathed in the villagers' blood in the belief that such a practice would keep her complexion youthful.[17]

In her invaluable book *Bodies: Sex, Violence, Disease, and Death in Contemporary Legend*, Gillian Bennett demonstrates that many of the current organ-theft legends parallel older rumors that have long circulated in Europe, focusing on child abduction. These accounts include the waves of anti-Semitic rumors that held that Jews were kidnapping and killing Christian children in order to use their blood in religious rituals.[18] A ballad, "Sir Hugh and the Jew's Daughter" (Child ballad number 155), widespread in both Great Britain and North America, describes a young boy lured into a secret room by a beautiful lady:

> The first she offered him was a fig
> The next a finer thing
> The third a cherry as red as blood
> And that enticed him in.
>
> She set him down in a chair of gold
> And gave him sugar sweet
> She laid him on a dresser board
> And stabbed him like a sheep

Despite being repeatedly debunked, these stories continued to be spread through the centuries. In Paris in 1750, during a panic about disappearing children, frightened city dwellers, echoing Pliny, claimed that King Louis XV, allegedly leprous, had children kidnapped to use their blood as a cure. Twenty years later in Lyons, France, townspeople claimed that surgeons kidnapped a child each night to amputate his or her arm and sew it on the torso of a one-armed prince.[19]

As this complex of rumors developed, one especially stable detail was the appearance of an unusual vehicle. In one nineteenth-century version, this was the "Bloody Coach at Antwerp," described as "a wonderfully beautiful carriage with four horses," into which a finely clad lady entices young children "with sweetmeats and dainties." Those unwise enough to enter are taken far away to a castle, where their great toes are cut off and their blood extracted to fill a bath for a "great king…suffering from a grievous malady."[20] A hundred years later, Polish and Russian communities were galvanized by the rumor that a "Black Volga" (a stylish Russian-made car) bearing strangers traveled around the countryside, abducting and murdering children.

In a 1977 Polish version, a woman dressed as a nun is the one who entices the child, this time to enter an empty house. Later, the child's corpse, drained of blood, is discovered. "I heard the blood is taken to West Germany to cure leukemia," one informant said. The story was also current in Russia as well. There, a sister and brother "on holiday" (i.e., visiting a tourist spot) meet a nice-looking couple, who gives them sweets and lures them away: "They were found dead in a place one hundred kilometers away with their eyes plucked out." According to this variant, the kidnappers were eventually caught, "but they worked for a well-known oculist and the whole thing was hushed up.

Nothing came of it."[21] These culprits are not royalty, but wealthy patrons, who paid the kidnappers to steal children to treat leukemia or eye diseases.

In 1990, a similar complex of rumors emerged in Sicily, focusing on a mysterious "black ambulance driving around the city trying to kidnap our children." Initially, suspicion rested on Gypsies, whom for centuries have been suspected of carrying off small children to swell their ranks. But as the rumor developed, the perpetrators were increasingly described as men "disguised as medical workers" who come to a school in a mysterious car and attempt to get children to come with them, explaining that their parents have been admitted to a hospital. The children were then supposedly taken to the outskirts of Rome. Once a month a team of foreign surgeons flies in to harvest the children's organs, hired by a mysterious international organization that sells the organs on the black market.[22]

As is true with other bundles of belief, some rumors that deal with globalization touch on the same racial themes as tales in the United States. This recognition echoes the rumor of "The Snake in the Greens," discussed in chapter 6. Global rumors can have domestic parallels, transforming fears of the exotic into fears of racial dominance and the reverse. A related and disturbing rumor had been common in previous decades in African American communities in the United States. In its early "Night Doctor" forms, the vehicle was an ambulance, and the perpetrators were medical students who would slip up behind a lone black man in the street and immobilize him with a poisoned needle. The students then would whisk the victim into the ambulance and take him to a hospital to be dissected or made the unwilling subject of medical experiments.[23] These rumors were later given social credence in the aftermath of the Tuskegee syphilis experiment in which black men with advanced stages of venereal disease were left untreated so that government physicians could observe the damage done to their bodies by the illness.

Rumors in the aftermath of the Atlanta child murders from 1979 to 1981 constitute a particularly dramatic instance that demonstrates how black bodies, particularly children's bodies, are perceived to be medically valuable. In this case, dozens of African American children in this Southern city were murdered. For a long period the FBI and the Atlanta police did not arrest anyone, and as a result rumors spread widely. Folklorist Patricia Turner describes the fears in her book *I Heard It through the Grapevine: Rumor in African-American Culture:*

> Many informants who claim that the FBI was responsible for the
> Atlanta child murders elaborate by reporting that the bodies were

taken to the Centers for Disease Control in Atlanta for biological experiments. A college-aged African-American female said, "I remember hearing that the killings in Atlanta were related to the genocide of the black race. The FBI was responsible and using the bodies for interferon during research:"…Two informants even went on to say that the desired substance was removed from the victims' genitals with a syringe….As one African-American male…claimed, "I heard it was the CIA or the government who was killing the children for experimenting with their bodies, blood, etc. It's been said that only black children's biology was the source of human flesh needed for these experiments."[24]

As Fine and Turner later emphasize in their discussion of racial rumors in the United States, claims that at first glance appear paranoid or racist depend on collective memories of real, historical events.[25] This is not to suggest that a grain of truth can be found in every story, but the stories are based on historical particulars that make them plausible. Historian Luise White, discussing African body-part abduction rumors, stressed that such claims "conform to standards of evidence; they do not seem false, fanciful, unlikely, or even unreasonable to those who tell them and those who hear them."[26]

Body Parts From Colonialism to Globalization

Claims of organ thefts from tourists are distressing, but another class of rumors is even more powerful: those that suggest that third-world children are killed and kidnapped for their body parts. In contrast to our focus on rumors widely spread in the United States and Europe, these rumors are often heard in the developing world and suggest that agents of villainy are connected to the powerful and wealthy West. These rumors turn the tables on the developed world, spreading among powerless groups to the detriment of those who dominate them. As Véronique Campion-Vincent[27] argues, kidney-theft stories reflect animosity toward "evil elites," which is frequently a form of anticolonialism or resistance to foreign control. In recent decades this has typically involved anti-Americanism. In societies in which many children are killed, are kidnapped, or run away, these stories displace the anger and grief of parents onto malicious and dangerous outsiders, while also serving as a vivid warning to children to stick close to home, not to be tempted by strangers, and to obey their parents.

Discontent in China

One of the first widely discussed rumors of this type emerged in China in the 1860s in response to increased colonial activity by Western countries. In Yangzhou, anonymous handbills asserted that Europeans "scooped out the eyes of the dying, opened foundling hospitals to eat the children, cut open pregnant women (for the purpose of making medicine of the infants), etc." In 1870, rumors emerged in the wake of local discontent over the activities of French Christian missionaries in Tianjin (Tientsin). At a large church, built on the site of a local temple the previous year, the Sisters of Mercy had set up an ambitious orphanage, devoted to the care of homeless children. To encourage the local population to let them care for unwanted infants, they let it be known that they would give a small fee to anyone bringing them a child. As many abandoned children were already seriously and chronically ill, it soon became obvious that the mortality rate in the orphanage was distressingly high. That in turn fostered rumors that Christians were collecting children for medical purposes.

A particularly widespread and vivid rumor held that the nuns removed the eyeballs of the dead children, preserving them in jars, either for medicine or, in one version, to be used in photographic processing. On June 21, 1870, a mob attached the Christian community, destroying the church and killing 21 foreigners, including the French consul and 12 priests and nuns. The Tianjin Church Incident, as it became known, led to a serious confrontation between the West and the Chinese government, which was forced to pay compensation. Similar rumors continued to circulate for many years, leading to additional attacks on missionaries.[28]

Countering Colonialism in East Africa

A set of narratives from East Africa, known as wazimamoto stories, well documented by historian Luise White,[29] suggests that the fear of white vampires and their African agents reflected the tensions and contradictions of colonialism. Often these vampires gathered children while driving red fire trucks. White colonial authorities and their African agents symbolically represented the vampire, sucking the life juices from those they oppressed. In one especially prevalent local variant—what folklorists call an *ecotype*—the abduction is tied to the *femme fatale* theme, similar to the themes found in "The Wandering Kidney" versions discussed earlier. White presents a typical version:

> I heard that a long time ago the wazimamoto was in Mashimoni
> [a Nairobi neighborhood noted for prostitution], even those peo-
> ple who were staying there bought plots with the blood of some-
> body. I heard that in those days they used to dig the floors very
> deep in the house and they covered the floor with a carpet. Where
> it was deepest, in the center of the floor, they'd put a chair and the
> victim would fall and be killed. Most of the women living there
> were prostitutes and this is how they made extra money, from the
> wazimamoto. So when a man came for sex, the woman would say,
> "Karibu, karibu" [Welcome, welcome], and the man would go to
> the chair, and then he would fall into the hole in the floor, then at
> night the wazimamoto would come and take that man away. When
> they fell down they couldn't get up again.[30]

This narrative is similar to the European versions in which a male victim,
child or adult, is enticed into a dangerous place by an attractive woman who
offers a treat—such as an offer of sex, or the symbolically similar chocolate,
apple, or cherry.

We must be cautious, however, to assume that similarity in content
marks some kind of meaning intrinsic to all of them. "Stories and rumors are
produced in the cultural conflicts of local life," White comments, and so "they
mark ways to talk about the conflicts and contradictions that gave them
meaning and power."[31] She argues that the vampire stories are grounded in a
variety of local conflicts: the often insensitive way in which Western medicine
was introduced, the ambiguous economic role of women in enlarging African
cities, religious conflicts caused by Catholic missionaries' efforts to supplant
traditional religious beliefs, and class struggles caused by labor disputes in
the African Copperbelt. Nevertheless, common to all these stories is the disorientation created by colonialism—an early form of globalism—in a traditional culture, whether the ambiguity was caused by rapid urbanization,
aggressive missionary activities, or the imposition of Western-style health
practices with little sensitivity to indigenous medical knowledge.[32]

Some rumors could and did become deadly as in Tianjin. Sociologist
William H. Friedland describes a riot that occurred in a suburb of Dar es
Salaam, Tanzania, in 1960. It took place at a stone (i.e., European-style)
house, where it was suspected that Africans were taken to be slaughtered for
medical purposes. Earlier in the day a disturbance had taken place, and
three African policemen were sent to investigate. Although the situation

had settled down by the time they arrived, they took one local resident into custody, and soon after a story spread that he, too, had been abducted for his blood. The three policemen returned to the scene in the evening and were surrounded by a mob; one was cornered and beaten to death on the spot. Friedland concludes that the vampire rumor functioned much like those in Western contexts, isolating one cultural group from others. Such a claim, he argues, "serves to maintain social distance for a group which feels itself at the mercy of another group," adding, "At the same time, it delineates the original group as the 'safe' one in which members of the society can find security."[33] Dramatic rumors about blood sucking, vampires, and kidnapping by Western agents, along with the presence of a gray or black market in human organs, fuel the widespread belief in body-part thefts that have been spread throughout the third world. Among other things, they neatly explain how body parts became available, given purported shortages. As with other rumor cycles, we need not assume that large numbers of people are convinced definitively that body parts are stolen against the will of the donor, but only that they are prepared to entertain the possibility.

Although most of the specific rumors that we examine in this chapter are almost certainly false, their falsity is hard to demonstrate conclusively, and a disturbing and all too real trade in organs has been well documented by crusading anthropologist Nancy Scheper-Hughes as well as by journalists.[34] Organs are bought and sold; sometimes poor people mine their own bodies under threat or financial pressure. Given the reality of the unseemly and often cruel global trade in human organs, one must be cautious in separating grisly legend from brutal criminality. To analyze a body of rumor texts is not to deny the dark reality that lies behind these rumors and which the rumors build upon to demonstrate their plausibility.

The Latin American Baby-Parts Panic

The essential elements of the medical abduction rumors reached Latin America as early as 1889, when a British merchant reported a "reign of terror" that erupted in the port city of Pernambuco, Brazil. A dozen children, rumor held, had recently disappeared, supposedly to help cure wealthy people with leprosy, "for which disease there is no cure, but an old superstition is that it may be done if persons attacked eat heart, liver, and kidneys of a young, healthy child, wash themselves with its blood, and make grease of its body also for anointing their bodies." Figures in the black market allegedly paid the equivalent of £10 sterling for such a child. "It seems really too horrible to be true; anyway a panic exists, and hardly any children are now seen out," the observer commented, adding, "Some people who were supposed to have bought some children had their carriage stopped in the street, and were stoned."[35]

As we describe in the story opening this chapter, these stories continue to the present day in a variety of locations ranging from Mexico to Peru. This situation is reflected in an account by Nicole Maxwell from the Amazon circa 1958:

> A rumor had spread like plague along the rivers of the whole area, terrifying the natives into panicky hostility. Gringos (Americans, English, any blond foreigners) were said to be prowling the forests and shooting their inhabitants, then melting their bodies down to extract the fat. This operation is known in Peru as pishtaco. Human fat, according to the story, is an essential ingredient of atomic weapons, and the United States had contracted for vast quantities to be sent from the local jungles.... Dr. [Ray] Isbell said that back in the sixteenth century, lard was commonly used by the Spanish conquistadores to polish their armor and preserve it from rust. Unable to find pigs or any other suitable domestic animals in the New World, a few of the boys melted down some Indians to use their fat for this purpose. The Indians weren't Christians, they reasoned; maybe they weren't really human. That's not the sort of thing Indians forget.[36]

This tradition was still active in 1995, as the British travel writer Nicholas Shakespeare found when he visited Peru. On visiting a remote region, he became aware that the locals were treating him with extreme suspicion, fearing that he was a *pistaco*. Making inquiries, he determined that a *pistaco* was thought to be a tall foreigner who ambushed Indians and boiled down their bodies for grease, which was essential to run the machines of industrial countries; likewise, weapons of war required human fat to make them work efficiently. "The space shuttle Challenger," Shakespeare was told, "had blown up because it lacked this *aceite humano*." He was informed that the practice went back to the conquistadores, who learned to use an ointment made from Indians' body fat to treat an otherwise incurable disease. The ethnicity of these kidnappers was debated. Some said they came from the neighboring country of Argentina; others, that they were Swiss. In any case, it was assumed that they were hired by the current president of Peru, who had agreed to the murder of thousands of Indians for their body fat in exchange for canceling his country's foreign debt. No one went out after dark without a noisemaker, and he was told that the last white person to visit the town had been attacked by a mob, his head crushed ("because you can't shoot a *pistaco*") and his eyes torn out.[37]

Adoption or Dismemberment?

Similar stories became widespread in Latin America during the 1980s and 1990s. In these stories, children were allegedly to be adopted by wealthy couples in North America or Europe; however, the children were taken to medical clinics and dismembered, and their organs used for transplants. A related, earlier instance concerns the attempt of black singer Josephine Baker to adopt a child in the days before international adoptions were common:

> There had been trouble, too, in Colombia, where [Baker] had orig-
> inally fastened upon a different child from the one she eventually
> adopted [circa 1954]. The villagers seemed upset when she took
> the child from its mother, and later there were angry demonstra-
> tions. Her lawyer told her that according to local superstition,
> white people stole black babies to drink their blood. Baker replied
> in astonishment that she was black herself. But the lawyer explained
> that to the natives she was not. Her wealth made her white.[38]

According to Campion-Vincent, it was symptomatic that the international versions of the kidney theft rumor exploded during this same
period of increased international adoption. Desperate Americans were
clamoring for third-world babies. Perhaps they wished for the whole
child, not their organs, but the symbolic parallel was clear. Local residents
could see that babies were being shipped from their poor communities to
wealthy Americans, but for what reason? Was it plausible that white,
wealthy American parents had suddenly decided that they wished to raise
dark-skinned children? Perhaps it was more believable to suggest that
these children were used for the medical needs of the wealthy.

Latin American body-part rumors were first widely reported in 1986,
asserting that wealthy Americans were paying exorbitant sums for the

organs cut from murdered Hispanic children.[39] Anna Pukas[40] suggests that the rumors first focused on a "death strip" of Brazilian road that stretched between São Paulo and Rio de Janeiro, where children were deliberately hit by drivers so that their organs could be removed. However, the story became popular when it was tied to international adoption from Central America. The claim that children are transferred to secret nurseries where they can be fed prior to adoption—called *casas de engorde* ("fattening houses")[41]—contributed to this sense of outrage. In January 1987, a Honduran newspaper alleged that such a fattening house had been discovered where 13 handicapped children who had been abducted or bought from poor families were awaiting adoption. The story claimed that there would be no adoptions. The children were to be sold for $10,000 for organ transplants.[42]

Soon afterward, a similar story emerged in neighboring Guatemala. Here, 14 children in a fattening house were to be sold for $20,000 each. A Guatemalan police officer claimed to have discovered an illegal adoption network where children were being sold for $75,000 apiece by Israeli conspirators. In another case, a judge from Paraguay claimed that Brazilian infants were held in an orphanage until they could be dissected in American hospitals with their organs placed in cold storage for later use.[43]

A Blinding Trade

In July 1987, the "strange vehicle" motif emerged again in Colombia with the emphasis on the theft of children's eyes, organs for which fattening is presumably not required:

> A group of children were playing soccer in a poor neighborhood of Medellín.... All of a sudden a shiny Cadillac broke into the open space. The children's curiosity was excited by the unusual sight and stopped their game. Some people got out of the car; they didn't say a word. They immobilized one of the children and fled with squealing tires. Several days later the child returned with a medicated bandage over one eye: a doctor determined that a skilful surgeon had removed his cornea.[44]

The accounts that focused on adoption blazed brightly in the late 1980s and then became dormant for a time. When they re-emerged soon thereafter, eye theft became the dominant focus. Children, it was alleged, were having their eyes (or corneas) stolen. A pair of accounts captures the ghoulish details of these stories that swept through Central America, Brazil, and the Andes:

> The rumors typically told of abductions followed by mutilations: the child reappeared blinded, scarred, or missing a kidney. In its pocket was a sum of money (sometimes a substantial amount, sometimes only a derisory sum) and a note saying "thank you for your eyes" (or kidneys or organs). The abductions were said to have been carried out by strangers dressed in black leather and armed with machine guns who burst out of big black shiny cars or red ambulances. The rumors spreading in Brazil were usually more somber. In these stories, the child did not survive and the crime was discovered only when the body was unearthed and the eyes, heart, lungs, or liver were found to be missing.... The fear was so acute that children were kept out of school, sent away to relatives in the country, or locked up while their parents went to work. For about ten days at the end of 1988, Lima, the capital of Peru, was invaded by rumors of eye thefts. It was said that groups of men dressed like doctors but carrying machine guns were driving around the poor districts of the city abducting children. The children were later found wandering around with bandages over their eyes and thank you notes in their pockets. The eyes were allegedly being sold to pay off the national debt.[45]

> Residents of Alto de Cruzeiro, the Brazilian shantytown ... reported sightings of large vans (the rumors even agreed the vans were blue and yellow) driven by American, or sometimes Japanese, agents scouring poor neighborhoods in search of stray youngsters. People whispered that children would be nabbed and shoved into the back of the vans and that their discarded bodies, minus heart, lungs, liver, kidneys, and eyes, would turn up by the side of roads or in hospital dumpsters.[46]

One graphic detail reported from Mexico concerned a "traveling salesman who boarded a bus with a leaky suitcase. When a suspicious bus driver opened it, he found it full of children's eyes and kidneys, wrapped in plastic and chilled with melting ice."[47] Headlines suggested, "20,000 Kidnappings Each Year in Tijuana and Cuidad Juárez."[48] Whenever children were found

dead or missing, these stories re-emerged, often pointing to medical authorities or Americans as villains, such as an Associate Press story about the
deaths of 61 babies at a Mexican hospital, allegedly because of an organ
racket.[49]

Understandably, governmental agencies, including the U.S. Information
Agency, vehemently denied these claims, suggesting that they were part of
communist disinformation campaigns, aimed to spread anti-Americanism.
Admitting its vigor and suggesting the perceived political impact of the
rumor, Todd Leventhal, writing for the U.S. Information Agency in 1994,
notes that since 1987:

> [A] totally unfounded, horrifying rumor has swept the world
> press. The ghastly—and totally untrue—charge is that Americans,
> or sometimes Europeans, Canadians, or Israelis, are adopting or
> kidnapping babies from Latin America or other locations, and
> butchering them in order to use their body parts for organ trans-
> plants. This gruesome story has been reported hundreds of times
> by newspapers, radio, and television stations throughout the
> world.[50]

A Political Twist

Often these rumors have political implications, expressing resentment of
advanced, Western nations, particularly the United States.[51] On April 5,
1987, *Pravda* reported that "thousands" of children were being transported
from Central America to the United States, where they were used as the
source of transplant organs for wealthy families. The story, never formally
retracted by the Russian news service, circulated widely for several years in
pro-Soviet media.[52] Other groups critical of American hegemony, such as
the International Association of Democratic Lawyers, have also actively
spread the rumor. The Cuban government has introduced resolutions
calling for investigation of the baby-part rumors at United Nations
human-rights meetings.[53]

The rumors were so robust that they even targeted Cuba itself, according to the British newspaper *The Observer* in 1995: "Strange rumors are
circulating in Havana. Children are being snatched from their mothers by
men on motorcycles and their bodies found days later without their internal organs. Tourists are being kidnapped, butchered, and sold as pork for

New Year celebrations…. Some Cubans are saying that the children's organs have been stolen for transplants; others fear that believers in Santeria…require them for sacrifice."[54] That this belief is found within Cuba must be seen as particularly ironic if these stories were indeed encouraged by a Soviet-based disinformation campaign. However, much the same reaction was expressed by westerners in the wake of the 1870 Tianjin Church Incident, blaming the riots on manipulation of the masses by intellectuals with a grudge against European culture. Perhaps some of these beliefs resulted from political disinformation campaigns, but they could not have spread widely without being fundamentally plausible.

Even the European Parliament has suggested that the story might be true. Leventhal notes:

> On February 25, 1993, the European Parliament's Committee on the Environment, Public Health, and Consumer Protection issued a report on prohibiting trade in transplant organs. The report… included the unsubstantiated claim that "there is evidence that fetuses, children, and adults in some developing countries have been mutilated and others murdered with the aim of obtaining transplant organs for export to rich countries." The report, drafted by the distinguished French oncologist and European member of Parliament Leon Schwartzenberg, stated that "to deny the existence of such trafficking is comparable to denying the existence of the ovens and gas chambers during the last war." On September 14, 1993, the European Parliament adopted a resolution on prohibiting trade in transplant organs based on this report.[55]

Subsequently, Dr. Schwartzenberg revealed that the source for his allegations suggesting that organ trafficking was akin to Auschwitz was merely a provocative journalistic account.

Fact or Fiction?

Still, it is well documented that the babies of poor women were bought in Central and South America for adoption, sometimes for small amounts, and some babies were likely marketed without the full consent or understanding of their parents. "Everything about the baby-parts story is true," said Francisco Goldman, a Guatemalan activist, "except for gringos and baby parts." She added: "Children get stolen all the time in Guatemala. But not for their organs and not by foreigners." Even the U.S. Embassy in Guatemala City conceded that in at least 30 cases per year, the alleged "birth mother" giving a child to adoption brokers for export to North America was not in fact the child's parent but an imposter.[56] In some cases, then, the child might well have been kidnapped and sold for profit. It is inarguable that body organs are in high demand, and some people in Paraguay and Guatemala were in fact arrested for involvement in the organ trade,[57] although convictions are rare. Further, there remains much human smuggling across the southern border of the United States. Given this web of crimes, the argument that the laws of the United States did not permit such organ theft and that hospitals closely monitored transplantation rang hollow. Perhaps the clinics were as illegal as the rest of the trade, filled with unethical and rapacious physicians.

Rumors Run Amok

As disturbing as this rumor complex seems, its main effect was to provoke vigilance among parents and children. However, when the media and government officials promoted the rumor, it caused mob action, and not for the first time. Gillian Bennett notes that legends assert that Jews accused of ritually murdering William of Norwich in 1144 were protected from mob violence only when the local sheriff allowed them to enter the Royal Castle.[58] The Jews of Lincoln were less fortunate; 18 were executed, the first of many to be judicially murdered because of the rumor. The Tianjin Church Incident was another bloody consequence of body-part rumors. So it was not surprising that, in the 1990s, the rumor again proved robust enough to provoke violence.

This instance of rumor seems to have first appeared in the press when Leonardo Villeda Bermudez, the former secretary general of the Honduran Committee for Social Welfare, described the body-part rumors so as to make it seem that he believed them. He soon issued a retraction, as did other Honduran officials, but within a month the story had migrated to Guatemala and shortly it was being reported in Europe as well.[59]

Early in 1993, Guillermo Carranza Targena, a high-ranking official in Guatemala's Public Health Ministry, endorsed the belief that Americans stole children for their organs, and *Prenza Libre*, Guatemala's most popular daily, published an article headlined "Purchase of Children for Mutilation

Has Become Frequent." The progovernment newspaper, citing "official documents," informed Guatemalans that "Dozens of foreigners...who come as tourists have been detected in activities that could be part of the black market in human organs, kidnapping and sale of children. This despicable type of merchant, coming from Europe or the U.S., acts with incredible impunity, with the obvious consent of Guatemalan authorities."[60] The going price for a transplantable liver was $150,000 U.S. dollars, while a heart or lung could bring $100,000. The most sensational details were soon spread to a wider audience by TV and radio. An American tourist visiting ruins at Santa Lucia Cotzumalguapa was mobbed by residents who had become convinced that she had come to steal children. Authorities took her into custody and were able to evacuate her unharmed, but army units had to be called in to restore order. Another Swiss man was injured soon after when his tourist group was attacked by villagers.

Less fortunate was another American tourist, Alaska resident June Weinstock, nearly a martyr to rumor, who came to San Cristóbal Verapáz to see the village's colorful Easter decorations. She attracted unwelcome attention after she photographed a group of children. John Shonder reported:

> Tourists sometimes do not realize that their presence is seen by many as a mixed blessing. While the economic benefits of tourism cannot be denied, the presence of so many automobiles, buses, and strange people can cause problems in cultures which have a traditional suspicion of outsiders. Many times I have seen tourists in small villages giving candy to children, patting them on the head, and filming them with video cameras. During an Easter procession in Antigua, at the height of the baby-stealing paranoia, I watched a middle aged American woman coo at a little indigenous boy, chuck him on the chin and rub his hair. The child's mother was clearly uncomfortable, and dragged him away by the hand.[61]

Apparently Ms. Weinstock had made the cultural blunder of snapping pictures of local children and even caressing the head of one. An observer noted later that the *Prensa Libre* article denouncing American tourists as child snatchers was posted prominently on the wall of a local store.

Suddenly a local woman realized that her 8-year-old son was no longer by her side. The word passed quickly through the crowd, and at this moment Weinstock attempted to board the tourist bus to leave. A mob prevented her, accusing her of having the child's organs in her backpack. Authorities quickly escorted her to the police station, where not even the safe recovery of the child or the public unpacking of Weinstock's backpack could restore peace. At the end of a frightening four-hour siege, which was recorded on video cameras by bystanders and reporters,[62] the mob broke down the doors of the police station, dragged Weinstock outside, and beat her unconscious with clubs and metal pipes. Only when the chief of police (falsely) pronounced her dead were authorities able to restore order.[63] The day after the attacks the U.S. State Department warned Americans "to defer nonessential travel to Guatemala at this time....We urge that US citizens who remain in Guatemala avoid crowds, avoid traveling alone, and exercise utmost caution."[64]

Others have been attacked in Guatemala as well, including a Swiss volcanologist, a visiting Salvadoran family, foreign assistance workers, and backpackers. Later, an American living in Guatemala was mobbed when she attempted to board a bus in Guatemala City with her (legally) adopted baby; she was forced to flee to the U.S. Embassy to escape the angry crowd.[65] For several anxious months, the Guatemalan public was in a state of near panic while the country's Public Ministry reported that six children were being reported missing daily.[66]

The rumors were so vigorous that not only the United States but also the nations of Central and South America have had to deny them publicly. After all, infants and children adopted by American families are immigrants, too, though they are rarely treated as such, and if the adoption is tainted with shady and even criminal activities in the source country, they are illegal immigrants and the hopeful parents, their traffickers.

Adoptions and Rumor

If illegal workers can slip across America's borders, why not babies? On May 29, 1993, a multilateral treaty intended to check the most serious baby-smuggling abuses was issued in The Hague. A year after the Weinstock attack, the United States signed the Hague Convention, and the subsequent Congressional Intercountry Adoption Act of 2000 was intended as the first step in making American adoption policies compliant with the convention's goals.

Still, while historian Anne Collinson notes that this convention, combined with the negotiated end of Guatemala's generation-long civil war, reduced many of the tensions fueling the mob violence of 1994, the essential mechanics of transnational adoption have not substantially changed. Fewer children are born in the United States than are desired, and an insistent demand exists for adoptions among couples wanting a family; conversely, women in Latin American countries have little access to birth control, "and placement abroad may be the only chance their child will have at an education and a life outside of the poverty endured by their biological family."[67] While some feel that sufficient monitoring and regulation are built into American medical institutions so that adoptions for organ transplants are improbable, others allude to medical clinics that service a few very wealthy patients who will stop at nothing. However, at issue is not whether the story might be true or whether the claims that are pictured could possibly happen, but what the existence and vigor of the story suggest about attitudes toward globalization among those who see themselves as victims. Such rumors have not disappeared, although their contents have shifted over time.

On April 30, 2000, a Guatemalan tour bus brought a group of Japanese tourists to the remote village of Todos Santos Cuchumatan. The tour organizers were unaware that rumors were active that "a satanic leader from Los Angeles" was coming to town to abduct children and remove their hearts during an occult ritual at the local soccer stadium. When the visitors emerged from the bus, which was unusually large and had tinted windows, and began taking photographs in the town's market, a mob formed and attacked them. Tetsuo Yamahiro, 40, was killed, his head crushed, while the Guatemalan tour bus driver was hacked to death with machetes and his body burned with gasoline.[68]

Scheper-Hughes found similar potential for anticolonial violence in the slums of Brazil and South Africa, where body snatchers are perceived as fearsome threats in a context of institutional corruption and an absence of attention to human rights.[69] As Campion-Vincent demonstrates, kidney-theft rumors take many forms, but they depend on the recognition of a fundamental and unbridgeable chasm between the first and third worlds. A set of real social problems—those that involve the pressured sales of body organs and the sometimes hidden and distressing forms of international adoption[70]—is transformed into rumors that challenge a medical regime in which transplantation is increasingly common and demanded. Children, like the organs in one's own body, are internationally exportable commodities, and poor people are led to perceive their own body and the fruits of their body as sources of income.

Organ Thefts and Weapons of the Weak

People—wealthy or impoverished, modern or traditional—must interpret complex worlds in which truth is often cloudy or opaque. In the aftermath of illness or disappearance, the question frequently arises as to how to explain the mystery. As is so true of rumor, people make an effort after meaning. In a world where body parts have value for persons other than those in whose bodies they originate, motivated kidnappings seem plausible. Just as tourists' rumors commonly describe unwary sightseers whose purses are slit and their contents stolen, so perhaps the furtive removal of a valuable organ is possible. And as the residents of third-world countries realize that extractive industries remove metals and agricultural produce from their land for the benefit of wealthy nations, perhaps mining human bodies is the next step. Once an account is accepted, it becomes a template for explaining future mysteries. Stories are to be found within hierarchies of plausibility, quickly recalled when other, mundane explanations do not easily apply.

As we described, organ-theft rumors with similar content may be found in varied social locations. Both the comfortable and the impoverished fear that their organs could be stolen in circumstances in which they lack control. These situations may involve tourism, sex, sleep—or poverty.

The theft of organs after erotic activity is a subtype of rumors spread about tourism, much like legends of AIDS infection. Sexual intimacy can produce poor judgment or the absence of conscious thought, and sex can be used as a come-on by the unscrupulous. In some ways these stories are as much about sleep as about sex, for it is during sleep that the villainous can vanish or can anaesthetize the victim. For the middle class, this lack of control is equivalent to the powerlessness of the poor.

The dynamics of the second set of rumors are quite different and their implicit politics are distinct as well. In the case of baby thefts, the lack of control is structural. Poor people (and their infants) are powerless against mighty forces that are arrayed against them. Men in vans, ambulances, and limousines cannot be stopped, except possibly by collective action, but even crowds are often ineffective. These stories constitute a cry of rage and anger, as the children of the poor are stripped from them. As Scheper-Hughes argues,[71] these rumors reflect and transform the real conditions of difficult lives. Babies die needlessly and they may be removed from parents by powerful or wealthy men. If infants are not literally cut into pieces, they may be metaphorically butchered. These narratives are attempts to speak truth to power.

Terry Ann Knopf asserts that rumor "creates a 'common culture' within which leadership, mobilization, and concerted action can occur spontaneously. By crystallizing, confirming, and intensifying hostile beliefs while linking them to actual events, rumors often provide the 'proof' for mass mobilization."[72] Folklorist David Samper puts the matter pungently: "The produce of the third world now includes children, who fall under the same category as coffee, bananas, sugar, and even cocaine…children who are bought and sold, children who are exported in a global marketplace."[73] These rumors are situated within the complex political structure of domination. As Gonzalo Maisch, Isidro Valentin, and Soraya Irogoyen recognized in examining the sacaojos scares in Lima, Peru:

> That the rumor reached plausibility in several Latin American countries points to a matrix of shared history, a common sensibility: that of feeling oneself to be a victim of the metropolis. Perhaps here we can find the emotional roots of the resurgence and success of the so-called dependence theory. Its fundamental hypothesis is that poverty and riches mutually explain each other.[74]

Put another way, as political scientist James Scott maintains, these stories are "weapons of the weak." They are everyday practices that constitute acts of resistance, voiced through the seemingly informal, and perhaps trivial and impotent, forms of discourse such as rumors, gossip, folktales, jokes, and songs. Yet, even in their mundane quality, they set the terms through which people view their world.

Yet, as this chapter demonstrates, such weapons are not necessarily weapons of the "weak" alone, but are weapons of all those—strong and weak alike—who feel frightened and aggrieved. Those who need answers embrace rumor. Kidneys can be stolen for many reasons by many agents, and it is the lot of those who feel themselves at risk to interpret their danger and improvise the solutions. This public desire feeds the politics of plausibility.

8

Whispers on the Borderline

In our complex and virtual world, rumors speed across the globe, knitting individuals into an international network, even if it is a community of the mind rather than of place. Previously, rumors and legends have been studied in terms of face-to-face interaction between members of a "community" or "folk group" who shared a common physical world. But with the emergence of this new, borderless information community, many of the old social factors that we took for granted now need to be reconsidered. As the communications web becomes global in reach, participants increasingly use it to help them understand how the world system influences their lives and shapes their prospects. The politics of plausibility and the politics of credibility, once linked closely to one's places of employment, residence, and play, are now negotiated in a global arena. This creates new challenges for those of us who encounter such rumors. We must judge messages that relate to experiences we have not had, and from people we have not met. The local grounding that had characterized face-to-face communication is being superseded by claims from distant others, and the verbal intonations and body language of oral expression give way to the more complex visual rhetoric and graphic enhancements of a silent message on our computer screen. Local communities still judge stories and beliefs, of course, and oral discourse remains alive and well. But the information that these groups must judge now is increasingly provided by faraway, uncertain sources. This broadening of horizons has made the world of rumors a more fast-paced, multiculturally based realm, and so it is little wonder that internationalism has emerged as one of its predominant themes in recent years.

As with the interpretation of rumor generally, issues of trust remain salient and consequential. But in the case of rumors that target issues of globalization, trust is not constructed through the evidence of our own eyes and our direct memories of how people we know have acted in the past. We must use our imagination to create a mental image of how distant others live. It is through this "mind's eye," not our literal senses, that we now judge topics and speakers that reside outside of our close, comfortable world of action. This internal construction of the globe is prone to stereotyping and error, and so complex are the issues involved that even normally authoritative sources can sometimes commit serious factual errors or even brazen misrepresentations of the truth. Hence, individuals must use rumoring as one mental tool among others to gain a clearer sense of global issues. We can no longer marginalize the topic as the study of popular misconceptions. Rumors may be true, and to circulate they must contain a grain of truth, however distorted. Further, those who spread rumors are not always the ignorant and misinformed. The active circulation of a rumor does not reveal much about the extent to which participants believe it. In such a context, people spread rumors not just because they consider them "news," but because they find them amusing or hope to have them confirmed or denied through communal discussion.

Crisis Rumors and the Communal Construction of Reality

We began by examining rumors about the events on September 11, arguing that rumors helped to address the emotional concerns that Americans felt as they came to assume what terrorists are like, even though the messages were often contradictory and sometimes based on stereotypes rather than direct contact with Middle Easterners. A visit to the Web site Snopes.com in the section on rumors that relate to September 11 is daunting, reminding us of the astonishing diversity of rumors that even a single storyline can generate. As of early 2008, over 165 rumors were chronicled. Taken together, these assertions revealed the fractured beliefs inspired by the attacks. Rumors appeal to different audiences. These rumors, with all their varied forms, emotions, contexts, and factual claims, underscore the diversity of talk in conditions of ambiguity and crisis. Research on rumor began with the study of rumor in crisis—in war or after disaster—and September 11 rumors fit this pattern, as they mixed hope, fear, and anger. Not since World War II have we had such a profusion of rumors that generated such conflicted emotions. That war represented beginnings of serious research into rumor. Social scientists were drafted into service in order to limit rumor claims, warning the public that the enemy might be behind such "lies," sapping our resolve (although the allies spread rumors with as much vigor as the axis). Even when the stories contained valid information, we were warned that "Loose lips sink ships."

One of the most prominent of these rumor researchers was Robert Knapp,[1] head of rumor control for the Massachusetts Committee of Public Safety. Knapp recognized the diversity of rumors, so evident after September 11, classifying them as fear (bogie) rumors, pipe-dream (wish) rumors, or wedge-driving (aggressive) rumors, the latter most common in Knapp's nonrandom sample. These same common-sense themes apply today. Shopping malls are to be attacked, cyanide has been stolen, or dirty bombs have been secreted in American cities. Such rumors reflect our fears. Others, suggesting that Jews were warned ahead of time, that the government used the attack to justify an attack on Iraq, or that the fire chief in Berkeley removed American flags from local fire trucks, create divisions in society. Still others, reflecting our hopes, report that bin Laden has been secretly captured or is soon to die, or that a dog, Daisy, led many World Trade Center workers to safety. As in Knapp's sample, rumors of hope are less common than rumors of fear. Rumors can reveal the diversity of raw emotions. As Knapp understood, taken together, rumor provides a means through which we can measure the temperature and pulse of society. Granted, this is a metaphor of the society as a person, but we can recognize that what people believe is plausible and what sources they believe are credible, even if these judgments are never made explicit.

Knapp's groundbreaking work developed into the traditional model of rumor diffusion more than 60 years ago.[2] Rumor diffusion, as seen by social psychologists, results from the multiplicative effect of importance, ambiguity, and an absence of critical ability. The emergence of rumors into academic study was followed a decade later by anthropologists' and folklorists' early awareness of similar traditions. Even though these researchers were often unaware of each other's work, they came to similar conclusions about rumor. (Again, we assume that "rumor" encompasses "urban legend" as well.)

First, researchers understood that a rumor was not simply a particular kind of ignorant statement that was unlikely to be true, but the result of a ubiquitous, socially beneficial communal process of fact finding. A rumor is a means of understanding what many see as a new, potentially risky, and poorly understood social reality. The process produces statements and stories, but in the context of active debate, in which one rumor is challenged and countered by another in an interactive conversational context and modified in light of what a culture defines as plausible. In so doing, rumors develop a vocabulary and set of images that allow people to work toward understanding a potentially disorienting situation. As rumors develop, change, and merge with others, they constitute a larger body of thoughts, beliefs, and activities that constitute what some label a "subversion myth."[3] The history and function of an individual rumor cannot be understood without understanding the much larger and more diffuse body of knowledge that informs them.

These same forces continue to generate beliefs about conspiracies behind traumatic events. Conspiratorial beliefs circulate around most major disturbing events, whether the crucifixion of Jesus, the Black Death, the Japanese attack on Pearl Harbor, the assassination of President Kennedy, the origin and spread of the HIV virus, or the World Trade Center attacks. The concerns with evil elites, as well as with disdained conspirators, are together part of our cognitive makeup and part of the structure of a complex society.[4] These emblematic events demand explanations that uncertainty or randomness cannot properly provide. And, so, as groups construct meaning communally through rumor, they construct an alternative version of contemporary history.

Second, researchers understood that the rumor process becomes most intense when cultures that lack a regular means of communicating with each other come into close contact. In such a situation, rumors often emerge in a dialectic relationship, with the two neighboring cultures generating and circulating legends about each other that never come to the other's attention.[5] As Gary Fine and Patricia Turner saw in *Whispers on the Color Line: Rumors and Race in America*, it is tempting to dismiss the others' network of myths, beliefs, and rumors as the result of ignorance and malice. This is itself a misconception, and one that often blocks full understanding of the social response to a crisis.[6] Researchers see that rumors by no means circulate exclusively among uneducated or backward subcultures, but are active among groups of well-educated, economically and politically powerful policy makers. As the rumor process moves toward forming agendas of actions intended to protect a culture against a potential threat, it contributes to political decisions that, for better or worse, can lead to long-lasting social consequences. On a small scale, local acts of ostension or rumor panics have to be considered as rumors performed not just in the form of spoken or digitally transmitted texts, but as collective, ritualized behavior.[7]

If rumor is "essentially political in nature," as Bill Ellis argued, so, too, choosing to look systematically at rumors (and, conversely, refusing to do so) is likewise an "equally and inescapably political" act.[8] For this reason, much recent research on rumor and legend has examined its role in policy making. Diane Goldstein's work on AIDS rumors showed how pervasive and influential they were in defining a community's response to this new, threatening public health issue,[9] while Ellis and Gillian Bennett have shown that rumors and legends concerning "Satanism" had deep influence on international networks of social workers, psychotherapists, and police forces in ways that motivated high-profile acts of intervention, later shown to be ill-founded and unproductive.[10] Thus, salient events and the rumors associated with them are inevitably linked to debates over the validity of trust and the health of the public sphere.

Rumors reveal important features of civil society. An important goal of an active civil society is to ensure that citizens have access to information that will help them shape their lives and that will simultaneously contribute to shaping the worlds in which they participate. By this we mean that the worldviews of all Americans should essentially agree on how things *really* are. However, such an optimistic and happy picture is often undercut in practice. Some of this lack of consensus is a result of widely diverging religious and ethnic belief systems; some of it also results when subcultures cannot easily communicate, due to language barriers, or choose not to listen to each other because of underlying suspicion. And yet another factor is the increasing popularity of conspiracy beliefs, building on Americans' bitter experiences of the effects of secretive government action.

Our analysis of terrorism rumors did not attempt to address the more complex and contentious writings of those who treat the attacks as cynical acts of government, such as the 9/11 Truth Movement. Still, the smaller-scale rumors that we did address embodied similar concerns, suggesting that the very individuals and institutions that we trust to protect ourselves were either incompetent or even complicit in the attacks. This is no surprise, as rumors have always tended to place moral blame onto disfavored groups in times of crisis. The willingness to cast aspersions reveals that trust, that core building block in the social order, is not unconditionally or absolutely given. Although the awarding of trust typically assumes good intentions of those to whom it is given, it is also possible to *trust* evil or malicious forces to act in accord with their contrary beliefs. Trust can imply that we admire and identify with our heroes or can imply a cynical confidence that evil elites always act in their own self-interests, even when such actions are hostile to the smooth functioning of society. The preponderance of rumors about the attacks in New York and Washington identify few heroes, but finger many potential villains.

To suggest that all rumors about terrorism relate to September 11 is to misstate the case, transforming these attacks into a more unique event than is accurate. Terrorism is a tactic, not an ideology, and has been used since ancient times for many reasons. Even contemporary terrorism has a longer history than is suggested by a single-minded focus on September 11 as residents of London, Belfast, Madrid, Bologna, Beirut, Nairobi, Mumbai, Jakarta, Jerusalem, or Oklahoma City will all attest. While the rumors that refer to the events on September 11 are based on the local events of that morning, nevertheless, the *themes* that are evident in other rumors about terrorism, attacks prior to 2001 and those after, are largely similar.

All acts of terrorism are efforts to disrupt a culture by undercutting the feelings of trust that citizens feel toward their state and by forcing them to alter the routines of their lives. To that extent, when a society responds in a dysfunctional way to a terrorist attack, turning on itself and its core institutions, the terrorist's victory is more complete. If the public no longer feels confident in its pattern of living and when their routines become problematic, acceptance of the status quo is challenged. Rumors that address terrorist attacks interpret these disruptions, and depending on their content and on their narrators, can either bolster confidence or lead to a belief that the social order has been irreparably breached. So when rumors about cause and conspiracy arise more quickly and remain active longer than rituals of solidarity and constructive changes to prevent future attacks, as with the September 11 rumors, then we can be sure that many citizens no longer have trust in the stability and longevity of the social order.

Strangers in Our Midst

Although violent attacks demonstrate how the global political system can shake local communities, other globalized connections also generate rumor. Rumors are not always caused by disasters; the uncertainty of change is sufficient to shake confidence. In the case of changes in the global economy and political instability in the third world, the transit of workers from one nation to another can generate enough anxiety to spark rumor. The presence of migrants in a community—naturalized citizens, legal immigrants, or undocumented workers—is often a source of tension and strain. When these migrants are perceived as fundamentally different, and when, as we have seen, communication between them and the existing community is difficult, their presence may lead long-time residents (some of whom may have been the children of migrants themselves) to believe that the community they once saw as stable and comfortable is in danger of being destroyed. In the history of large-scale immigration, we know that residents often ask: Who are these people? What are they like? Why are they here? How long will they stay? Are they dangerous? Will our government keep them in place, or give them special treatment? Many Western societies, notably the United States, are mosaics of immigrants and so immigrants are welcomed and shunned simultaneously. The vibrancy of this foreign culture may in time be welcomed through restaurants, festivals, or music, but in the short run their presence may be seen as increasing competition for jobs, new demands for welfare, or both simultaneously. It was ironic, but not surprising, that when the Mexican immigrant Luis Ramirez was beaten to death by a mob of teenagers shouting anti-Latino slurs, Shenandoah, the town where this happened, was preparing a "Heritage Day" festival honoring the many ethnic cultures already present in the community.

Typically, migrants begin their new lives on the lowest rung economically, and must scrape to get by. Some do engage in illegal activities, though, the ACLU claims, undocumented migrants, because of their fear of peremptory deportation, may be less likely to commit crimes than documented migrants or native-born Americans.[11] Still, their presence generates claims that they are dirty, deviant, immoral, or even dangerous. The belief that immigrants spread exotic diseases, infecting the body politic, is one traditional rumored fear that still arises, but other rumors, such as immigrants kill pets for food, reflect similar claims of moral distance. Rumors of migration emphasize the boundaries between insiders and outsiders.

Over time, the rumors wane as communication increases between the newcomers and the older community and the salient differences among groups become less noticeable. The recognition of ethnic, racial, or religious groups as different never entirely vanishes, but as in the case of Irish, Japanese, Polish, Greeks, or Norwegians, rumors that emphasize fundamental and essential differences give way to jokes. When rumors persist about Italians (Mafiosi), Jews (control of banks), Cubans (animal sacrifice), or Vietnamese (eating dogs), they are certainly less potent in inciting hate crimes than they once had been. The content of such rumors remains latent in memory, ready to depict the latest migrants—the ones pouring across the border right now—as dangerous invaders bent on the destruction of all we hold sacred. While the boundaries of who are proper citizens continually expand, in time incorporating new groups as they acculturate and recognizing them as fundamentally similar to previous residents, the essential reaction to newcomers remains one based on suspicion, fear, and, in the worst cases, justifications for hate crimes.

Trading on Uncertainty

Rumors that track international trade are among our most vibrant narratives. While trade is claimed by economists to benefit consumers, products from abroad are exported without the control that characterizes local production. These products—natural or manufactured—can harm naïve purchasers, or so rumors tell us. And some claims are fully justified. Today, we find legitimate concern about imports from China, including seafood, medicine, and toys. Rumors track concerns that may be genuine or fantastic, or an amalgam of both. These dangers can be of various kinds: either botanical in the case of plants like yuccas or manufactured as in the case of beer or blankets. And the dangers can be willful or unwitting. In these stories foreign workers may sabotage a product, such as urinating in a vat of beer, or simply may not care sufficiently to check overcoats for scorpions. In either case the consumer is at risk.

Fear cuts against shared confidence in the marketplace. Objects that appear safe in sleek stores can gain a patina of peril when consumers recognize that they have an exotic place of origin. Consumers can no longer assume that the objects they buy, or even consider buying, are as safe as they appear on the surface. When this trust is violated, global trade becomes problematic. Such a belief benefits those who manufacture domestic products, and sometimes mercantile rivals, such as American beer distributors, may encourage the spread of stories impugning the purity of foreign imports. But more often the fear is simply the inchoate, unexpressed anxiety that comes from a lack of confidence in the values of foreigners. Of course, domestic manufacturers have their problems as well: with every bite of peanut butter one remembers the horrifying images of filth that came out of the 2009 exposé of the Peanut Corporation of America.[12] There are enough scandals to make that clear. But generally these scandals are seen as the fault of individual greed, not ethnic inferiority.

Innocents Abroad

The final domain involves the exposure of Americans and citizens of other advanced nations to the third world through tourism and travel. A body of rumor has blossomed over the past several decades to recount dangers from visits to exotic realms. Although travel is portrayed in advertisements with bright colors and happy faces, rumors suggest a darker side. In traveling to a third-world nation, the tourist is an innocent abroad. Anything might happen. What appears safe and similar on the surface—a cute dog, an elegant hotel room—must be approached with caution. Things are not as they appear, providing a warning to stick to the tried and true, investing global contact with a frisson of fear. Once one is abroad, the facade of the routine rapidly crumbles. Yet, from the domestic side, these rumors are often awash in humor. Travel is not as troubling as terrorism or migration: one doesn't have to leave the country on vacation, after all, and often the stories advise prudent watchfulness and a modicum of familiarity with local customs.

Body Snatchers

A more dramatic and politically active body of stories that incorporate both trade and tourism involves the belief that Western visitors in fact trade in human organs, taken from kidnapped children in their own country. While some rumors involve mysterious crimes in which kidneys are surgically removed after a torrid night of lovemaking, the most troubling rumors are based on the claim that the trade involves the intentional murder and medical experimentation on children. Of course, as has been revealed by Nancy Scheper-Hughes,[13] an international trade in body parts exists and involves social malignancies, and the stories' credibility is based on other abuses, such as a trade in impoverished children for adoptions. But the rumors go well beyond medically plausible scenarios, capturing core beliefs about conspiratorial, elite power structures. These rumors have often led to break-downs in trust, undermining confidence in the West's moral ability to lead and even causing, as chapter 7 detailed, the serious injury and even death of some unlucky tourists.

Coping With Global Rumor

The rumors we survey are, on the face of it, disheartening and pessimistic. In a world as fractured as ours and so rife with disorienting change, is consensus remotely possible? To be sure, trust is grounded on the plausible and the credible; change challenges what is known and believed. But even as one change challenges trust in one arena, open-minded exposure eventually builds it in another, especially when contact occurs spontaneously between equals. When we learn more, stability triumphs, and when novelty is defined as progress, something new is embraced as usual or enjoyable. In the case of rumor, most hostile stories fade with time.

Still, we should do more than simply pause until bad memories vanish. Some rumors undercut social harmony and others hurt vulnerable individuals, even if not attacked personally. In any case, if not challenged, a rumor used against one class of immigrants may, in the next generation, return as a useful weapon against the latest threatening newcomer.

While the dynamics of global rumor operate somewhat differently from the rumors that motivated race riots in the United States or, in an earlier time, anti-Semitic violence,[14] the need to confront rumor still applies. A sharp division exists between rumors that were found in the black community and rumors found among whites. Blacks and whites live in two separate knowledge communities. The chasm based on trust is still wide and deep. However, at this point, while rumors that deal with globalization are pungent, they do not target a single group. Some rumors target Hispanics, others Afro-Caribbeans, East Asians, people from the Indian subcontinent, and those from the states of the former Soviet Union; an increasing number are aimed at Arabs. Some villains are defined as foreigners and others as hyphenated-Americans.[15] As with many rumors found in racial situations, where whites and blacks may stereotype each other in similar ways, the target of one rumor may be spreading another, or even the very same rumor with the target group altered to ensure that the teller and audience find the attack plausible. While these rumors are not the claims of genocide found along the color line, they have the potential to shape public policy. In the case of rumors about terrorism and illegal migration, anger and bitterness may result.

Given the potential of these claims to undercut communal trust, we must carefully monitor our responses. We would be deceived if we pretended that rumor can be halted—or even that it should be. The presence of rumors suggests that our culture finds new situations worth clarifying, and that the future of society matters. This was apparent in the attempts after the attacks on the World Trade Center to find villains and to place blame. While most Americans rejected attacks on Arabs or Arab Americans, some hostility—both verbal and physical—resulted toward innocent people linked to the attacks only through their ethnicity or religious beliefs. The case of the Hazleton anti-immigrant crusade, as we noted in chapter 4, was motivated by entirely understandable concerns over the safety of residents' young people and the future of their neighborhoods. And, as it was impossible to determine how many illegal immigrants did reside in the area, or what their intentions in doing so were, it was impossible to discount rumors that attempted to clarify the situation. Referring to those who credited these sets of claims as "racist" or "xenophobic" slurred the community in a way that did not attempt to understand the intense stress that fear of future attacks or changes in demographics produce.

Nevertheless, in the short term, rumors can create deadly mischief. The beating death of Luis Ramirez, like many lesser, unreported acts of intimidation in the area, was an expression of the anger and desire to confront the stresses of immigration head on, as was the occasional attack on Arab Americans who were assumed to share the political beliefs of radical jihadists. Throughout the book we have seen similar acts of group violence, from the burning of Catholic convents in the early nineteenth century to the vigilante activities on the Mexican border aimed at rumored attacks by Central American gangs. Sometimes the result is literally violent, but even linguistic violence will sow the seeds of long-lasting resentment that can emerge in later years, perhaps with a new target. The "micks," "wops," and "polacks" of America endured the invective of exclusion during their postimmigrant days, and so it is only human that they would generate a new set of abusive terms—"spics" or "towel heads"—to exclude the Latinos or Arabs who came after them. We describe a deeply ingrained human tendency, and so simply describing these claims as "mistaken" is not sufficient. We propose five elementary rules that can caution and direct us when confronted with stories of global change, helping to edge us into a surprising future.

Question Easy Truth Claims

A crucial step in understanding rumor is to question those claims that seem too good to be false. These claims seem simultaneously strange and believable. Rumor is not a claim that presents itself as definitively true or false; by contrast, it is a statement that is plausible, at least in the minds of those who circulate it. The immediate political situation faced by local communities can determine if a rumor will be widely entertained. For instance, in a town where Latinos have lived for many years near a local meat processing plant, a rumor that violent gangs are at work may be met with skepticism, while residents of Hazleton, with little previous contact with Hispanic immigrants, may be easily panicked by the same claim. Often, in a climate of rapid change and crisis, we espouse stories about which we should be skeptical, wishing to show solidarity with the neighbors we know rather than put ourselves at risk at the hands of strangers. Yet, skepticism comes hard precisely because these narratives embody values that we hold to be precious, even sacred. We do not insist that we be given evidence for much of what we are told, and on most occasions we are prudent to accept what we hear. It is precisely those things that we are most ready to accept on faith that we should challenge. Proof is most essential whenever our hearts suggest that proof is unnecessary.[16]

A good rule of thumb is that we should discount stories that depend on the condemnation of a group that we found troublesome prior to the telling. Even when information appears highly specific, naming precise locations and giving the names of authoritative officials, it still may be false. There is an aesthetic to the performance of a rumor, one founded on the skillful formulation of convincing statements. Presenting precise details that bolster the claim is one of these skills, and so those very details may be of doubtful accuracy. Inquiring after the source of a story may not always help. Tellers may recall having read a rumor in a responsible media outlet, even though the information had been debunked or whispered by a colleague or friend. Sometimes stories are spread through the media but have not been fully checked or are exaggerated. We need not assume that rumors are shaped or passed on maliciously; more frequently, the person who passes on the claim unconsciously omits accurate details that don't make the rumor plausible and creates others that do.

When confronting xenophobic rumors, we should accept negative information only provisionally. In Hazleton, immigrants did commit at least one murder, and probably two: that cannot be denied in the name of multicultural inclusivity. And at least two horrifying mass murders have been committed in recent years by Asian immigrants. Foreigners, for better or worse, are no better (or worse) than natives, and so we cannot simply discount stories of violent crime. Still, if the information is not easily verifiable from authoritative sources, it should be treated as unproven, and those who hear it should be hesitant to engage in moral crusades or vigilante actions until it is proven. Listeners who are aware of the range of rumors often discover that they have heard similar claims previously, perhaps with only a few details changed. The popular volumes on contemporary legends compiled by Jan Harold Brunvand and others over the past quarter century have led those who might otherwise be gullible listeners to recognize that a new story sounds "like an urban legend," increasing their critical ability. When we perceive that a story sounds like a rumor, our healthy skepticism is likely to be bolstered and prejudices curbed.

Accept Rumor as Part of Social Change

However, exercising skepticism about the credibility or plausibility of rumors is only half of the effort. William Blake famously said, "Every thing possible to be believ'd is an image of truth,"[17] and so it is as important to see what Dame Rumor gets right as to debunk the details that she (like most scholars and politicians) routinely gets wrong. Rumor is inevitable in times of change, especially when society evolves so rapidly that even the people and agencies that we look to for guidance are themselves overwhelmed with new facts. And so any observer of rumors that address issues of globalization must concede that these claims look to the future as frequently as they look to the past or present. The reality is that, like it or not, societies are never fixed, and so there is no infallible guide to determine what can and cannot happen in this world.

Not only can the clock not be set back, but also it cannot be stopped from ticking. Something new is always present and so people's comfort level from their routines may be shaken. And as soon as this new process begins, rumors will emerge as those most directly affected try to make sense of it. In a world with demands for cheap labor and in which workers desire to move for economic or political benefits, the character of national populations will shift. Likewise, in a world in which both trade and tourism are desirable, in which the global transport of goods is easy, and in which people search for new and novel experiences, the interchanges among nations will continue and, as more people have access to resources, are likely to expand. Nations are not islands: this metaphor is increasingly inapplicable to the reality of global connections. While the idea of national identity is not likely to disappear anytime soon, one can sense in the European Union the growth of larger supranational identities based on region, questioning the linkage between traditional culture and citizenship.

Finally, the threats of terrorist violence, no longer linked to disputes within national borders, reveal that the unipolar global stability that emerged after the end of the Cold War did not end history. While terrorist attacks, outside of certain hotspots such as Iraq and Afghanistan, remain blessedly rare, they reveal global political strains made all the more difficult to heal by the prevalence of hostile ethnic stereotypes reinforced by rumor. Similarly, no one would doubt that the United States needs to secure its borders. The currently dysfunctional immigration code needs to be revised, to provide fairer treatment of both legal and illegal immigrants in the context of protecting national borders. We cannot know whether groups such as Al Qaeda will rise or fall in prominence in the decades to come; however, it is likely that the world system in 2020 will have different strains than the world today. All of these pressures, inevitably, produce stress as cultures, neighborhoods, and families have to adjust to situations that they have never faced before. And with this stress comes the process of fact finding, expressed through newly minted rumors. If it is necessary to question these rumors, especially those that express prejudicial stereotypes, it is equally necessary to understand how they aid those who use them to understand the present as a process that leads to the future, not to the past.

Remember the Past

To survive, we must consider potential futures. But it is also essential that we examine the means by which we reached the point at which paths divide. Just as there are multiple futures that can be imagined and can be prepared for, there are also multiple explanations for how we came to be who we are now. Some of these pasts are invoked by politicians and taught with pride in our schools; others remain untold or recorded only in archives and back issues of crumbling newspapers. Yet, all of these pasts influence the present, and to celebrate some and forget others misrepresents the past and leaves us unprepared for the future.

For Americans, the beneficiaries of waves of immigration, images of multiculturalism come more naturally than is the case in many of the nations of Europe that depended on the solidification of a secure image of national ethnicity. America prided itself on being a "melting pot," even if, as has often been pointed out by critics of that toasty metaphor, the melting pot was in actuality more like a stew pot with ethnicity not fully melting into the idea of the "American." In general, Americans, proud of the Statue of Liberty, felt that migration defined them. On occasion immigration became a heated issue, as it currently is today, but the idea that immigration is healthy and that certain sorts of immigrants should be welcomed is embedded in the American self-image. This is a nation of immigrants from across the Bering Strait, from the religious persecutions of Europe, the forced Middle Passage, and today's nightly border crossings. This history of immigration, plus the image of the nation as a fortress secure from the outside world—the city on a hill—produces our ambivalence about globalizing pressures.

While alternatively welcoming and ostracizing immigrants, Americans have also been uncertain about attitudes toward international trade. During much of the late nineteenth century and early twentieth century, no issue had more political potency than tariffs. What surtax should be placed on goods entering the United States to compete with our own products, manufactured and agricultural? Of course, one's stance had a lot to do with one's economic self-interest, as consumers wanted low tariffs and manufacturers wished for high tariffs. Laborers and farmers had their own perspectives on which products required protection from international competition. This issue is still evident today as we debate the impact of NAFTA and CAFTA, and other movements toward free trade, asking free for whom? The history of trade, like tourism and immigration, shapes the rumors that we hear and how we respond.

Similarly, the rise of terrorism requires that we situate political violence in its historical context, seeing violence aimed at the state as directly traced to the nineteenth century. Al Qaeda belongs to a tradition that developed from theories of direct political action, linked to the complexities of relations between the West and the Islamic world. This relationship dates back to the Crusades and the Moorish invasion of Spain as well as, of course, to more recent examples of Western colonialism and oil-based imperialism throughout the Middle East.

The rumors that we face result from historical patterns, just as surely as they predict future directions. We gaze backward and forward as we attempt to understand the present. The process of learning to "think like a terrorist," as described in chapter 1, displays precisely such an effort. To counter enemies, the rumors suggest, we must first understand our enemies' way of thinking more fully, and we do this by imagining their backgrounds. This involves imagining them as similar to us and as very different: they are shaped by a history and biography that is like ours but also diverges. We must recognize that the individuals who engage in acts of terror are human beings, with private lives that include having girlfriends, standing in line ahead of us in a convenience store, and instinctively responding to good news by cheering, and also with a set of values. This does not make terrorists any less threatening: after all, American soldiers do the same things and are still trained to carry out missions that involve the destruction of lives and property. And the rumors, as did earlier ones about foreign-born anarchists and subversive Jewish "elders of Zion," still present the "others" as terrifyingly powerful and dangerous, perhaps more dangerous even in that they live among us. But it is precisely their "otherness" that makes them so terrifying. When we begin to understand the contradiction embodied in the rumors, that young Islamists with normal human emotions can still be induced to carry out random acts of violence against innocent people, against the explicit teaching of the Koran,[18] then we begin to move past stereotypical thinking. Rumor is rarely the whole truth, but it can be an essential first step toward a fuller understanding of the complex world in which we live.

Build Strengths

To respond to rumor requires that we recognize our strengths as a society. While diversity has social costs, heterogeneity also has many benefits as compared to homogeneous societies. Diverse national and ethnic groups carry ideas, traditions, customs, and behavior, providing an enlarged and enriched toolkit of action. Yet, arriving in this country, immigrants often find themselves unable to communicate with their new neighbors. Confronted with hostility, they may turn back into themselves, as did earlier waves of immigrants, unintentionally forming ghettoes that rely on common knowledge of an indigenous culture and tacitly deter contact, even friendly contact, from the older community. The town of Georgetown, Delaware, has recently experienced many of the same changes as Hazleton, though without the bitterness of the Pennsylvania community's reaction. Home of one of Perdue Farms' largest poultry processing plants, the town has seen its blue-collar district grow predominantly Latino, nearly all of them Guatemalans from one local region, early settlers buying up property and then inviting relatives to travel north for the ready jobs.

The Delaware town has largely escaped the worst of the anti-Latino rumor mill (though a locally circulated statement that 4,000 illegal immigrants lived there seems unlikely, as official census figures show only 5,000 residents total, Anglo and Latino). But a recent profile of the area revealed a strong undercurrent of frustration. The new population was benefiting the area by opening new businesses, the director of the local chamber of commerce admitted. "It would be remiss or inappropriate if we didn't recognize the businesses that are developing and becoming part of the fabric of the Georgetown community," she said. "But right now, these businesses are just serving their own populations, and the problem we keep running into is the language barrier." As in Hazleton, the new stores posted signs in Spanish only, and curious residents visiting freshly opened restaurants and markets found business done in the immigrants' language only. The town's former mayor agreed, and then added: "It's not just the language, but if you can't communicate with someone, you're instantly suspicious of them.... Really, there's no interaction." This creates concern among residents about the new residents' agenda for the town.

Hazleton's abortive Illegal Immigrant Relief Act, which included a requirement that all city business be conducted in English, proved counterproductive. But, like even the most hostile anti-Latino sentiments, it had a germ of sense. When groups can communicate, both in vocabulary and customs, they often learn that they have more similarities than differences. Sergio Escalante, one of the Georgetown shop owners, narrated a typical American dream story to the reporter—but in Spanish. He conceded that he and others ought to learn and speak more English, but "never had time to really study." Surrounded by immigrants from his Guatemalan home district, who work for Spanish-speaking foremen in the Perdue plant, Escalante and others find learning a new language, for the moment, unnecessary.[19]

It is overly optimistic to assume that new arrivals will simply pick up the communication skills they need to assimilate or that the existing population will learn about what immigrants have to offer by casual contact. What is required here, and in many other places, is a proactive plan that provides language support and translation on both sides, so that the stories and values of the immigrants are fairly put on the record. Too often respect for ethnic background focuses on traditions that seem the most exotic and different from those natives are familiar with. It was telling that when Hazleton's Latino residents were interviewed by Spanish-speaking researchers from Zogby International, they expressed values identical to those who were concerned about the changes that newcomers might bring: fear of crime, concern for family, and desire for solidarity.[20] By embracing the inevitability of globalization and the value of diversity, we provide protection against the most malign forms of rumor, particularly those that are targeted at the poorest and weakest. Not all forms of globalization should be embraced with lusty abandon, but the reality of global interconnection provides benefits for American citizens and others alike. We need to determine cautiously and carefully which forms of globalization strengthen us, without assuming thoughtlessly that the breaking of walls and the breaching of boundaries is dangerous.

Unity Comes with Time

Perhaps the most important aspect of the attempt to confront and control rumor is the recognition that rumors are not easily mastered. Their control takes time, and sometimes they retreat when they become widely known. As a result, little new evidence is reported so that they become boring. Part of the justification for the spread of rumor is its vibrancy and diversion. When rumors stagnate, they lose their conversational value.

In examining American history, the boundaries of citizenship have expanded over generations, as has our openness to the moral standing of those different from established ethnic groups. The dividing line between *us* and *them*, while not erased, has become smudged, and campaigns to have Americans "buy local" or "buy American" have rarely met with great success, whether the target is motels or automobiles, shoes or shirts.

The passage of time helps us adjust to new social arrangements, and this is surely the case in regard to the topics of these rumors. Yet, as citizens become adjusted to the benefits and drawbacks of new social relations, a deepened well-spring of good feeling can be found. We do not suggest that there will not be rumors and false beliefs after a deadly terrorist attack, a rapid increase in migration, or the recognition of a new economic threat. These events alter what is considered plausible and who is considered credible. Still, over time, the boundaries of the exotic shift, incorporating more persons and more possibilities. In time, we edge toward embracing that core belief on which our republic rests: *E pluribus unum*: Out of many, One.

Beyond a Culture of Rumor

Despite our hesitancy to condemn, this is not a manifesto that supports the status quo. The beliefs that we have about alien others—those within our society and those outside—can be dangerous to the others and, more fundamentally, to ourselves. Robert Frost, hearing a neighbor repeat what he took as self-evidently true traditional wisdom that "good fences make good neighbors," perceptively countered:

> Before I built a wall I'd ask to know
> What I was walling in or walling out,
> And to whom I was like to give offence.
> Something there is that doesn't love a wall,
> That wants it down.[21]

In a world of deep, powerful, and lasting connections, we need good neighbors, even if we recognize that strains and competition cannot be casually erased. And we do not make our neighbors better, either the old ones or the new, by erecting walls that exclude.

Although we have not emphasized those rumors that target America, they exist and they can be noxious. These rumors, too, are grounded in history and look to an imagined future based on benevolent values. But how can we build an America that is a better place for our friends and our children if the building blocks, though they seem sound, are in fact made of fear, distrust, and surface impressions? The same is true for others: Latinos who are complacent in maintaining isolated communities must learn that their wall building contributes to the problem.

While we focus on the rumors that Americans transmit, Americans are not fonder of rumors than are others. The world is a rumor bazaar. And these rumors, whether about terrorism, imperialism, capitalism, or political dominance, must be confronted as vigorously as rumors that spread in our own land. As far as rumors go, every culture has a *street* on which talk is cheap. Today, for a variety of political, cultural, and economic reasons, America and Americans are seen as a source of mischief or evil, a belief as destructive as the others we examine.

Ultimately, the examination of rumor involves uncovering through the truth claims of rumor what beliefs and values the public embraces. Rumor can quicken our pulse and raise our temperature. That's good sometimes. The fact that rumors claim to be about facts and events permits them to spread values and feelings. Our goal is not to discover whether rumors are present—they are and will be—but to learn which themes are most common and what concealed sentiments they reveal. In doing this, the examination of rumors on the borderline will, we hope, shape the course of our lives *together*.

Notes

INTRODUCTION

1. The core of the legend's aesthetic, folklorist Linda Degh has said, "is in the skillful formulation of convincing statements." See her "Folk Narrative," pp. 53–83 in *Folklore and Folklife: An Introduction*, ed. Richard M. Dorson (Chicago: University of Chicago Press, 1972), 74. Traditionally, both sociologists and folklorists have tried to justify distinguishing legends from rumors. However, Dan E. Miller, in "Rumor: An Examination of Some Stereotypes," *Symbolic Interaction* 28, no. 4 (2006): 505–519, after surveying some standard definitions of the term in the light of fieldwork, concluded that the distinction "is not completely supported by empirical evidence... as urban legends become situated in communicative acts in social situations, they behave in the same way that rumors do" (p. 509). A similar insight had been made as early as 1982 by folklorist Paul Smith, in "On the Receiving End: When Legend Becomes Rumour," pp. 197–215 in *Perspectives on Contemporary Legend: Proceedings of the Conference on Contemporary Legend, Sheffield, July 1982*, ed. Paul Smith (Sheffield, UK: The Centre for English Cultural Tradition and Language, 1984). Smith called attention to the "fluidity" of legend/rumor texts, shifting both in detail and in form from person to person and even from one telling to the next by the same informant. Smith suggested that distinguishing "rumor" from "legend" on purely textual grounds limited understanding and proposed a focus "on discovering how, when, where and why" contemporary legends are told and used.

2. Ralph Rosnow and Gary Alan Fine, *Rumor and Gossip: The Social Psychology of Hearsay* (New York: Elsevier, 1976); Gary Alan Fine, *Manufacturing Tales: Sex and Money in Contemporary Legend* (Knoxville: University of Tennessee Press, 1992); Gary Alan Fine, "Accounting for Rumor: The Creation of Credibility in Folk Knowledge," pp. 123–136 in *Folklore*

Interpreted: Essays in Honor of Alan Dundes, ed. Regina Bendix and Rosemary Zumwalt (New York: Garland, 1995).

3. Bill Ellis, *Aliens, Ghosts, and Cults: Legends We Live* (Jackson: University of Mississippi Press, 2001), xiv, 235. Ellis was hardly the first scholar to make this observation. An earlier instance was a paper by sociologist William H. Friedland, which was presented at a meeting of social scientists in Lusaka, Northern Rhodesia (now Zimbabwe). Coining the term "urban myth" to discuss such materials, he stressed that "myth is not being used here in the sense of a 'false belief' but as a set of ideas which can be utilized as a basis for action" (p. 85). A myth, he contended, is a set of beliefs that may or may not be true; what makes a myth a myth is the extent to which it is used in a group to interpret events. See Friedland, "Some Urban Myths in East Africa," pp. 83–97 in *Myth in Modern Africa: The Fourteenth Conference Proceedings of the Rhodes-Livingstone Institute for Social Research*, ed. Allie Dubb (Lusaka: Rhodes-Livingstone Institute, 1960). For an overview of the context of this paper, see Bill Ellis, "The Roots of 'Perspectives on Contemporary Legend': 'Urban Myths' in the 1960 Rhodes-Livingstone Institute for Social Research Conference," *Contemporary Legend* NS 8 (2006): 1–40.

4. See chapter 2 in Gary Alan Fine and Patricia Turner, *Whispers on the Color Line: Rumor and Race in America* (Berkeley: University of California Press, 2001).

5. Bill Ellis, "Contemporary Legendry—'The Pale Cast of Thought?' An Editorial," *FOAFTale News* 21 (March 1991): 7–8; John Stauber and Sheldon Rampton, "How PR Sold the War in the Persian Gulf," in *Toxic Sludge Is Good For You: Lies, Damn Lies and the Public Relations Industry* (Monroe, ME: Common Courage Press, 1995), http://www.prwatch.org/books/tsigfy10.html; Tom Regan, "When Contemplating War, Beware Babies in Incubators," *Christian Science Monitor*, September 6, 2002, http://www.csmonitor.com/2002/0906/p25s02-cogn.html; Mitchel Cohen, "How the War Party Sold the 1991 Bombing of Iraq to US," Antiwar.com, December 30, 2002, http://www.antiwar.com/orig/cohen1.html (accessed June 22, 2008).

6. Notably, the future U.S. senator Daniel K. Inouye (D-Hawaii) was present as a medical volunteer at Pearl Harbor and later received the Congressional Medal of Honor for his military heroism in Italy after Japanese American soldiers were permitted to serve in the European theater of World War II.

7. Quoted in *Personal Justice Denied: Report of the Commission on Wartime Relocation and Internment of Civilians* (Seattle: University of Washington Press, 1994), 221–222.

8. Tamotsu Shibutani, *Improvised News: A Sociological Study of Rumor* (Indianapolis: Bobbs-Merrill, 1966), 128.

9. Gordon Allport and Leo G. Postman, *The Psychology of Rumor* (New York: Holt, 1947).

10. Stephan Lewandowski, Werner G. K. Stritzke, Klaus Oberauer, and Michael Morales, "Memory for Fact, Fiction, and Misinformation: The Iraq War 2003," *Psychological Science* 16, no. 3 (2005): 190–195.

11. David Maines, "Information Pools and Racialized Narrative Structures," *Sociological Quarterly* 40 (1999): 317–326.

12. Eric Holder, "Remarks as Prepared for Delivery by Attorney General Eric Holder at the Department of Justice African American History Month Program," http://www.usdoj.gov/ag/speeches/2009/ag-speech-090218.html (accessed May 5, 2009).

13. A. Chorus, "The Basic Law of Rumor," *Journal of Abnormal and Social Psychology* 48 (1953): 313–314.

14. James Scott, *Weapons of the Weak: Everyday Forms of Peasant Resistance* (New Haven, CT: Yale University Press, 1987).

CHAPTER 1

1. Ann Swidler, "Culture in Action," *American Sociological Review* 51 (1986): 273–286.

2. Jenny Kitzinger, "Media Templates: Patterns of Association and the (Re)construction of Meaning Over Time," *Media, Culture & Society* 22 (2000): 61–84.

3. See, for instance, Raymond A. Bauer and D. B. Gleicher, "Word-of-Mouth Communication in the Soviet Union," *Public Opinion Quarterly* 17 (1953): 297–310.

4. Bill Ellis, *Aliens, Ghosts, and Cults: Legends We Live* (Jackson: University Press of Mississippi, 2001), 11.

5. "The Fall Guy," http://www.snopes.com/rumors/survivor.htm (accessed April 14, 2006).

6. Dexter Filkins, "After the Attacks: Alive; Entombed for a Day, Then Found," *New York Times*, September 13, 2001, http://query.nytimes.com/gst/fullpage.html?res=9 B01E0DB1038F930A2575AC0A9679C8B63.

7. Susan Wells and Jack Maher, "AP Photographer Stands by His Work," http://9news.com/newsroom/13294.html (accessed December 19, 2005).

8. E-mail dated September 25, 2001. "'Satan in the Smoke' Emails," *The September 11 Digital Archive*, Fairfax, VA: Center for History and New Media, George Mason University), http://911digitalarchive.org/parser.php?object_id=3420. This digital archive was subsequently (2003) accepted as a permanent collection by the Library of Congress, Washington D.C, which currently maintains it.

9. Daniel Wojcik, "'Polaroids from Heaven': Photography, Folk Religion, and the Miraculous Image Tradition at a Marian Apparition," *Journal of American Folklore* 109, no. 432 (1996): 129–148.

10. E-mail dated September 21, 2001. "'Satan in the Smoke' Emails," http://911digitalarchive.org/parser.php?object_id=3265.

11. E-mail dated September 25, 2001. "'Satan in the Smoke' Emails," http://911digitalarchive.org/parser.php?object_id=3536.

12. E-mail dated September 21, 2001. "'Satan in the Smoke' Emails," http://911digitalarchive.org/parser.php?object_id=3132.

13. John R. Groch, "September 11, In Theory," *Journal of American Studies of Turkey* 14 (2001): 105–109, p. 105.

14. Karen Cerulo (ed.), *Culture in Mind: Toward of Sociology of Culture and Cognition* (New York: Routledge, 2002); Eviatar Zerubavel, *Social Mindscapes* (Cambridge, MA: Harvard University Press, 1997).

15. Jeffrey Olick and Joyce Robbins, "Social Memory Studies: From Collective Memory to the Historical Sociology of Mnemonic Practices," *Annual Review of Sociology* 24 (1998): 105–140.

16. Thierry Meyssan, *9/11: The Big Lie* (London: Carnot, 2001); Thierry Meyssan, *Pentagate* (London: Carnot, 2002); Webster Griffin Tarpley, *9/11 Synthetic Terror: Made in USA* (Joshua Tree, CA: Progressive Press, 2005).

17. A related rumor was that the "Israeli Defense Agency" sent a film crew to distribute candy in Palestinian areas to create the appearance of a celebration. This story is

also apparently false ("False Footaging," http://www.snopes.com/rumor/cnn.htm [accessed April 17, 2006]). These rumors were likely seen as plausible by those who wished to preserve the moral stature of Palestinians, not wishing to believe that they would so joyously support a terrorist attack.

18. Diane Goldstein, "A Little Knowledge Is a Dangerous Thing," unpublished manuscript, 2002.

19. Another variant has the terrorist issuing a warning not to drink Pepsi or Coca-Cola after a certain date.

20. Felicity Barringer, "The Rumor: A False Challenge to News Photos Takes Root on the Web," *New York Times*, September 24, 2001, C9; Christopher Callahan, "Anatomy of an Urban Legend," *American Journalism Review* (November 2001): 13.

21. Heather MacDonald, "Keeping New York Safe from Terrorism," *City Journal* (Autumn 2001): 58–68.

22. Irfan Khawaja, "The Celebrating Arabs of Paterson, NJ: An Episode in Contemporary Legendry," unpublished manuscript, 2002.

23. Ralph L. Rosnow and Gary Alan Fine, *Rumor and Gossip: The Social Psychology of Hearsay* (New York: Elsevier, 1976), 11.

24. The *Washington Post* reported that "law enforcement authorities detained and questioned a number of people who were allegedly seen celebrating the attacks and holding tailgate-style parties on rooftops" in Jersey City, watching the destruction. See Serge F. Kovaleski and Frederick Kunkle, "Northern New Jersey Draws Probers' Eyes; Many in Area Fell Wrongly Targeted," *Washington Post*, September 17, 2001, A6. Aside from this article, we could find no other information about this event.

25. Jeffrey Zaslow, "Arab's Restaurant is Nearly Ruined by Rumor of Celebration on Sept. 11," *Wall Street Journal*, March 13, 2002, A1.

26. Nicole Gaudiano, "Scares, Hoaxes, and False Alarms," *Bergen Record*, September 14, 2001, A19.

27. Anthony Colarossi, "Critics: Radio Shows Fuel Hate," *Orlando Sentinel*, September 14, 2001, D1.

28. Marilynn S. Johnson, "Gender, Race, and Rumors: Re-Examining the 1943 Race Riots," *Gender and History* 10 (1998): 252–277.

29. Goldstein, "A Little Knowledge Is a Dangerous Thing."

30. Press release, Federal Bureau of Investigation, October 15, 2001, http://www.fbi.gov/pressre101/101501.htm.

31. See http://chnm.gmu.edu/ematters/issue6/911exhibit/emails/halloween.htm.

32. See http://www.snopes2.com/rumors/mallrisk.htm.

33. Bill Ellis, *Making a Big Apple Crumble: The Role of Humor in Constructing a Global Response to Disaster*. Special issue of *New Directions in Folklore* 6 (June 2002), http://www.temple.edu/isllc/newfolk/bigapple/bigapple1.html.

34. Goldstein, "A Little Knowledge Is a Dangerous Thing."

35. Bruce Wiltshire, *Role Playing and Identity: The Limits of Theatre as Metaphor* (Bloomington: Indiana University Press, 1982).

36. Posted on the listserv alt.folklore.urban, by Sian Massey on March 7, 2000, in the thread "IRA reconnoitre Trafford Centre." http://groups.google.com/group/alt.folklore.urban/browse_thread/thread/77d67db5e536b409?hl=en. Massey headed the story by saying, "This morning I had coffee with a group of other mums in Hale (a suburb of Manchester, U.K.) One of them recounted the following story." After giving the variant above, she added, "Another mum then said she'd heard the same story, only it

happened to her friend's auntie's daughter's friend, and the man had been in front of her in the queue, and short of change to pay for his meal, and she had helpfully made up the shortfall. This sounded very like an urban legend to me..."

37. "Urban Myths—Police, Armed Forces and Commercial Capers," *Dragonqueen's Humor Story Collection*, February 21, 2003, http://www.shartwell.freeserve.co.uk/humor-site/corporate-myths.html.

38. Barbara Mikkelson, "Stalk Tip," *Urban Legends Reference Pages*, October 12, 2001, http://www.snopes.com/rumors/warning.htm.

39. "Urban Myths—Police, Armed Forces and Commercial Capers." Ellis received a version of this version by private e-mail, dated Wednesday, October 10, 2001, 7:32 P.M., and ending with a reminder that "Thursday is tomorrow."

40. David Emery, "Soda Pop Terrorist Warning," *Urban Legends and Folklore*, August 28, 2002, http://www.urbanlegends.about.com/library/bl-soda-pop-terror.htm.

41. "Tainted Coke," *Urban Legends*, 102.7 WGNI (Wilmington, NC), October 9, 2002, http://wgni.com/html/legends.htm.

42. alt.folklore.urban, September 18, 2002.

43. William J. Bennett, *Why We Fight: Moral Clarity and the War on Terrorism* (Washington, D.C.: Regnery, 2003), 18–19, 67–68.

44. Fouad Ajami, "Out of Egypt," *New York Times Magazine*, October 7, 2001, 19.

45. Peter Callero, "From Role-playing to Role-using: Understanding Role as Resource," *Social Psychology Quarterly* 57 (1994): 228–243; Walter Contu, "Role-playing vs. Role-taking: An Appeal for Clarification," *American Sociological Review* 16 (1951): 180–187.

46. J. L. Austin, *How to Do Things with Words* (Cambridge, MA: Harvard University Press, 1975).

47. Fred Siegel, "Radical Islam at War With America," *New York Post*, September 14, 2001.

48. See http://www.uscj.org/njersey/w-orange/rav/5762_Sermons_High_Holy_Days/First_Day_Rosh_Hashana_5762_htm.

49. Robert Knapp, "A Psychology of Rumor," *Public Opinion Quarterly* 8 (1944): 22–37.

50. Drew Limsky, "America's Course: Of War," *Los Angeles Times*, September 23, 2001, M2.

51. Robert Grant, "Yelling Fire in a Packed Theater," *Bergen Record*, October 1, 2001, 16.

52. John Chadwick, "Battling Rumors—and Hatred," *Bergen Record*, September 13, 2001, A8.

53. See http://chmn.gmu.edu/ematters/issue6/911exhibit/emails/halloween.htm.

54. See http://www.snopes2.com/rumors/mallrisk.htm.

55. Ibid.

56. Ibid.

57. Many later texts (from November 3 on) add "and white powder," presumably referring either to drugs or to bioweapons. Concern over anthrax contamination was then at its height in the United States.

58. This version was posted by "Andrew P" [i.e., Andrew Porter, radio coordinator for Kingston Hospital Radio] on the listserv uk.local.surrey on the afternoon of October 15 in the thread "Arab man warned me off," http://groups.google.com/group/uk.local.surrey/browse_thread/thread/6e446654ac6d01ba?hl=en. In a follow-up post to the

related listserv alt.local.london, (October 18), Porter (posting as "ACP") admitted authorship of the parody, commenting that the spoof had been "inspired by the hoax email that has swept the nation." See the thread "OMG—Fame from this newsgroup," http://groups.google.com/group/uk.local.london/browse_thread/thread/b21584867b796daf?hl=en.

59. Posted by "Cerberus—The Dog of Hell" in the thread "Stay Away from New Jersey" to the listserv alt.humor on March 3, 2003. http://groups.google.com/group/free.jokes/browse_thread/thread/78f242d0f04a5db0?hl=en.

CHAPTER 2

1. In fact, box cutters and small knives were found on other flights on September 11, but these may have been left innocently by a previous passenger or a mechanic, as before September 11 they did not receive great concern. See "Box Cutters Found on Other September 11th Flights," http://edition.cnn.com/2001/US/09/23/inv.investigation .terrorism/ (accessed May 9, 2009).

2. David Frankfurter, *Evil Incarnate: Rumors of Demonic Conspiracy and Ritual Abuse in History* (Princeton, NJ: Princeton University Press, 2006), 7.

3. John Hewitt and Peter Hall, "Social Problems, Problematic Situations, and Quasi-Theories," *American Sociological Review* 38 (1973): 367–374.

4. Gary Alan Fine and Patricia Turner, *Whispers on the Color Line: Rumor and Race in America* (Berkeley: University of California Press, 2001), 74. We draw on this analysis for the material in this section.

5. J. L. Austin, *How to Do Things with Words*, 3rd ed. (Cambridge, MA: Harvard University Press, 1975), 98–99.

6. C. Wright Mills, "Situated Actions and Vocabularies of Motives," *American Sociological Review* 5 (1940): 905–913; Marvin Scott and Stanford Lyman, "Accounts," *American Sociological Review* 33 (1968): 46–62.

7. Véronique Campion-Vincent, "From Evil Others to Evil Elites: A Dominant Pattern in Conspiracy Theories Today," pp. 103–122 in *Rumor Mills: The Social Impact of Rumor and Legend*, ed. Gary Alan Fine, Véronique Campion-Vincent, and Chip Heath (New Brunswick, NJ: Aldine Transaction, 2005), 107.

8. David Bromley, "The Social Construction of Subversion: A Comparison of Anti-Religious and Anti-Semitic Cult Narratives," pp. 49–69, in *Anti-Cult Movements in Cross-Cultural Perspective*, ed. Anson Shupe and David Bromley (New York: Garland, 1994), 55–61.

9. Campion-Vincent, "From Evil Others to Evil Elites," 105.

10. Marina Abalakina-Paap, Walter G. Stephan, Traci Craig, and W. Larry Gregory, "Belief in Conspiracies," *Political Psychology* 20 (1999): 637–647.

11. Ted Goertzel, "Belief in Conspiracy Theories," *Political Psychology* 15 (1994): 731–742; Carl F. Graumann, *Changing Conceptions of Conspiracy* (New York: Springer-Verlag, 1987); Richard Hofstadter, *The Paranoid Style in American Politics and Other Essays* (New York: Knopf, 1965); Robert Robins and Jarrold Post, *Political Paranoia: The Psychopolitics of Hatred* (New Haven, CT: Yale University Press, 1997).

12. Campion-Vincent, "From Evil Others to Evil Elites," 115–117.

13. Patricia Turner, *I Heard It through the Grapevine: Rumor in African-American Culture* (Berkeley: University of California Press, 1993).

14. "Fare Whether Friend," http://www.snopes.com/rumors/taxi.htm (accessed December 19, 2005).

15. Ibid.

16. Ibid.

17. Erik C. Nisbit and James Shanahan, "Special Report: Restrictions on Civil Liberties, Views of Islam, & Muslim Americans," The Media & Society Research Group, Cornell University, December 2004, http://www.comm.cornell.edu/msrg/report1a.pdf.

18. "Faces in the Cloud," http://www.snopes.com/rumors/wtcface.htm (accessed December 19, 2005).

19. James Toedtman and Charles V. Zehren, "America's Ordeal: Profiting From Terror?: Worldwide Probe of Surge in Trades Days Before Attack," Newsday, September 19, 2001, 39; Judith Schoolman, "Probe of Wild Market Swings in Terror-Tied Stocks," New York Daily News, September 20, 2001, 6.

20. "International Probe of Unusual Trading before Attacks," http://www.ict.org .il/spotlight/det.cfm?id=675 (accessed May 17, 2006).

21. "Put Paid," http://www.snopes.com/rumors/putcall.asp (accessed December 19, 2005).

22. Norman Cohn, Warrant for Genocide: The Myth of the Jewish World-conspiracy and the Protocols of the Elders of Zion (New York: Harper and Row, 1967).

23. Arthur Wailer, "The Protocols of the Elders of Zion in the 21st Century," http:// www.holocaustresearchproject.org/essays&editorials/protocols.html (accessed May 9, 2009).

24. See Bill Ellis, Raising the Devil: Satanism, New Religions, and the Media (Lexington: University of Kentucky Press, 2000), 120–142.

25. The Protocols have been made available online by a variety of religious and conspiracy-minded organizations. We have used the translation by Victor E. Marsden and originally published in London in 1921. This is available on several Web sites, including one maintained by the Australian anti-Semitic organization Bible Believers: http://www.biblebelievers.org.au/przion1.htm. As this text is available from several sources, we simply refer to it by Protocol numbers.

26. Nesta Webster, World Revolution: The Plot against Civilization (London: Constable and Company, 1921), 305–306.

27. Adolf Hitler, Mein Kampf, vol. 1 (München: Zentralverlag der N.S.D.A.P. Franz Eher Nachf., G.M.B.H., 1935), chap.XI, 307–308 (Mannheim translation).

28. "The 4,000 Jews Rumor," http://usinfo.state.gov/media/Archive/2005/Jan/14– 269033.html (accessed December 7, 2005).

29. Ibid.

30. Yossi Melmen, "5 Israelis Detained for 'Puzzling Behavior' After WTC Tragedy," http://www.haaretzdaily.com/hasen/pages/ShArt.jhtml?itemNo=75266&con trassID=2&subContrassID=1&sbSubContrassID=0&listSrc=Y (accessed May 16, 2006).

31. "The White Van: Were Israelis Detained on Sept. 11 Spies?" http://web.archive .org/web/20020802194310/http://abcnews.go.com/sections/2020/DailyNews/2020_ whitevan_020621.html (accessed May 16, 2006).

32. Brian McWilliams, "Instant Messages to Israel Warned of WTC Attack," http:// web.archive.org/web/20011005221245/http://www.newsbytes.com/news/01/170583 .html (accessed May 16, 2006).

33. Neil Mackay, "Five Israelis Were Seen Filming as Jet Liners Ploughed into the Twin Towers on September 11, 2001," http://www.sundayherald.com/37707 (accessed May 16, 2006).

34. Michael Slackman, "Iranian Letter: Using Religion to Lecture Bush," *New York Times*, May 10, 2006, 1.

35. Thierry Meyssan, *Pentagate* (London: Carnot, 2002).

36. "FEMA Was in New York the Night Before 9/11," http://www .whatreallyhappened.com/fematape.html (accessed May 17, 2006).

37. "9/11 Truth Movement," http://en.wikipedia.org/wiki/9/11_Truth_Movement (accessed May 17, 2006).

38. Ibid.; "LIHOP," http://www.halexandria.org/dward255.htm (accessed May 17, 2006); Mark Jacobson, "The Ground Zero Grassy Knoll," *New York Magazine*, March 27, 2006, 31.

39. "Small Things Amuse," http://www.snopes.com/rumors/osama.htm (accessed December 19, 2005).

40. Originally posted by "99mickey237" in the thread "OT: A creative solution to Osama," on the listserv rec.crafts.metalworking, October 3, 2001. http://groups.google .com/group/rec.crafts.metalworking/msg/387ee389fa652396?hl=en. Quoted in Bill Ellis, *Making a Big Apple Crumble: The Role of Humor in Constructing a Global Response to Disaster. New Directions in Folklore* 6 (June 2002), http://www.temple.edu/english/isllc/ newfolk/bigapple/bigapple1.html.

41. Susan Block, "We're All Afghans Now: Why We Should Support RAWA, Afghan Women and a Less Terrorized Global Future," October 30, 2001, http://www .counterpunch.org/block2.html (accessed May 5, 2008).

42. "Does Osama bin Laden Own Snapple?" http://urbanlegends.about.com/ library/blsnapple.htm (accessed December 19, 2005).

43. See "Snapple Rumor," http://www.snopes.com/rumors/snapple.htm (accessed December 19, 2005); "Citibank Rumor," http://www.snopes.com/rumors/citibank.htm (accessed December 19, 2005).

CHAPTER 3

1. See "Great American Boycott," http://en.wikipedia.org/wiki/Great_American_ Boycott (accessed May 6, 2008).

2. Barbara and David P. Mikkelson, "Talking Shoplifting," *Urban Legends Reference Pages*, http://www.snopes.com/politics/immigration/shoplift.asp (accessed May 13, 2006). As this site points out, these statistics were completely fabricated. One of the first persons to post the claim (on May 11, 2006, in the thread "OT—Boycot [*sic*] Results" on the public listserv rec.outdoors.rv-travel) in fact conceded that it "could have been a joke, never know" (http://groups.google.com/group/rec.outdoors.rv?travel/msg/ 71e83a09dfb0c87a?hl=en.). Another early circulator of the claim, "Chuck," who posted it on alt.smokers.cigars on May 13, 2006 under the thread "Boycott Results," added skeptically, "Snopes will have this one up shortly, I'm sure." After several other participants had criticized him for passing on unreliable information, "Chuck" returned later in the thread to stress, "NO it was not EVER presented as truth, but purely as humor" (http:// groups.google.com/group/alt.smokers.cigars/browse_thread/thread/28f0e5d6393c 569d/6b2865a3ce32bb7c?hl=en#6b2865a3ce32bb7c). However, the more detailed list of

statistics, allegedly from the Los Angeles County Sheriff's office, was posted seriously by "Iconoclast" on the listserv alt.politics.immigration on May 7, 2006 under the thread "White Guilt" (http://groups.google.com/group/alt.politics.immigration/msg/3a97b9972e23c5b8?hl=en).

3. Benedict Anderson, *Imagined Communities* (London: Verso, 1991).

4. Talk show transcripts quoted in "Paranoia Pandemic: Conservative Media Baselessly Blame Swine Flu Outbreak on Immigrants," *Media Matters for America*, April 27, 2009, http://mediamatters.org/research/200904270037 (accessed July 8, 2009).

5. Lauren R. Harrison, "With Swine Flu, Hispanics Worry about Racism," April 30, 2009, http://www.chicagobreakingnews.com/2009/04/with?swine?flu?hispanics?worry?about?racism.html (accessed May 10, 2009).

6. Transcript quoted in "O'Reilly Agreed with Caller Who Labeled Immigrants 'Biological Weapon[s],'" *Media Matters for America*, April 19, 2005, http://mediamatters.org/mmtv/200504190002 (accessed July 8, 2009).

7. As in so many instances, the language that one uses to refer to a group indicates cultural attitudes. A vast symbolic chasm exists between speaking of these men and women as "undocumented workers" as opposed to "illegal aliens." Neither one is precisely wrong, but they convey different messages that affect what claims are judged to be plausible. They make a statement about the moral character of the rumor target and the amount of trust that we should award them.

8. Hemant Shah, "'Asian Culture' and Asian American Identities in the Television and Film Industries of the United States," *Studies in Media & Information Literacy Education* 3, no. 3 (August 2003), http://www.utpjournals.com/jour.ihtml?lp=simile/issue11/shahX2.html#t.

9. "CBS Contributor Dobbs Defends False Leprosy Claim after Confrontation by CBS' Stahl," *Media Matters for America*, May 11, 2007, http://mediamatters.org/research/200705110004 (accessed July 8, 2009). Records kept by the U.S. Department of Health and Human Services, by contrast, recorded 8,490 cases of Hansen's disease from 1966 to 2005, with 431 recorded in the last 3 years, about a third less than the 40-year average rate.

10. Randy Shilts, *And the Band Played On: Politics, People, and the AIDS Epidemic* (New York: St. Martins, 1987).

11. Marc Lacey and Andrew Jacobs, "Even as Fears of Flu Ebb, Mexicans Feel Stigma," *New York Times*, May 4, 2009, http://www.nytimes.com/2009/05/05/world/asia/05china.html (accessed May 10, 2009).

12. Aristotle, *Politics*, section 1253a.

13. "Analogy of the Body Politic," *The Dictionary of the History of Ideas: Studies of Selected Pivotal Ideas*, ed. Philip P. Wiener (New York: Charles Scribner's Sons, 1973–1974), http://etext.virginia.edu/cgi-local/DHI/dhi.cgi?id=dv1–11.

14. Florence E. Baer, "'Give Me…Your Huddled Masses': Anti-Refugee Lore and the 'Image of Limited Good,'" *Western Folklore* 41 (1982): 275–291; Roger Mitchell, "The Will to Believe and Anti-Refugee Rumors," *Midwestern Folklore* 13 (1987): 5–15.

15. Baer, "'Give Me…Your Huddled Masses,'" 278.

16. Ray Allen Billington, *The Protestant Crusade: 1800–1860: A Study of the Origins of American Nativism* (New York: Quadrangle Books, 1964), 362.

17. Ibid., 67.

18. Ibid., 99ff.

19. Ibid., 361–362.

20. Mary Ann Irwin, "'White Slavery' as Metaphor: Anatomy of a Moral Panic," *Ex Post Facto: The History Journal* 5 (1996), http://www.walnet.org/csis/papers/irwin-wslavery.html.

21. Alan Hunt, "Anxiety and Social Explanation: Some Anxieties about Anxiety," *Journal of Social History* 32 (1999): 509–528.

22. Edward J. Bristow, *Prostitution and Prejudice: The Jewish Fight against White Slavery, 1880–1939* (Oxford: Clarendon Press, 1982), 82.

23. Ibid., 44.

24. State of Massachusetts, "Report of the Commission for the Investigation of the White Slave Traffic, So Called" (1913). Rpt. in *Prostitution in America: Three Investigations* (New York: Arno Press, 1976), 22.

25. Ibid., 44–45.

26. Ernest A. Bell, *Fighting the Traffic in Young Girls: or, War on the White Slave Trade* (Nashville: Southwestern Company, 1910), 18.

27. Hunt, "Anxiety and Social Explanation," 516.

28. Ibid.

29. Edgar Morin, *Rumor in Orléans* (New York: Random House, 1971).

30. David Frankfurter, *Evil Incarnate: Rumors of Demonic Conspiracy and Satanic Abuse in History* (Princeton, NJ: Princeton University Press, 2006), 137.

31. Peter Landesman, "The Girls Next Door," *New York Times Magazine*, January 24, 2004, 32.

32. Michael Specter, "Contraband Women—A Special Report," *New York Times*, January 11, 1998, http://www.michaelspecter.com/times/1998/1998_01_11_nyt_contraband.html.

33. Victor Malarek, *The Natashas: Inside the New Global Sex Trade* (New York: Arcade Publishing), 2003.

34. William Pierce, "Jews and the White Slave Trade," *Free Speech* 4, no. 2 (February 1998), http://www.natvan.com/free-speech/fs982a.html.

35. Alison Bateman-House and Amy Fairchild, "Medical Examination of Immigrants at Ellis Island," *Virtual Mentor* 10:4 (April 2008): 235–241, http://virtualmentor.amaassn.org/2008/04/mhst1-0804.html (accessed December 5, 2009). A list of these chalk markings and their meanings is a much-photographed display at the current Ellis Island museum.

36. Howard Markel and Sam Potts, "American Epidemics, a Brief History," *New York Times*, May 2, 2009, http://www.nytimes.com/2009/05/03/opinion/03markel.html?emc=eta1 (accessed May 3, 2009).

37. Paul Farmer, *AIDS and Accusation: Haiti and the Geography of Blame* (Berkeley: University of California Press, 1993).

38. For additional discussion of concerns about black immigrants spreading disease, see Barbara Browning, *Infectious Rhythm: Metaphors of Contagion and the Spread of African Culture* (New York: Routledge, 1998).

39. The Chicago Historical Society and Northwestern University, "The Official Report," *The Great Chicago Fire and the Web of Memory*, last revised October 1, 1997, http://www.chicagohs.org/FIRE/oleary/report.html.

40. Willis Fletcher Johnson, *History of the Johnstown Flood* (Philadelphia: Edgewood Publishing Co., 1889), http://prr.railfan.net/documents/JohnstownFlood/chapter17.html.

41. David McCullough, *Johnstown Flood* (New York: Peter Smith, 1987), 210–212.

42. Melvin Lerner, *The Belief in a Just World: A Fundamental Delusion* (New York: Plenum, 1980).

43. Carl Smith, *Urban Disorder and the Shape of Belief* (Chicago: University of Chicago Press, 1995).

44. Adrienne Mayor, "The Nessus Shirt in the New World: Smallpox Blankets in History and Legend," *Journal of American Folklore* 108 (1995): 54–77.

45. This is an instance in which there is strong evidence (in the form of letters) to support a rumor about a particular instance of biological warfare, although there is no evidence that smallpox-infected blankets were widely used or used in the nineteenth century. But during the French and Indian War, in response to Pontiac's rebellion in western Pennsylvania, General Lord Jeffrey Amherst seriously discussed distributing smallpox-infected blankets and his troops likely did so. We do know that shortly after the discussions, smallpox was spreading widely among the local Indians. See, for instance, Peter D'Errico, "Jeffrey Amherst and Smallpox Blankets: Lord Jeffrey Amherst's Letters Discussing Germ Warfare against American Indians," http://www.nativeweb.org/pages/legal/amherst/lord_jeff.html (accessed May 10, 2009).

46. Tacitus, "...haud proinde in crimine incendii quam odio humani generis convicti sunt," *Annals* 15.44.

47. Carl Lindahl, "Katrina Stories, The David Effect, and The Right to Be Wrong," unpublished manuscript (2006).

48. Dionizjusz Czubala, "Mongolian Contemporary Legends: Field Research Report, Part Two. Political Rumors and Sensations," *FOAFTale News* 29 (March 1993): 5.

49. Tetsuya Ozaki, "Buddha's Teachings and the Possibility of 'Globalization,'" http://rhizome.org/artbase/2398/fear/ozaki.html (accessed October 24, 2005).

50. Vernon Stauffer, *New England and the Bavarian Illuminati* (New York: Columbia University Press, 1918), 268.

51. Ibid., 299–303.

52. Protocol 1.

53. Protocol 10.

54. Radio show transcript quoted in "Paranoia Pandemic."

CHAPTER 4

1. This "quote" is coauthor Bill Ellis's distillation of many comments made to him personally or to groups in his presence during the hot period of controversy. The chapter documents most of these claims as they appeared in local media or were recorded by opinion pollsters; however, this quote is an imaginative effort to reflect how these rumors actually appeared in the daily life of Hazleton residents.

2. Debbie Burke, "Packing's 'Case-ready Revolution' Results in Hazleton Plant," *Northeast Pennsylvania Business Journal*, December 1, 2001, http://www.allbusiness.com/periodicals/article/983777–1.html.

3. *Total Impact: Citizenship Report* (Minneapolis: Cargill Public Affairs, 2003), 14, http://www.cargill.com/files/br_citizenship.pdf.

4. As documented by an extensive survey conducted by Zogby International, Michael Calogero et al., *Greater Hazleton Area Civic Partnership* (Utica, NY: Zogby International, August 2007), 81, 92. Only 1% of respondents said they had come to Hazleton directly from a foreign country, however; most had lived first in other U.S. locations.

5. The African American population in Hazleton is miniscule, under 1%.

6. Michael Vitez, "Small Town, Big Conflict: Latinos Have Helped Hazleton Come Back. Now, the Poconos City Is Targeting Illegal Aliens," *Philadelphia Inquirer*, June 23, 2006, http://www.philly.com/mld/inquirer/news/local/14881261.htm. This article provoked a large number of outspoken comments from readers, which were posted on Philly.com Article Comments: Thread #559: "Small town, big conflict," http://pod01 .prospero.com/n/pfx/forum.aspx?nav=printDiscussion&webtag=krphillytm&tid=559 (accessed December 4, 2009). These readers' reactions are cited below simply as "Philly. com Comments" and by the number and date of their posting.

7. "Philly.com Comments," no 46, posted June 23, 2006.

8. Ann Swidler, "Culture in Action: Symbols and Strategies," *American Sociological Review* 51 (1986): 273–286.

9. Angeline Francisci, "Whispers on the Color Line 1," undergraduate student contribution to an online discussion forum on urban legends, Penn State Hazleton, April 15, 2004. Francisci comments: "This story comes up in the midst of much tension in Hazleton. There is a lot of tension, especially in the older community, with the new increase in the Puerto Rican population. This story illustrates how they are trying to make the other group out to be a bad person. This shows that they are making the Puerto Ricans out to be an intimidating group who are only out to cause problems. This makes it seem credible because there is a large group of people who feel this same way."

10. Robert W. Balch and Margaret Gilliam, "Devil Worship in Western Montana: A Case Study in Rumor Construction," pp. 249–262, in *The Satanism Scare* ed. James Richardson, Joel Best, and David Bromley (New York: Aldine de Gruyter, 1991).

11. As determined by the Zogby survey's analysis of officially reported crimes and arrests. See Calogero, *Greater Hazleton Area Civic Partnership*, 23–24. While overall rates of reported crime declined during the period, the survey found, overall arrests of Latinos did grow in proportion to other ethnic groups. Arrests, of course, do not always result in convictions and may simply represent the greater vigilance local authorities showed as a result of the controversy.

12. Although two Latinos, both illegal immigrants, were charged with the May 2007 crime, on July 6, 2007, the charges were dropped because of the unreliability of witnesses. Prosecutors claimed that although they would not press charges, they were not convinced of the innocence of the two men (Associated Press, "Murder Case Fails against Immigrants in Pennsylvania City," *New York Times*, July 8, 2007, http://www .nytimes.com/2007/07/08/us/08hazleton/html?ref=us [accessed July 8, 2007]).

13. Vitez, "Small Town, Big Conflict."

14. "Philly.com Comments," no 38, posted June 23, 2006.

15. Vitez, "Small Town, Big Conflict."

16. "Philly.com Comments," no 126, posted June 24, 2006.

17. "Philly.com Comments," no 57, posted June 23, 2006.

18. John Bonner, "Rumors about Latino American," undergraduate student contribution to an online discussion forum on urban legends, Penn State Hazleton, April 16, 2004.

19. Kalen Churcher, "Documents Show Large Scope of Drug Ring," *The* [Scranton/ Wilkes-Barre] *Times-Leader*, November 16, 2003.

20. The photo, published the next day in the *Hazleton Standard-Speaker*, showed the handcuffed suspect holding out his first two fingers in a "V" sign, perhaps a "victory" sign signifying his that he would be cleared of the crime, or, since the photo shows him with the back of his hand out, perhaps a variation of a gesture known to have

contemptuous obscene significance in Europe since the 1600s. See "Foreign Fingers," *Ooze Magazine*, December 4, 2004, http://www.ooze.com/finger/html/foriegn.html (accessed May 11, 2009).

21. Shawn M. Kelly, "Hazleton Officials Relay Concerns about Gang Activity," *Hazleton Standard-Speaker*, December 5, 2005.

22. Matt Conlon, "Rumors about Latinos," undergraduate student contribution to an online discussion forum on urban legends, Penn State Hazleton, December 7, 2006.

23. Jolene Busher, "Out of Box 3," undergraduate student contribution to an online discussion forum on urban legends, Penn State Hazleton, December 12, 2007.

24. Bill Ellis, *Aliens, Ghosts, and Cults: Legends We Live* (Jackson: University Press of Mississippi, 2003), 47–50. This legend type in fact dates to antiquity, as a variety of new religions, including Christianity, were said to hold initiations by kidnapping and murdering children or Roman citizens.

25. Daniel Knappenberger, "Out of the Box," undergraduate student contribution to an online discussion forum on urban legends, Penn State Hazleton, December 11, 2007.

26. Ellis, *Aliens, Ghosts, and Cults*, 213–214.

27. The affair and the ensuing legal actions were heavily covered in the Hazleton area and widely discussed in private accounts of what "really" happened on that evening. A good summary of the event and its context is David Montgomery, "Melting Point: A Small Immigrant Town Simmers in the Wake of a Brutal Murder," *The Washington Post*, September 2, 2008, C01, http://www.washingtonpost.com/wpdyn/content/article/2008/09/01/AR2008090102869_pf.html (accessed July 7, 2009). A revealing and often graphic verbatim eyewitness account of the brawl was posted as "Mexican Immigrant Beaten to Death in Shenandoah, Pennsylvania," *Democracy Now Reports*, July 24, 2007, http://www.democracynow.org/2008/7/24/friend_of_mexican_immigrant_beaten_to (accessed July 7, 2009).

28. This, too, was widely covered in the local press; the most detailed account was Leslie Richardson, "Verdict Surprises Many," [Wilkes-Barre] *Citizen's Voice*, May 3, 2009. National coverage included Michael Rubinkam, "Luis Ramirez Killers Found Not Guilty after Beating Mexican Immigrant to Death," *Huffington Post*, May 2, 2009, http://www.huffingtonpost.com/2009/05/04/luis-ramirez-killers-foun_n_195535.html (accessed July 8, 2009); and Ian Urbina, "After Trial, Tensions Simmer over Race," *New York Times*, May 17, 2009.

29. David Neiwert, "Jury Finds Teens Not Guilty of Hate Crime in Beating Death of Latino," *AlterNet*, May 6, 2009, http://www.alternet.org/story/139827/ (accessed May 17, 2009).

30. Richardson, "Verdict Surprises Many."

31. Richard Bauman, *Verbal Art as Performance* (Prospect Heights, IL: Waveland Press, 1977).

32. Erving Goffman, *Encounters* (Indianapolis: Bobbs-Merrill, 1961).

33. Kristen Lechner, "Vanishing Child," undergraduate student contribution to an online discussion forum on urban legends, Penn State Hazleton, December 2, 2004.

34. Jan Harold Brunvand, *The Choking Doberman and Other "New" Urban Legends* (New York: Norton, 1984), 78–82; Jan Harold Brunvand, *The Mexican Pet: More "New" Urban Legends and Some Old Favorites* (New York: Norton, 1986), 148–156.

35. Jean-Bruno Renard, "LSD Tattoo Transfers: Rumor from North America to France," *Folklore Forum* 24, no. 2 (1991): 3–26.

36. There is an extensive literature on issues of impression management within sociology, but the classic study is Erving Goffman, *Presentation of Self in Everyday Life* (Garden City, NY: Anchor, 1959).

37. Lechner, "Vanishing Child."

38. Gillian Bennett, "The Color of Saying: Modern Legend and Folktale," *Southern Folklore* 50 (1993): 19–32.

39. Lechner, "Vanishing Child."

40. David Messick and Roderick Kramer, "Trust as a Form of Shallow Morality," pp. 89–117, in *Trust in Society*, ed. Karen Cook (New York: Russell Sage Foundation, 2001).

41. Carol Heimer, "Solving the Problem of Trust," pp. 40–88, in *Trust in Society* ed. Karen Cook (New York: Russell Sage Foundation, 2001).

42. Reported in "Dashborder Crossing," http://www.snopes.com/photos/dashboard .asp (accessed November 21, 2005).

43. Reported in "Bent Out of Shape...Illegal Aliens Caught in Desperate Attempts to Cross U. S. Border," *U. S. Customs Today* 37, no. 9 (September 2001), http://www.cbp .gov/xp/Customs Today/2001/September/other/custody_bent.xml (accessed February 9, 2006).

44. Linda Dégh and Andrew Vázsonyi, "Does the Word 'Dog' Bite? Ostensive Action: A Means of Legend Telling," *Journal of Folklore Research* 20 (1983): 5–34.

45. "Palestinians and al Qaeda Bond through Ship Container," DEBKAfile Special Report, March 17, 2004, http://www.debka.com/article.php?aid=807 (accessed May 11, 2009).

46. The same source contained a number of claims supporting the controversial argument that Iraq's Saddam Hussein was seeking bomb-grade uranium and attempting to manufacture weapons of mass destruction, claims that proved untrue but which were at the time taken as authoritative by American foreign policy makers. DEBKA is an Israeli-based military online intelligence broker with ties to neo-conservative politicians in the United States; it relies on anonymous sources, and, while it asserts that its reports are "80 percent correct," its reliability is discounted by professional intelligence officers.

47. William I. Thomas and Florian Znaniecki, *The Polish Peasant in Europe and America* (Chicago: University of Chicago Press, 1918–1920), 1545–1546.

48. "Philly.com Comments," no 58, posted June 23, 2006.

49. "Philly.com Comments," no 72, posted June 23, 2006.

50. An extensive search turned up a number of court cases in which alleged MS-13 gang members had killed or assaulted females thought to be informers, most notably the May 2005 trial of four males in Alexandria, Virginia, for murdering 17-year-old Brenda Paz, who had been providing federal prosecutors with information on the gang. However, no information could be found of a murder trial in which the courtroom had been dominated by gang members trying to intimidate the jury.

51. Ned Martel, "Taking a Long Look at a Latino Gang Named for Fire Ants," *New York Times*, February 11, 2006, http://www.nytimes.com/2006/02/11/arts/television/ 11mart.html?ex=1151899200&en=dcaea406fc7742d0&ei=5070 (accessed May 11, 2009).

52. Luis J. Rodriguez, "Gang of Our Own Making," *New York Times*, March 28, 2005, http://www.nytimes.com/2005/03/28/opinion/28rodriguez.html?ex=12696660 00&en=14b0ac1b86bcf2ef&ei=5090&partner=rssuserland (accessed May 11, 2009).

53. Jerry Seper, "Gang Will Target Minuteman Vigil on Mexico Border," *Washington Times*, March 28, 2005, http://www.washingtontimes.com/national/20050328-125306-7868r.htm (accessed February 9, 2006).

54. David Holthouse, "Arizona Showdown: High-powered Firearms, Militia Maneuvers and Racism at the Minuteman Project," Intelligence Report, Southern Poverty Law Center (Summer 2005), http://www.splcenter.org/intel/intelreport/article.jsp?pid=917 (accessed May 11, 2009).

55. Martha Zoller, "A 'Comprehensive' Solution to Illegal Immigration," Americans for Legal Immigration PAC Web site, posted April 10, 2007, http://www.holdtheirfeettothefire.org/news/index.shtml (accessed July 9, 2009). In an attached biography, Zoller is described as a conservative talk show host for a radio station in Gainesville, Georgia, who also appears on Rightalk Radio.

56. For an overview of such claims, see Jeffrey S. Victor, "Satanic Cult Rumors as Contemporary Legend," *Western Folklore* 49 (1990): 51–81, and *Satanic Panic: The Creation of a Contemporary Legend* (Chicago: Open Court, 1993); Robert D. Hicks, *In Pursuit of Satan: The Police and the Occult* (Buffalo, NY: Prometheus, 1991); and Ellis, *Aliens, Ghosts, and Cults*, 199–219.

57. "Philly.com Comments," no 58, posted June 23, 2006.

58. William Finnegan, "New in Town: The Somalis of Lewiston," *The New Yorker*, December 11, 2006, 46–58, p. 48.

59. Web page of Congressman Todd Russell Platts, "Internet Rumors," http://www.house.gov/platts/casework/internet-rumors.htm (accessed January 26, 2006).

60. Edwardo Porter, "Illegal Immigrants Are Bolstering Social Security with Billions," *New York Times*, April 5, 2005, http://www.nytimes.com/2005/04/05/business/05immigration.html?ex=1270353600&en=78c87ac4641dc383&ei=5090&partner=rssuserland (accessed May 11, 2009).

61. "Philly.com Comments," no 94, posted June 23, 2006.

62. "Philly.com Comments," no 98, posted June 23, 2006.

63. "Tax Holidays for Immigrants," http://www.snopes.com/business/taxes/immigrants.asp (accessed November 21, 2005).

64. Ibid.

65. Ibid.

66. Ibid.

67. Ibid.

68. Johann Hari. "Unions? Ban Them! Cyclists? Fascists!" *New Statesman* (October 7, 2002), http://www.newstatesman.com/200210070014 (accessed January 28, 2010).

69. Summarized from online news reports (no longer accessible) in *Irish Independent*, February 1 and February 4, 2002; *Irish Times*, January 29 and February 1, 2002; *Sunday Independent*, January 27, 2002; *Irish News*, January 28, 2002; and *Irish Examiner*, February 2, 2002.

70. "Foreign Business Owners," http://www.freakzonline.com/forums/showthread.php?t=299975 (accessed February 5, 2005).

71. The double-1 in "hell" is deliberately replaced by two numeral ones, a device used to defeat automated moderators intended to prevent people from posting profanity-laced messages.

72. Philly.com Comments," no 29, posted June 23, 2006.

73. Lornet Turnbull and Florangela Davila, "Rumors Fuel Immigrant Fear: Illegal Residents Hiding to Avoid Deportation," *Seattle Times*, July 25, 2004, http://www.seattletimes.nwsource.com/html/localnews/2001988098_roundup25m.html (accessed January 26, 2006).

74. Naomi Haveln, "Immigration Rumor Causes Some Latinos to Miss Work," *Aspen Times*, July 13, 2004, http://www.aspentimes.com/article/20040713/NEWS/10713 0002&SearchID=73233611757965 (accessed January 26, 2006).

75. Wendell Edwards, "Hispanic Community Still Suspect of Immigration Rumor," KHOU News, April 7, 2004, http://www.khou.com/news/local/stories/khou040427_ds_ ImmigrationRumor.168ce872b.html (accessed January 26, 2006).

76. Michele R. Marcucci, "Immigration Roundup Rumors Are All Talk," *Oakland Tribune*, April 27, 2006, http://findarticles.com/p/articles/mi_qu4176/is_20060427/ai_ n16227048 (accessed on July 7, 2007).

77. Austin Jenkins, "Rumors and Panic Follow Immigration Raids," Northwest Public Radio, June 27, 2007, http://nwpr.org/07/HomepageArticles/Article.aspx?n=3035 (accessed on July 7, 2007).

78. David Ovalle, "President's Immigration Proposal Stirs Rumors," *Miami Herald*, February 2, 2004, http://72.14.207.104/search?q=cache:dufjNjqhAhIJ:www .miami.com/mld/miamiherald/7852013.htm+David+Ovalle+President%27s+immigr ation+proposal+Miami+Herald&hl=en&gl=us&ct=clnk&cd=2 (accessed on February 3, 2006).

79. A. Chorus, "The Basic Law of Rumor," *Journal of Abnormal and Social Psychology* 48 (1953): 313–314.

80. Gordon Allport and Leo Postman, *The Psychology of Rumor* (New York: Holt, 1947), 5.

81. Neiwert, "Jury Finds Teens Not Guilty."

CHAPTER 5

1. Bennett Cerf, *Good for a Laugh* (Garden City, NY: Hanover House, 1952), 203–204.

2. However, lalw6001, a participant in the discussion group soc.culture.celtic, commented, "As someone who lives in Blarney, and has worked in the Castle Estate, I find the...tale highly unlikely. The castle itself has, as any visitor will know, a large steel door. This is locked and cross-bolted every night. Then there is the high security presence within the grounds at night (dogs etc.), rendering this escapade dangerous as well as unlikely. Finally the Stone IS washed each morning, but to remove any unsavoury particles that may have wafted across from Sellafield or such (i.e. pollution)" (posted on February 6, 1995).

3. Irish Mike, "Don't Bother, You Won't Understand Anyway," posted on rec.gam-bling.poker, February 11, 2004 (accessed April 19, 2006).

4. John Ciardi, "Manner of Speaking," *Saturday Review*, November 27, 1965, 18.

5. Gillian Bennett, "Legend: Performance and Truth," pp. 13–36 in *Monsters with Iron Teeth: Perspectives on Contemporary Legend III*, ed. Gillian Bennett, Paul Smith, and J. D. A. Widdowson (Sheffield, UK: Sheffield Academic Press, 1988); and "The Color of Saying: Modern Legend and Folktale," *Southern Folklore* 50 (1993): 19–32.

6. Nathaniel Hawthorne, *The English Notebooks*, ed. Randall Stewart (New York: Russell & Russell, 1962), 55. A similar story, but without the "tourist" element, was recorded by Art Linkletter in 1967: a woman accidentally gets a price tag stuck to her dress in a store. She then walks around town with her posterior tagged "Bargain price—$6.95" (*Oops! or, Life's Awful Moments*. Garden City, NY: Doubleday, 1967, 77).

7. Hawthorne, 197, 281.

8. "Unicode Humor," http://www.i18nguy.com/humor/unicode?humor.htm (accessed February 20, 2006).

9. "Prostitution Medallion," http://www.snopes.com/risque/hookers/medal.htm (accessed November 21, 2005).

10. Barbara Mikkelson, in "Bite the Wax Tadpole" (http://www.snopes.com/cokelore/tadpole.asp), suggests that this story may be based on truth, though in this case the "mistake" was that of the first Chinese vendors introducing the beverage to the country, who may have used pictograms that would sound like "ko-ka-ko-la" but could mean all sorts of silly things. ("la" does mean "wax" in most Chinese dialects.) In any case, when the firm officially trade-marked a Chinese logo in 1928, they researched the options and carefully chose characters that could be read as "to allow the mouth to be able to rejoice."

11. By contrast, Barbara Mikkelson, in "Come Alive!" (http://www.snopes.com/business/misxlate/ancestor.asp [accessed May 12, 2009]), could find no corroboration for this widely circulated factoid.

12. Joel Martinsen, "Beijing Cleans up Its Sign Translations," posted on Danwei: Chinese media, advertising, and urban life on September 6, 2005, http://www.danwei.org/trends_and_buzz/beijing_cleans_up_its_sign_tra.php (accessed April 19, 2006).

13. "Hanzi Smatter: Dedicated to the Misuse of Chinese Characters in Western Culture," http://www.hanzismatter.com (accessed February 21, 2006).

14. "Chinese Tattoos Article," http://www.cantonese.sheik.co.uk/phorum/read.php?1,387,page=1 (accessed February 21, 2006).

15. Ibid.

16. Ibid.

17. "Prostitution Medallion."

18. Georgina Littlejohn, "The Ugly Truth about This Badly Drawn Boy," *Metro*, June 6, 2002, 8.

19. This is a fictitious name, though, perhaps suggested by the award-winning American graphic novel artist Stan Sakai, whose series *Usagi Yojimbo* (Rabbit Bodyguard) is one of the relatively few highly respected Japanese-style manga drawn in English by an American author.

20. The story specifies that Smith wanted Chinese characters tattooed, but that Sakai objected to Americans who asked for Japanese characters, a contradiction indicating that the story is not to be believed: "Disgruntled Asian Tattoo Artist Inks His Revenge," http://www.soufoaklin.com/tattooartist.html (accessed February 21, 2006).

21. Jan Harold Brunvand, *The Choking Doberman and Other Urban Legends* (New York: Norton, 1984), 96. As Barbara Mikkelson notes, however, these narrative touches describe Western-style haute cuisine rather than the simpler stir-fry approach that a real Hong Kong chef might conceivably take to serve a cooked poodle. See "Poodle with Noodles," http://www.snopes.com/critters/edibles/tourist.htm (accessed April 19, 2006).

22. Florence E. Baer, "'Give Me…Your Huddled Masses': Anti-Vietnamese Refugee Lore and the 'Image of Limited Good,'" *Western Folklore* 41 (1982), 275–291.

23. Jan Harold Brunvand, *The Vanishing Hitchhiker: American Urban Legends and Their Meanings* (New York: Norton, 1980), 62–64. He notes that the story first came to his attention ca. 1976. Early versions had a wet cat as the victim, but poodle variants appeared by 1978 and had become the dominant version by 1979.

24. Jan Harold Brunvand, *Encyclopedia of Urban Legends* (New York: W. W. Norton, 2002), 16.

25. Quoted in Brunvand (*Vanishing Hitchhiker*, 67) from an archival text in the Brigham Young University folklore archive, Provo, Utah.

26. Brunvand, *Encyclopedia of Urban Legends*, 16.

27. "Anti-Abortion Rally," Linuxinit, January 28, 2008, http://linuxinit.net/site/?id=156 (accessed April 16, 2008).

28. "Reports of Contemporary Cannibalism in China. Here Be Cannibals," *The Heretical Press*, last updated February 3, 2005, http://www.heretical.com/cannibal/china.html (accessed April 19, 2006). This news story supposedly appeared in the April 12, 1995, issue of *Eastern Express*, but while the newspaper and the reporter in the byline do exist, it has never been shown that this story actually was published. From its tone, it seems likely that the original was a spoof rather than an actual news story, as with several of the stories discussed previously. However, information from it was represented as authentic and circulated by a variety of right-wing evangelical organizations promoting pro-life agendas, notably Focus on the Family (August 1995 Newsletter).

29. Christian Life Resources, "Investigation Called for on Consumption of Fetal Tissue as Health Food," *LifeWire*, May 5, 1995, http://www.christianliferesources.com/index.php?/news/view.php&newsid=302 (accessed May 11, 2009).

30. David Emery, "Do They Eat Babies in China?" *Urban Legends and Folklore* 2 (October 2005), http://urbanlegends.about.com/library/weekly/aa080601a.htm. Barbara Mikkelson, "Fetus Feast," 19 (June 2001), http://www.snopes.com/horrors/cannibal/fetus.htm (accessed May 12, 2009).

31. In Europe, a similar story is known as "The Turkish Pet," as Turkey serves as the gateway to the third world for Europeans and is a frequent tourist location. Sometimes the "dog" is found in the border of the United States, where it has escaped from ports docking in American harbors. The rat is sometimes described as a "Hong Kong wharf rat." Other rats taken as pets are said to be native to Haiti, Sumatra, Belgium (!), Pakistan, Guatemala, Australia, Cambodia, Korea, or China.

32. Mike Kelly, "Love Leads into Rattrap," *Austin American Statesman*, September 23, 1983.

33. Art Linkletter recorded a "true-life" embarrassing story in which a lady smuggled a pet Chihuahua into a motel that did not allow animals by wrapping it in a beach towel and pretending it was her baby (*Oops! or Life's Awful Moments*. Garden City, NY: Doubleday, 1967, 147–148).

34. Jan Harold Brunvand, *The Mexican Pet: More "New" Urban Legends and Some Old Favorites* (New York: Norton, 1986), 22.

35. "I don't hate illegal immigrants...," *America Is Screwed*, http://americaisscrewed.com/gpage4.html (accessed July 8, 2009).

36. Véronique Campion-Vincent, "Complots et avertissements: legends urbaines dans la ville," *Revue française de sociologie* (1989), 91–105, p. 104. The translation is Campion-Vincent's.

37. A parallel legend concerns the existence of the "Buffo Frog" in South Florida in the early in early or mid-1960s. According to Farley Snell, who resided in South Florida at this time: "Someone's dog bit or attacked this frog and then died, so that the assumption was that it was poisonous" (Collected Taylor, Texas, March 1989). The bufo frog (Bufo marinus), more commonly known as the cane toad, was rumored to have arrived with Cuban immigrants but was actually introduced through an accidental release of a dealer's stock at the Miami airport in 1957.

38. "Hatian [sic] rats?," e-mail to alt.folklore.urban, May 18, 1995 (accessed April 19, 2006).

39. "The Mexican Pet: An Urban Legend," *Urban Legends and Folklore*, http://urbanlegends.about.com/library/blpet.htm (accessed April 19, 2006). This variant is attributed to Lorraine Lovely and is dated September 9, 1999, on other Web sites.

40. Martin van Beynen, "Rat Rumour Baffles MAF," *The Press* (Christchurch, New Zealand) 22 (May 1998), posted on alt.folklore.suburban, http://members.tripod.com/~SaraAnnette/lore/ratnews.html (accessed April 19, 2006).

41. "Russian Rat Legend," E-mail to folklist@magnus.acs.ohio-state.edu, August 18, 1996.

42. Jan Harold Brunvand, *The Baby Train and Other Lusty Urban Legends* (New York: Norton, 1993), 55. Some European versions, interestingly, place the crime in Florida, Hawaii, New York, or other American resort communities.

43. Untitled, from Joe Harrington to alt.folklore.urban, April 18, 1991. Reported in Bill Ellis and Alan E. Mays, "The Toothbrushes in the Anus Photo," *FOAFTale News* 30 (June 1993), 2.

44. Ibid., 2.

45. "Jamaican Thieves Legend," from Kevin McEntee to alt.folklore.urban, April 16, 1992. Reported in Ellis and Mays, "The Toothbrushes in the Anus Photo," 3.

46. "The Parisian Bellboy," from ebestrom to alt.folklore.urban, April 22, 1992. Reported in Ellis and Mays, "The Toothbrushes in the Anus Photo," 3–4.

47. Albert B. Friedman, "The Scatological Rites of Burglars," *Western Folklore* 27 (1968), 171–179.

48. Rolf Wilhelm Brednich, *Das Huhn mit dem Gipsbeim* (Munich: C. H. Beck, 1993), 37–38.

49. Diane E. Goldstein, *Once Upon a Virus: AIDS Legends and Vernacular Risk Perception* (Logan, UT: Utah State University Press, 2004), 101.

50. "Bad Mary Has AIDS so Use Protected Sex Please!", submitted by luckygurl2003@excite.com to Forward Garden, http://www.forwardgarden.com/forward/29429.html.

51. Gary Alan Fine, "Welcome to the World of AIDS: Fantasies of Female Revenge," *Western Folklore* 46 (1987): 192–197.

52. "Legends in the Tabloids," *FOAFtale News* 18 (June 1990), 10, based on an article in *The Sun* (March 6, 1990).

53. Jean-Nol Kapferer, "The Persuasiveness of an Urban Legend: The Case of 'Mickey Mouse Acid,'" *Contemporary Legend* (1993): 85–101.

54. Paradoxically, Kapferer found that 6% of his sample who said that they "did not believe [it] at all" nevertheless passed it on, a rate actually higher than those who "wholly believed" it (Ibid., 95–96).

55. Ibid., 94.

CHAPTER 6

1. Jill Lepore, "It's Spreading: Outbreaks, Media Scares, and the Parrot Panic of 1930," *The New Yorker*, June 1, 2009, 46–50, p. 46. Material in this section is taken from Lepore's article.

2. Ibid., 50.

3. The most recent figures, reported by the U.S. Department of Commerce, put the May 2009 trade deficit at only $29.0 billion.

4. See "Cane Backed," http://www.snopes.com/medical/toxins/candycane.asp (accessed April 19, 2008); "Chopsticks," http://www.snopes.com/medical/toxins/chopsticks .asp (accessed April 19, 2008).

5. See Patrick Mullen, "Department Store Snakes," *Indiana Folklore* 3 (1970): 214–228; George Carey, *Maryland Folk Legends and Folk Songs* (Cambridge, MD: Tidewater Publishers, 1971); Xenia Cord, "Department Store Snakes," *Indiana Folklore* 2 (1969): 110–115; Ann Carpenter, "Cobras at K-Mart: Legends of Hidden Danger," *Publications of the Texas Folklore Society* 40 (1976): 36–45; Frederick Koenig, *Rumor in the Marketplace: The Social Psychology of Commercial Hearsay* (Dover, MA: Auburn House, 1985), 85–86.

6. Christine Schiavo, "Burlington Can't Button Rumor of a Snake up Its Coat Sleeve; Whitehall Twp. Retailer Says Some Are Beginning to Believe the Hidden Serpent Story," *Allentown Morning Call*, November 24, 1997, B1.

7. Paul Smith, *The Book of Nasty Legends* (London: Routledge and Kegan Paul, 1983), 58–59.

8. Jan Harold Brunvand, *The Vanishing Hitchhiker: American Urban Legends and Their Meanings* (New York: Norton, 1981), 161.

9. Keith Faur, "Snake-in-Coat Tale Called Folklore Fantasy," *Omaha World-Herald*, April 4, 1991, 1, 10, p. 1.

10. "The Snake in the Store," http://urbanlegends.about.com/library/blsnakestore .htm (accessed December 7, 2005).

11. Gary Alan Fine, "The Goliath Effect: Corporate Dominance and Mercantile Legends," *Journal of American Folklore* 98 (1985): 63–84.

12. Schiavo, "Burlington Can't Button Rumor of a Snake up Its Coat Sleeve."

13. The text, collected from a maid in Shropshire, England, reads: "The lady of the house, her husband has brought her a very beautiful fur coat . . . direct from India where he's a high-ranking soldier out there. . . . She takes it out of the wardrobe and gloats over it and lays it flat on the bed ready to wear and while she's getting dressed, she looks at the coat and to her horror, it's moving up and down, and it stops moving and she gets a bit scared, puts it back in the wardrobe and as she puts it in the wardrobe, she sees the sleeves waggling as if there's an arm in it, screams and shuts the wardrobe door and sort of runs out. Later, persuaded that she's imagined it all, goes to put the coat on, puts her arm down the sleeve and out slithers a great big huge snake." One wonders if the text reflects the troubles the British were having with their colony in India, where a movement for independence was gathering. Cited by Gillian Bennett and Paul Smith (eds.), *Urban Legends: A Collection of International Tall Tales and Terrors* (Westport, CT: Greenwood Press, 2007), 230–231.

14. Gary Alan Fine, "Evaluating Psychoanalytic Folklore: Are Freudians Ever Right?" *New York Folklore* 10 (1984): 5–20.

15. Up until the mid-1960s, the phrase "Made in Japan" was a joke to indicate a poor-quality item, but by the end of the 1960s that had changed dramatically.

16. Patrick Mullen, "Department Store Snakes," *Indiana Folklore* 3 (1970): 214–228, p. 228.

17. Jan Harold Brunvand (*Curses! Foiled Again! The Hottest Urban Legends Going* [New York: Norton, 1989], 38) cites an account of amusement park merry-go-round horses imported from India that contain poisonous snakes that bite unsuspecting children. The

theme of the snake in the amusement park is a common one (e.g., Mullen, "Department Store Snakes," 224–226), even when no explicitly foreign origin for these exotic animals is named.

18. Mullen, "Department Store Snakes," 228.

19. Some of the changes in trade balance have been truly startling. For instance, from the period 1990 to 2000, our trade deficit with India increased from $704 million to $7.0 billion. Our trade deficit with Costa Rica increased from $16.7 million to $1.1 billion, and with Pakistan our surplus of $534 million became a deficit of $1.7 billion. These figures further increased as manufacturing expanded in Asia and South and Central America (statistics from the Office of Trade and Industry Information, Manufacturing and Services, International Trade Administration, U.S. Department of Commerce, 2005).

20. Brunvand, *The Mexican Pet: More "New" Urban Legends and Some Old Favorites* (New York: Norton, 1986), 83–84.

21. Véronique Campion-Vincent, "Complots et Avertissements: Légendes Urbaines dans la Ville," *Revue Français de Sociologie* 30 (1989): 103.

22. Bengt af Klintberg, "Legends and Rumors About Spiders and Snakes," *Fabula*, 26 (1985): 274–287, p. 281.

23. The story was widely known in Kalamazoo, according to the manager of Frank's Nursery and Crafts (collected in March 1989). In his version, the workers are always "two men in white suits." He insists that while tarantulas can live in desert cacti, they purchase their cacti from greenhouses in Florida, emphasizing that they are American grown. He added that some women have been afraid to enter the store because of a fear of tarantulas. In line with the Goliath effect in which rumors and mercantile legends attach themselves to the largest or most prestigious businesses, Frank's is part of the largest nursery chain in the United States, and this store is the largest nursery in Kalamazoo.

24. Geoffrey M. Miller, personal communication to Jan H. Brunvand, 1989.

25. Brian O'Neill, "Tarantula Rumor Gives Cactus Customers the Creeps," *Pittsburgh Press*, May 23, 1990, B1.

26. "Cactus and Spiders," *New York Times*, November 30, 1993, C11.

27. Véronique Campion-Vincent, "Complots et Avertissements," 91–105, p. 103.

28. Klintberg, "Legends and Rumors about Spiders and Snakes," 275.

29. "Frequently Asked Questions about Spiders," http://www.puyallup.wsu.edu/plantclinic/faqs/faqs_spdrs.html (accessed December 12, 2005).

30. R. Gane, "The Respiration of Bananas in Presence of Ethylene," *New Phytologist* 36, no. 2 (1937): 170–178.

31. George H. Townsend with Felix J. Levy, Harry G. Nicks, George Clinton Crandall, and Charles Phelps, *The Relation of Food to Health and Premature Death* (St. Louis: Witt Publishing Company, 1897), 181–183.

32. Herbert M. Shelton, *The Hygienic System, Vol. II, Orthotrophy,* 6th ed. (San Antonio: Dr. Shelton's Health School, 1975. First published 1935), chap. 9, http://www.soilandhealth.org/02/0201hyglibcat/020126shelton.orthotrophy/020126.ch9.htm.

33. "Killer Banana Rumor Grips China," May 25, 2007, http://news.bbc.co.uk/2/hi/asia?pacific/6691171.stm (accessed April 19, 2008); Clifford Coonan, "Do Bananas Spread Sars? China Gripped by Health Scare," May 25, 2007, http://www.independent.co.uk/news/world/asia/do-bananas-spread-sars-china-gripped by-health-scare-450288.html (accessed April 19, 2008).

34. Marina Warner, *Monsters of Our Own Making* (Lexington: University of Kentucky Press, 2007), 352.

35. Ibid., 373.

36. Hasia Diner, *Hungering for America: Italian, Irish, and Jewish Foodways in the Age of Migration* (Cambridge, MA: Harvard University Press, 2001), 63.

37. Ibid., 64.

38. Samuel Hopkins Adams, "The Poison Bugaboo," *Everybody's Magazine* 23, no. 4 (October 1910): 518–525, p. 522.

39. Jim Hiner, personal communication to Jan Harold Brunvand, 1982.

40. "The Banana Boat Song (Day-O)." The exact history of Belafonte's version and his immediate folk revivalist source remain disputed; however, all authorities agree that several recordings of the song preceded his, and that the tune and lyrics are based on a well-known traditional work song sung in Jamaica (not Trinidad, as often stated).

41. "CAB," electronic comment on "Black Widow Spider Found in Grapes," Entomology Forum, *Topix*, July 22, 2007, http://www.topix.net/forum/science/entomology/TOG55F7RF75T2UUJP (accessed September 25, 2007). A follow-up comment by "Katie" on August 4, 2007, added, "Seriously, this isn't uncommon at all. I work in a produce warehouse. We get them all the time. They come in with mangoes, bananas, grapes…From everywhere. Ask your produce workers the next time you shop. If they say they've never seen something like this, they're either incredibly new to the department or lying."

42. "Spider Bites Man in Supermarket," http://news.bbc.co.uk/2/hi/uk_news/wales/4080950.stm (accessed December 12, 2005).

43. "Frequently Asked Questions: Help! What to Do if You Suspect You've Got a Scorpion or Foreign Spider," *British Arachnological Society*, updated October 30, 2003, http://www.britishspiders.org.uk/html/bas.php?page=faq&faq=5 (accessed September 25, 2007). Worth noting, however, is the fact, acknowledged in the 2007 *Guinness Book of World Records*, that the South American "banana spider," also known as the Brazilian wandering spider (*Phoneutria* spp.), has the most potent venom of any known poisonous creature. It, too, hides in bunches of bananas but, luckily, uses its full complement of venom so rarely that deaths from its bites are uncommon.

44. Gary Alan Fine, "Redemption Rumors: Mercantile Legends and Corporate Beneficence," *Journal of American Folklore* 104 (1991): 179–181; Linda Dégh and Andrew Vázsonyi, "Does the Word Dog Bite? Ostensive Action: A Means of Legend-Telling," *Journal of Folklore Research* 20 (1983): 5–34.

45. Associated Press, "Black Widows Found in Red Grapes," *Portland Press Herald*, September 28, 1991; "You Are What You Eat," *Time*, July 22, 1991, 29; Linda Fullerton, "Stop'n'save Pulls Grapes from Shelves," *Portland Press Herald*, July 9, 1991, 1A, 8A.

46. Associated Press, "Less Pesticide Means More Bugs for Food Buyers," *USA Today*, November 26, 2003, http://www.usatoday.com/news/nation/2003-11-26-bugs_x.htm (accessed September 25, 2007).

47. Lindsay Jones, "'Nasty' Black Widow Spider Found on Grapes," *Halifax Daily News*, September 15, 2007, http://www.hfxnews.ca/index.cfm?sid=62702&sc=89 (accessed September 25, 2007).

48. Robert Detweiler, personal communication to Jan Harold Brunvand, 1983.

49. Dan E. Miller, "'Snakes in the Greens' and Rumor in the Inner City," *Social Science Journal* 29 (1992): 381–393.

50. Ibid., 385–335. Cf. Miller, "Rumor: An Examination of Some Stereotypes," *Symbolic Interaction* 28, no. 4 (2006): 516 and *passim*.

51. Miller, "Rumor," 512.

52. For more on this phenomenon, see the collections published by Alan Dundes and Carl R. Pagter, beginning with their groundbreaking *Work Hard and You Shall Be Rewarded* (Detroit: Wayne State University Press, 1974).

53. As argued by Bill Ellis in "Legend/AntiLegend: Humor as an Integral Part of the Contemporary Legend Process," pp. 123–140 in *Rumor Mills: The Social Impact of Rumor and Legend*, ed. Gary Alan Fine, Véronique Campion-Vincent, and Chip Heath (New York: Aldine Transaction, 2005).

54. The first dated text we could find was dated January 10, 2000. By January 28, its circulation was so widespread that the Centers for Disease Control and Prevention publicly labeled it a "false report" (http://www.cdc.gov/ncidod/banana.htm [accessed February 23, 2006]). For a brief history of its circulation and the official responses, see David Emery, "The Great Internet Banana Scare of 2000," *Urban Legends and Folklore*, posted February 23, 2000, http://www.about.com (accessed September 25, 2007).

55. Centers for Disease Control and Prevention, January 28, 2000.

56. "False Internet Report about Bananas," http://www.cdc.gov/ncidod/banana .htm (accessed February 23, 2006).

57. Stephen Lemons, "Attack of the Flesh-Eating Bananas!" http://www.salon .com/health/log/2000/04/04/banana (accessed February 23, 2006).

58. Véronique Campion-Vincent, "From Evil Others to Evil Elites: A Dominant Pattern in Conspiracy Theories Today," pp. 103–122 in *Rumor Mills: The Social Impact of Rumor and Legend*, ed. Gary Alan Fine, Véronique Campion-Vincent, and Chip Heath (New Brunswick, NJ: Aldine Transaction, 2005).

59. The first dated text was posted on August 31, 1999, by "Judy Johnson" on the Usenet listserv alt.folklore.urban under the thread "Toilet Spiders" (http://groups .google.com/group/alt.folklore.urban/msg/bcd93f8574f211a6?hl=en). The site itself is devoted to debunking dubious stories, and the original post ended: "This was quickly debunked by Chuck Kristensen of the arachnology mail list (which I confirmed by similar searches); no such article in Medline, no such journal, no such spider."

60. "'The chappies' is a condition somewhat like hemorrhoids but on a more temporary basis. Chappies are usually caused by excessive ass wiping due to having the shits or by excessive moist farts causing a sore, irritated anal region." JUMA = "Jump Up My Ass!" "Someone annoys you? Just say to them…'JUMA Baby!'" (*Urban Dictionary*, http://www.urbandictionary.com [accessed September 26, 2007]).

61. Another anal reference: invert the "n" in "glutens" and you have "gluteus," the name for the three muscles that make up the mass of the buttocks.

62. Text as quoted in Richard S. Vetter and P. Kirk Visscher, "Oh, What a Tangled Web We Weave: The Anatomy of an Internet Spider Hoax," *American Entomologist* 46 (2000): 221–223, pp. 221–222. Nearly all Internet versions were verbatim accounts.

63. Jennifer Watson, "Spider Bites: Assessment and Management," *Journal of the American Academy of Nurse Practitioners* 11, no. 5 (May 1999): 216, http:// www.blackwell-synergy.com/doi/pdf/10.1111/j.1745–7599.1999.tb00566.x (accessed September 26, 2007).

64. Vance Randolph, *Pissing in the Snow and Other Ozark Folktales* (Urbana: University of Illinois Press, 1976).

65. Vetter and Visscher, "Oh, What a Tangled Web We Weave," 223.

66. "Blush Spider Arachnius Gluteus Is a Hoax," http://www.spiders.ucr.edu/ debunk.html (accessed February 22, 2006); "Toilet Spiders," http://www.snopes.com/ horrors/insects/buttspdr.htm (accessed February 22, 2006).

67. Eric Nagourney, "Toilet Spiders? Not Real, but Good for a Scare," *New York Times*, July 31, 2001, F6. There is a Greek-themed "Hart Restaurant" in the area, but there is no such town or district as "South Wilkes-Barre."

68. Nagourney, "Toilet Spiders."

69. In this we do not forget that many Americans are Mexican Americans, but even they hold different stereotypes of Mexico and Canada.

70. In 1992, the United States had a $5.4 billion trade surplus. By 1995, that had become a $15.4 billion trade deficit (statistics from the Office of Trade and Industry Information, Manufacturing and Services, International Trade Administration, U.S. Department of Commerce, 2005).

71. "The Gambrinus Company," *Company Histories*, http://www.fundinguniverse .com/company-histories/The-Gambrinus-Company-Company-History.html (accessed September 26, 2007).

72. Both of these beers—Tecate and Dos Equis—are Mexican beers, but the rumors have only attached themselves to Corona, the most popular Mexican beer.

73. This is a very common motif in corporate rumors, particularly since TV personalities and news features have strong credibility but, unlike the print media, are difficult for skeptics to check. Similarly, Liz Claiborne, like previous corporate executives, was said to have admitted on TV that her company supported satanic cults, but the name of the show on which she did this varied from teller to teller and ultimately was impossible to verify. See Gary Alan Fine and Patricia Turner, *Whispers on the Color Line: Rumor and Race in America* (Berkeley: University of California Press, 2001), 98–99.

74. Jonathan Peterson, "Brewer Will Battle False Rumor about Its Product," *Los Angeles Times*, July 28, 1987, 1–2, p. 1.

75. Ibid.; Scott Joseph, "Urine No Danger," *New Times*, July 29–August 4, 1987, 18.

76. Gary Alan Fine, "The Goliath Effect: Corporate Dominance and Mercantile Legends," *Journal of American Folklore*, 98 (1985): 63–84.

77. Lori Rozsa, "Corona Leaves 'em Foaming at the Mouth," *Miami Herald*, August 1987.

78. June Anderson, personal communication to Jan Harold Brunvand, 1988.

79. "The Gambrinus Company." Interestingly, A. H. Tellier (personal communication to Jan Harold Brunvand, 1987) computed the amount of urine that it would actually take to contaminate a vat of beer. Using a detection level of two parts per million and a beer vat 20 feet in diameter and 20 feet high, he estimates that it would take 75 bladders filled with urine to make a noticeable difference. Of course, this implies that so long as Mexicans did not urinate en masse into the vats, individuals could do so occasionally without fear of detection.

80. Harry Middleton Hyatt, *Hoodoo—Conjuration—Witchcraft—Rootwork: Beliefs Accepted by Many Negroes and White Persons These Being Orally Recorded Among Blacks and Whites* (Hannibal, MO: Memoirs of the Alma Egan Hyatt Foundation, 1970–1974), No. 10273. Collected in New Orleans.

81. See, e.g., the blog entry by "Robert," "ME CHINESE, ME PLAY JOKE: Exploring the Urban Legend of Soda Can Urination by Asian Men," http://retrocrush.buzznet.com/ archive2/coke/default.htm (accessed September 26, 2007). Robert recalls encountering the rhyme at several schools as his military family moved around the United States dur-

ing his childhood. Oddly, this very common rhyme seems to have escaped the attention of folklorists. A joke version often has the Chinese protagonist "topped" by an all-American cowboy who responds, "Me Cowboy, me shoot fast, me put bullet in your ass."

82. "The Gambrinus Company."

83. Contributed by "RFerrie" to alt.folklore.urban on June 24, 1996, http://groups .google.com/group/alt.folklore.urban/browse_thread/thread/e2253840d2f489ff/fdc3eb a549f14738?lnk=st&q=Corona+beer+urine&rnum=164#fdc3eba549f14738 (accessed September 26, 2007). See also "Corona (beer)" in *Wikipedia*, which mentions other similar explanations, such as the belief that the lime juice would "sanitize" the mouth of the bottle, making it safe for tourists to drink from. In fact, the custom of adding a fruit slice to a bottle or glass of beer is widely distributed internationally.

CHAPTER 7

1. John Barry, "Too Good to Check," *Newsweek*, June 26, 1995, 33.

2. Donald Joralemon, "Organ Wars: The Battle for Body Parts," *Medical Anthropology Quarterly*, New Series, 9, no. 3 (September 1995): 335–356, http://links .jstor.org/sici?sici=0745–5194%28199509%292%3A9%3A3%3C335%3AOWTBFB%3E 2.0.CO%3B2–0.

3. David Schreiberg, "Dead Babies," *New Republic*, December 24, 1990, 12–13, p. 12.

4. Jan Harold Brunvand, *The Baby Train and Other Lusty Urban Legends* (New York: Norton, 1993), 149.

5. Danusha Goska, "'Waking up Less than Whole': The Female Perpetrator in Male-Victim Kidney Theft Legends," *Southern Folklore* 54 (1997): 196–210, p. 199.

6. Jan Harold Brunvand, *Curses! Foiled Again! The Hottest Urban Legends Going* (New York: Norton, 1989), 195–202.

7. Gary Alan Fine, "Welcome to the World of AIDS: Fantasies of Female Revenge," *Western Folklore* 46 (1987): 192–197.

8. Elissa Henken, "Gender Shifts in Contemporary Legend," *Western Folklore* 63 (2004): 237–256.

9. Brunvand, *The Baby Train*, 152.

10. Ibid., 153.

11. Ibid., 152.

12. Kate Barry, "Kidney Theft Crosses the Border," posted on the listserv alt.folklore .urban, on December 20, 1996 (no longer available there); Archived at "Kidney Theft," *Don't Spread That Hoax!* http://www.nonprofit.net/hoax/catalog/Kidney_Theft/kidney1 .htm (accessed December 4, 2009).

13. Goska, "'Waking up Less Than Whole,'" 198.

14. Gillian Bennett, *Bodies: Sex, Violence, Disease, and Death in Contemporary Legend* (Jackson: University Press of Mississippi, 2005), 201.

15. Ibid., 199.

16. Véronique Campion-Vincent, *Organ Theft Legends* (Jackson: University Press of Mississippi, 2005), 31–33.

17. Placed under house arrest in 1610 by order of King Matthias, Báthory was never tried but instead bricked up in a special room in her castle, where she died four years later. See Raymond T. McNally, *Dracula Was a Woman: In Search of the Blood*

Countess of Transylvania (New York: McGraw Hill, 1983). In fact, scholars are divided as to whether Báthory was in fact a sadistic serial killer or simply an iron-fisted governor of her region, like her more notorious neighbor Vlad Tepes, aka "Dracula." In any case, no surviving legal document ever substantiated the blood-bathing rumor.

18. R. Po-chia Hsia, *The Myth of Ritual Murder: Jews and Magic in Reformation Germany* (New Haven, CT: Yale University Press, 1988); Miri Rubin, *Gentile Tales: The Narrative Assault on Late Medieval Jews* (New Haven, CT: Yale University Press, 1999).

19. Arlette Farge and Jacques Revel, *The Vanishing Children of Paris* (Cambridge, MA: Harvard University Press, 1991), 104–113.

20. Quoted in Bennett, *Bodies*, 191.

21. Dionizjusz Czubala, "'The Black Volga': Child Abduction Urban Legends in Poland and Russia," *FOAFTale News* 21 (February 1991): 1–3.

22. Giuseppe Stilo and Paolo Toselli, "The Kidnappers and the Black Ambulance: Child Abduction Legends from Sicily," *FOAFTale News* 23 (September 1991): 5–6.

23. Gladys-Marie Fry, *Night Riders in Black Folk History* (Knoxville: University of Tennessee Press, 1975), 196.

24. Patricia Turner, *I Heard It through the Grapevine: Rumor in African-American Culture* (Berkeley: University of California Press, 1993), 137, 144, 148.

25. Gary Alan Fine and Patricia Turner, *Whispers on the Color Line: Rumor and Race in America* (Berkeley: University of California Press, 2001).

26. Luise White, "Social Construction and Social Consequences," pp. 241–254 in *Rumor Mills: The Social Impact of Rumor and Legend*, ed. Gary Alan Fine, Véronique Campion-Vincent, and Chip Heath (New Brunswick, NJ: Aldine Transaction, 2005), 241.

27. Véronique Campion-Vincent, "From Evil Others to Evil Elites: A Dominant Pattern in Conspiracy Theories Today," pp. 103–122 in *Rumor Mills: The Social Impact of Rumor and Legend*, ed. Gary Alan Fine, Véronique Campion-Vincent, and Chip Heath (New Brunswick, NJ: Aldine Transaction, 2005), 117–18.

28. Véronique Campion-Vincent, "Organ Theft Narratives," *Western Folklore* 56 (1997): 1–37. For a fuller account of this incident, see John King Fairbank, "Patterns behind The Tientsin Massacre," *Harvard Journal of Asiatic Studies* 20, no. 3/4 (December 1957): 480–511, http://links.jstor.org/sici?sici=0073-0548%28195712%2920%3A3%2F4%3C480%3APBTTM%3E2.0.CO%3B2-G.

29. Luise White, *Speaking with Vampires: Rumor and History in Colonial Africa* (Berkeley: University of California Press, 2000).

30. Ibid., 167–168.

31. Ibid., 312.

32. This point is also made by Pamela Feldman-Savelsberg, Flavien T. Ndonko, and Song Yang, "How Rumor Begets Rumor: Collective Memory, Ethnic Conflict, and Reproductive Rumors in Cameroon," pp. 141–157 in *Rumor Mills: The Social Impact of Rumor and Legend*, ed. Gary Alan Fine, Véronique Campion-Vincent, and Chip Heath (New Brunswick, NJ: Aldine Transaction, 2005).

33. William H. Friedland, "Some Urban Myths in East Africa," pp. 93–96 in *Myth in Modern Africa: The Fourteenth Conference Proceedings of the Rhodes-Livingstone Institute for Social Research*, ed. Allie Dubb (Lusaka, Zambia: Rhodes-Livingstone Institute, 1960).

34. Nancy Scheper-Hughes, "The Global Traffic in Organs," *Current Anthropology* 41 (2000): 191–224.

35. Ache [a pseudonym], "Brazilian Superstition Respecting Leprosy," *Notes & Queries* N.S. 8 (August 24, 1889): 145–146, reported in *FOAFTale News* 30 (June 1993): 10.

36. Nicole Maxwell, *Witch-Doctor's Apprentice: Hunting for Medicinal Plants in the Amazon*, revised ed. (New York: Collier Books, 1975), 21–23.

37. Frank de Caro, "The Body Parts Panic and the Peruvian *Pistaco* Tradition," *FOAFTale News* 36 (January 1995): 1.

38. Phyllis Rose, *Jazz Cleopatra: Josephine Baker in Her Time* (New York: Doubleday, 1989), 237; see Barbara Katz-Rothman, *Weaving a Family: Untangling Race and Adoption* (Boston: Beacon, 2005), 136.

39. Brunvand, *The Baby Train*, 153.

40. Anna Pukas, "The Global Lie That Cannot Be Silenced," *Folklore Frontiers* 27 (1995): 16–17, cited by Bennett, *Bodies*, 194.

41. "Europeans Move to Tack Down Baby Traffickers," IPS—Inter Press Service, September 21, 1988.

42. Bennett, *Bodies*, 194.

43. Schreiberg, "Dead Babies," 12–13.

44. *Corriere della Sera* (July 13, 1987), quoted in Stilo and Toselli, "The Kidnappers and the Black Ambulance," 6.

45. Bennett, *Bodies*, 196–197.

46. Nancy Scheper-Hughes, "Truth and Rumor on the Organ Trail," *Natural History* 107 (1998): 48.

47. Schreiberg, "Dead Babies," 12.

48. Ibid.

49. "More Organ Sale Rumors," *FOAFTale News* 38 (December 1995): 8.

50. Todd Leventhal, "The 'Baby Parts' Myth: An Anatomy of a Rumor," http://tafkac.org/medical/organ.theft/baby.parts/baby_parts_myth.html (accessed May 14, 2009).

51. David Samper, "Cannibalizing Kids: Rumor and Resistance in Latin America," *Journal of Folklore Research* 39 (2002): 1–32, pp. 16–20.

52. Campion-Vincent, *Organ Theft Legends*, op cit., 6.

53. Samper, "Cannibalizing Kids," op cit.

54. Adrian Dimmick, "Cannibals and Stolen Organs," *Folk-Lore Society News* 21 (June 1995): 10.

55. Todd Leventhal, "The 'Baby Parts' Myth, op cit.

56. Bill Ellis, "Body Parts Panics in Guatemala," *FOAFTale News* 33–34 (June 1994): 17.

57. "Organ Trafficking and Child Theft Abounds," *IPS—Inter Press Service*, March 27, 1995; "Rumor and Rage," *People*, April 25, 1995, 78.

58. Bennett, *Bodies*, 257–258.

59. Ibid.

60. Quoted in Anne Collinson, "The Littlest Immigrants: Cross-Border Adoption in the Americas, Policy, and Women's History," *Journal of Women's History* 19 (2007): 132–141, p. 136.

61. John A. Shonder, "Organ Theft Rumors in Guatemala: Some Personal Observations," *FOAFTale News* 35 (October 1994): 2.

62. The footage was subsequently edited and broadcast by NBC's news program *Now* on August 17, 1994, as part of a study of the baby-snatching rumors and the adoption abuses at their core. Produced by Bert Medley and edited by Greg Bertrand, the feature was narrated by Mike Boettcher.

63. Weinstock survived, but was severely disabled (Collinson, "The Littlest Immigrants," n. 19). Thirty-five villagers were arrested for their parts in the attack, but were later released by a court, citing "lack of evidence" (GHRC/USA Human Rights Update, PEACENET Versions #4 & #5 [February 10, 1995], http://www.tulane.edu/~latinlib/RESTRICTED/Guatemala_Human_Rights_Update/1995_0210.txt [accessed May 14, 2009]).

64. Bulletin No. 94–013, quoted in *FOAFTale News* 33–34 (June 1994): 18. See also Trish O'Kane, "Dangerous Rumors," *Time*, April 18, 1994, 48.

65. Ibid.

66. Collinson, "The Littlest Immigrants," 136.

67. Ibid.

68. Ibon Villelabeitia, Reuters news report, May 4, 2000, http://www.latinamericanstudies.org/guatemala/japanese.htm (accessed May 14, 2009); Will Weissert, Associated Press news report, May 13, 2000, http://www.latinamericanstudies.org/guatemala/rumor.htm (accessed May 14, 2009). See also Robert Sitler, "Understanding Death in a Mayan Market," *Community College Humanities Review* 22, no. 1 (Fall 2001): 88–98, www.stetson.edu/~rsitler/TodosSantos/Ts.doc (accessed May 14, 2009).

69. Nancy Scheper-Hughes, *Death without Weeping: The Violence of Everyday Life in Brazil* (Berkeley: University of California Press, 1992), 233–258; Scheper-Hughes, "Truth and Rumor on the Organ Trail," 48.

70. Steven L. Varnis, "Regulating the Global Adoption of Children," *Society* 38 (January/February 2001): 39–46.

71. Scheper-Hughes, *Death without Weeping*, 233–258.

72. Terry Ann Knopf, *Rumors, Race, and Riots* (New Brunswick, NJ: Transaction Books, 1975), 168.

73. Samper, "Cannibalizing Kids," 19.

74. Gonzalo Portocarrero Maisch, Isidro Valentin, and Soraya Irigoyen, *Sacaojos: Crisis Social y Fantasmas Coloniales* (Lima, Peru: TAREA), 35, translated by David Samper, "Cannibalizing Kids," 18.

CHAPTER 8

1. Robert Knapp, "A Psychology of Rumor," *Public Opinion Quarterly* 8 (1944): 22–37.

2. Gordon Allport and Leo G. Postman, *The Psychology of Rumor* (New York: Holt, 1947).

3. See Ellis, *Raising the Devil: Satanism, New Religions, and the Media* (Lexington: University of Kentucky Press, 2000), 124–125. The term was initially introduced by David G. Bromley in his discussions of movements devoted to alleged "Satanic cults" that were responsible for a wide variety of social evils in the 1980s and early 1990s. See his "Constructing Subversion: A Comparison of Anti-Religions and Anti-Satanic Narratives," pp. 49–76 in *Anti-Cult Movements in Cross-Cultural Perspective*, ed. Anson Shupe and David G. Bromley (New York: Garland Publishers, 1994).

4. Véronique Campion-Vincent, "From Evil Others to Evil Elites: A Dominant Pattern in Conspiracy Theories Today," pp. 103–122 in *Rumor Mills: The Social Impact of Rumors and Legends*, ed. Gary Alan Fine, Véronique Campion-Vincent, and Chip Heath (New Brunswick, NJ: Aldine Transaction, 2005).

5. This is an insight first made by Janet Langlois in "The Belle Isle Bridge Incident: Legend Dialectic and Semiotic System in the 1943 Detroit Race Riots," *Journal of American Folklore* 96 (1983): 183–199, and since developed into the Topsy/Eva principle, a central concept in the work done on black/white folklore by Patricia A. Turner in *I Heard It through the Grapevine* (Berkeley: University of California Press, 1993) and extended in Gary Alan Fine and Patricia A. Turner, *Whispers on the Color Line: Rumor and Race in America* (Berkeley: University of California Press, 2001).

6. Fine and Turner, *Whispers on the Color Line*, 224–225.

7. This argument was first made by Sylvia Grider at the 1982 Sheffield Seminar, concerning the widespread belief that at Halloween children are at risk of receiving booby-trapped trick-or-treat goodies, such as apples with razor blades concealed inside. Although no authenticated case ever emerged (other than a father who poisoned his own child for insurance purposes, then tried to use the story as a smokescreen to mislead police), the story resulted in widespread collective actions across the United States to protect youngsters against this potential threat. See her "The Razor Blades in the Apples Syndrome," in *Perspectives on Contemporary Legend: Proceedings of the Conference on Contemporary Legend, Sheffield, July, 1982*, ed. Paul Smith (Sheffield, UK: CECTAL, 1984), 128–140, and Bill Ellis, " 'Safe' Spooks: New Halloween Traditions in Response to Sadism Legends," pp. 24–44 in *Halloween and Other Festivals of Death and Life*, ed. Jack Santino (Knoxville: University of Tennessee Press, 1994).

8. Bill Ellis, *Aliens, Ghosts, and Cults: Legends We Live* (Jackson: University Press of Mississippi, 2003) 243.

9. Diane E. Goldstein, *Once Upon a Virus: AIDS Legends and Vernacular Risk Perception* (Logan: Utah State University Press, 2004).

10. Ellis, *Raising the Devil*; Gillian Bennett, *Bodies: Sex, Violence, Disease, and Death in Contemporary Legend* (Jackson: University Press of Mississippi, 2005).

11. Plaintiff's Post-Trial Proposed Findings of Fact and Brief, *Pedro, Lozano, et al. v. City of Hazleton*, Civil Action No. 3:06-cv-01586-JMM, dated May 14, 2007, p. 23.

12. One employee told reporters that it was common to find cockroaches in with the peanuts, and rodent droppings were commonly seen in the facilities. He even once saw a dead rat mixed in with the product, "dry roasting in the peanuts." See "Worker: I Saw Rat Roasting in Peanut Plant," *CBS News: The Early Show* (February 3, 2009). Available: http://www.cbsnews.com/stories/2009/02/03/earlyshow/health/main4771754 .shtml. Accessed: July 16, 2009. The story recalls Fine's "Cokelore and Coke Law: Urban Belief Tales and the Problem of Multiple Origins," in *Manufacturing Tales: Sex and Money in Contemporary Legends* (Knoxville: University of Tennessee Pres, 1992), pp. 79–85, which showed that cases of contaminated soft drink beverages were in fact common, particularly in the American South.

13. Nancy Scheper-Huges, "The Global Traffic in Organs," *Current Anthropology* 41 (2000): 191–224.

14. See Fine and Turner, *Whispers on the Color Line*, and Gillian Bennett's discussion of the role played by rumor and legend in both the medieval "blood libel" panics and the more recent "Satanic child abuse" claims, in *Bodies*, 247–303.

15. Woodrow Wilson famously said that "any man who carries a hyphen about with him carries a dagger that he is ready to plunge into the vitals of this Republic whenever he gets ready. If I can catch any man with a hyphen in this great contest I will know that I have got an enemy of the Republic." "Final Address in Support of the League of Nations," delivered September 25, 1919, in Pueblo, Colorado, *American Rhetoric: Top 100 Speeches*, http://www.americanrhetoric.com/speeches/wilsonleagueofnations.htm (accessed July 16, 2009).

16. Gary Alan Fine, "Rumor, Trust and Civil Society: Collective Memory and Cultures of Judgment," *Diogenes* 54 (2007): 5–18.

17. "Proverbs of Hell," *The Marriage of Heaven and Hell*, plate 8.

18. Sura 5 ("The Feast"), verse 32 reads: "anyone who murders any person who had not committed murder or horrendous crimes, it shall be as if he murdered all the people. And anyone who spares a life, it shall be as if he spared the lives of all the people."

19. Summer Harlow, "A Clash of Two Cultures: Native Residents, Georgetown Immigrants Still Living a World Apart," *The [Wilmington, DE] News Journal*, July 7, 2009, http://www.delmarvanow.com/apps/pbcs.dll/article?AID=/20090707/NEWS01/907070320 (accessed July 7, 2009).

20. Michael Calogero, et al. *Greater Hazleton Area Civic Partnership* (Utica, NY: Zogby International, 2007).

21. Robert Frost, "Mending Wall," *North of Boston* (New York: Henry Holt and Company, 1914), 12. Quoted from the Google books public domain edition, http://books.google.com/books?id=_dtaAAAAMAAJ&printsec=frontcover&source=gbs_v2_summary_r&cad=0#v=onepage&q=&f=false.

Index